Capitalism's Sexual History

Oxford Studies in Gender and International Relations

Series editors: J. Ann Tickner, American University, and Laura Sjoberg, University of Florida and Royal Holloway, University of London

CAPITALISM'S SEXUAL HISTORY

Nicola J. Smith

OXFORD
UNIVERSITY PRESS

OXFORD
UNIVERSITY PRESS

Oxford University Press is a department of the University of Oxford. It furthers
the University's objective of excellence in research, scholarship, and education
by publishing worldwide. Oxford is a registered trade mark of Oxford University
Press in the UK and certain other countries.

Published in the United States of America by Oxford University Press
198 Madison Avenue, New York, NY 10016, United States of America.

© Oxford University Press 2020

Library of Congress Cataloging-in-Publication Data
Names: Smith, Nicola Jo-Anne, author.
Title: Capitalism's sexual history / Nicola J. Smith.
Description: New York, NY : Oxford University Press, [2020] |
Series: Oxford studies in gender and international relations |
Includes bibliographical references and index.
Identifiers: LCCN 2020012845 (print) | LCCN 2020012846 (ebook) |
ISBN 9780197530276 (hardback) | ISBN 9780197545195 (paperback) |
ISBN 9780197530290 (epub)
Subjects: LCSH: Prostitution—Great Britain—History. |
Sex—Great Britain—Economic aspects—History. |
Capitalism—Social aspects—Great Britain. | Queer theory. |
Feminist theory. Classification: LCC HQ185.A5 S65 2020 (print) |
LCC HQ185.A5 (ebook) | DDC 306.740941—dc23
LC record available at https://lccn.loc.gov/2020012845
LC ebook record available at https://lccn.loc.gov/2020012846

CONTENTS

ACKNOWLEDGMENTS

The writing of this book has had a very long history, and I am indebted to a great many people who have offered me help, advice, and encouragement along the way. I would like to begin by thanking my colleagues in the Department of Political Science and International Relations and the School of Government at the University of Birmingham for their individual kindness and collective generosity as well as for the various conversations we have had about the research and writing process. I would also like to express my gratitude to Juanita Elias, Penny Griffin, Sarah Kingston, Mary Laing, Donna Lee, Milly Morris, Lucy Neville, Katy Pilcher, Adrienne Roberts, Heather Savigny, Dani Tepe-Belfrage, Tiina Vaittinen, Julia Welland, and Heather Widdows for their intellectual, practical, and moral support for this project. Special thanks to Tendayi Bloom, Nicola Pratt, and Nick Wheeler for reading and commenting on the draft materials, and to Lisa Downing not only for her feedback on the manuscript but also for making the writing of it a lot less lonely and a lot more enjoyable than it otherwise would have been.

I owe a huge debt of thanks to Angela Chnapko for making this book possible, for her enthusiasm for and guidance on the project, and for leading me through the publication process—it has been such a wonderful experience to work with her and her colleagues at Oxford University Press. I am also beholden to J. Ann Tickner and Laura Sjoberg as series editors for all their help in bringing this book to life, as well as the two anonymous readers for their invaluable feedback on the manuscript—I hope I have done justice to their very careful and constructive comments but any errors and omissions in the final text are of course mine alone.

Sections of text in the Introduction, Chapter 1, and Chapter 5 of this book draw from earlier chapters published elsewhere. Many thanks to Oxford University Press and Edward Elgar for granting me permission to reproduce material from the following publications: "Toward a Queer Political

Economy of Crisis" by Nicola Smith, in *Scandalous Economics: Gender and the Politics of Financial Crisis*, edited by Jacqui True and Aida Hozić (New York: Oxford University Press, 2016), 231–247; and "Queer Theory and Feminist Political Economy" by Nicola Smith, in *Handbook on the International Political Economy of Gender*, edited by Juanita Elias and Adrienne Roberts (Cheltenham, UK: Edward Elgar, 2018), 102–112.

Last but definitely not least, I would like to thank my family and friends—including my brother, Kieron Smith, my beloved friend Cathy Newman, and "soul restorers" Sophie Khan and Manita Rajgor—for listening to me, advising me, and cheering me on. I reserve particular thanks for my lifelong friend Emma Cooper, who has shared the journey of this book with me from start to finish, and who gives me immeasurable support for my writing and everything else besides. Above all, I would like to thank my mum and dad, Lesley and Greg Smith—who are there for me every day in every way and without whom I could never have completed this project—and my son, Tom, of whom I could not be more proud.

Introduction

What does capitalism have to do with sexuality? At one level, the relationship between economic and sexual practices could scarcely be more contested. When Amnesty International voted to support the decriminalization of consensual commercial sex in August 2015, for example, it did so in response to longstanding activism by sex workers globally. Yet its proposal was denounced as "unfathomable" in an open letter signed by hundreds of prominent figures from every region of the world.[1] Otherwise disparate voices from politicians to psychiatrists, religious sisters to truckers, and university professors to Hollywood stars were united in their condemnation of the notion that sex could in any way be understood as an economic activity.

At another level, though, the connections between economic and sexual life are often rendered invisible. Sexuality—especially but not only for women—is understood as intimate, sacred, the embodiment of love. That sexuality exists somewhere beyond economy is believed to be the natural order of things—an order that, for the most part, can go unnoticed but, when transgressed, must be fiercely defended. What Amnesty International's decision did was to confront deep-rooted assumptions that sexuality is inherently separable from capitalism, and that it can be taken as read that "the inside of a woman's body is not a workplace."[2]

The letter's use of the term "unfathomable" is telling, for it reveals how the intended effect of the moral outcry was not just to influence Amnesty International's policy position but also to set strict limits on how sexuality can and cannot be conceptualized. For sex to become work, and so for the sexual to become economic, was beyond the pale, beyond morality, beyond

Capitalism's Sexual History. Nicola J. Smith, Oxford University Press (2020). © Oxford University Press.
DOI: 10.1093/oso/9780197530276.001.0001.

comprehension. Yet, as this book explores, it is this very move—a move that removes sexuality from political economy through appeals to morality—that is, and has long been, extremely convenient for capitalism. It means that certain tricky questions can be taken off the table, and especially those regarding the close alignments between normative sexuality and prevailing economic logics. If the inside of a woman's body can never be thought of as a workplace, for instance, then it is easy to conclude that the labor of childbirth is not really "labor" at all. Similarly, if we protest against paid sex on the grounds that sexual exploitation for profit can never be tolerated, then the possibility that capitalism routinely appropriates *unpaid* sexual labor for profit can simply slide from view.

The overarching purpose of this book is to challenge these assumptions. More specifically, it aims to excavate and contest how sexuality has come to be regarded not only as distinct from political economy but as antithetical to it. Such an agenda is especially significant given that the field of inquiry devoted to the study of global capitalism, international political economy (IPE), is itself structured by the economy/sexuality dichotomy. As decades of feminist critique have shown, IPE's disciplinary legacies are not ones of embodiment, intimacy, and desire.[3] Historically, orthodox IPE was founded on the twin pillars of states and markets—two imaginary spheres that were understood to touch and, at times, collide but that remained clearly separable both from each other and from the mess and matter of everyday life.[4] Critical IPE has done much to tackle these dualisms and abstractions, exploring instead how states and markets are socially embedded and how it is in everyday life that the oppressions and struggles of global capitalism play out.[5] Yet critical IPE, too, remains in some important respects disembodied—both in rendering invisible actually existing human beings and in neglecting embodied social hierarchies such as gender, race, and sexuality.[6] Certainly, work on sexuality exists, but it is nevertheless regarded as marginal at best, and irrelevant at worst, in the vast majority of IPE scholarship.

Conversely, the prevailing field in sexuality studies, queer theory, has often come uncoupled from debates about global capitalism. As Judith Butler notes, queer theory is frequently consigned to the realm of the "merely cultural": as only interested in, and applicable to, "matters of cultural recognition" rather than those of political economy.[7] This move enables sexuality to be presented as both non-material and immaterial (i.e., as neither bound up with, nor relevant to the study of, economic structures). Although Butler argues against this depiction of queer theory, contending instead that it potentially has a great deal to say about material (in)justice, it is also the case that many queer scholars have overlooked—and many continue to overlook—exactly these kinds of questions. This is not least because queer theory has had a rather tetchy relationship with Marxism, with the former accusing the latter of erasing sexuality and the latter reproaching the former for ignoring materiality, and this has all too often played out as a series of dogged battles over meta-theory, the nature of social "reality," and the so-called material-discursive divide.[8]

Thus, rather than challenging the division between the economic and the sexual, both IPE and queer theory have often reinforced the sense that this division is somehow natural and neutral as opposed to contingent and contestable. This lack of engagement between the two fields matters very much, for it nurtures the illusion that the deployment of sexuality is anomalous, not endemic, to capitalism, and that it is on the outside of capitalism that the inside of women's bodies can naturally be found.

This is, of course, not to claim that there are no IPE scholars who engage with sexuality or no queer scholars who are interested in capitalism, for neither of these things are true.[9] Yet, despite the empirical presence of queer theory in political economy, and vice versa, sexuality is often placed on the constitutive outside of IPE. This is a function of disciplinary histories, for IPE was founded on a series of binaries and oppositions that continue to inform contemporary debates. These include the dualisms of states and markets, politics and economics, and national and international—all of which are treated as endogenous to IPE—as well as the boundaries that constitute the inside and outside of the field itself. Particularly important has been the separation between the public sphere (e.g., of government and work) and the private sphere (e.g., of household and family)—a move that has allowed intimate and domestic life to be bracketed off and treated as external to the discipline.[10] Associated with private/personal space in this way, sexuality has not even been written out of IPE since it was never written in to start with. The picture for queer theory is slightly different, for a major impetus has been to dismantle conceptual binaries and disciplinary boundaries rather than to maintain them. However, queer theory's own heritages (including its strong tradition in literary and cultural criticism) mean that it, too, has frequently replicated the economy/sexuality dichotomy. Thus, although intersections between queer theory and political economy do exist, the respective fields could nevertheless gain a great deal from closer dialogue with each other—and a central task of this book is to foster exactly this kind of engagement.[11]

This agenda is particularly warranted given that the economy/sexuality dichotomy does not just play out in disciplinary practice but, as the book examines, it is woven into the fabric of capitalism itself. Feminist scholars have illuminated how public space has been historically constituted (and privileged) as the "masculine" sphere of economic production, whereas private space has been constructed (and devalued) in terms of the "feminine" realm of social reproduction.[12] As Silvia Federici writes, capitalism has needed the creation, and concealment, of a sexual division of labor that is "above all a power-relation, a division within the workforce, while being an immense boost to capitalist accumulation."[13] This book focuses in on the *sexual* element of this equation by exploring how capitalist development has been sexual in the dual sense, for it has relied not only on the sexual division of labor but also on the cultivation and suppression of sexuality. Indeed, as the book interrogates, sexuality has played a crucial role in demarcating the public from the private, the productive from the reproductive, and the economic from the intimate. Thus, while this volume aims to bring queer theory more into conversation with political economy, it does so by drawing on and contributing toward the long-established tradition of feminist political economy—a project that is sometimes sidelined in IPE and largely ignored in queer theory, and without which no story of capitalism's sexual relations could be told.

In order to investigate these themes, the book takes up commercial sex as a site of particular relevance to the study of capitalism and sexuality. Indeed, there is arguably no other case in which the economy/sexuality dichotomy is both more apparent and more contested, even if debates are not explicitly articulated as such. Although sex work has received scant attention in queer theory,[14] it has attracted considerable interest in feminist scholarship and activism. For some, commercial sex is synonymous with sexual exploitation because it entails the sale and purchase of women's bodies and, hence, of their sexual selfhood. It is for this reason that abolitionist feminists call for the sex industry to be tolerated no longer, either legally or culturally.[15] For others, commercial sex can constitute a terrain of agency, subversion, and even radical politics. Some sex-positive feminists, for instance, have argued that sex work represents not a violation of bodily integrity but a reflection of an individual's property in their own body.[16] Such accounts are underpinned by the economy/sexuality dichotomy in that commercial sex is understood in terms of oppression or liberation that is first and foremost sexual rather than economic in nature.[17] Yet the emphasis on the sexual element of commercial sex has also been disputed, not least by sex workers themselves in demanding that their sexual labor be accepted as legitimate work, thereby rejecting conventional separations between sex and work and, hence, between sexuality and economy.[18]

This book strongly supports calls by sex workers to recognize and decriminalize their sexual labor but, in so doing, it follows the lead of Juno Mac and Molly Smith in refusing to "prioritize discussion on whether the sex industry, or even sex itself, is intrinsically good or bad."[19] Nor does it engage in philosophical or political deliberation about the essential "truth" of sex or sex work. As intuitively appealing as such debates are, their strong tendency is to divert attention away from the material conditions under which sex workers labor and so to produce distracting and polarizing effects that, ultimately, capitalism thrives on. As Michel Foucault brings to light, all of the "garrulous attention which has us in a stew over sexuality," and especially the quest for its underlying truth, can be understood as an apparatus of modern power.[20] Indeed, it is precisely this "garrulous attention" that the book seeks to interrogate, in particular by considering how the politicization of sexuality as a moral issue both requires and enables its depoliticization as an economic one. While it was a particularly high-profile example that garnered widespread interest internationally, the furor over Amnesty International's support for the decriminalization of commercial sex was underpropped by moralizing discourses that were neither distinctive nor new. Indeed, as the book will explore, the sex/work split has been constituted as much through the proliferation of discourses of sex work as it has been through the censoring of sex work, with these apparently incongruous energies working together to foster the *illusion* that sex work is fundamentally different from other intimate and economic relations. As we shall see, capitalism needs and allows sex work to be constructed as an aberration in order to naturalize the appropriation of unpaid sexual labor that takes place primarily, if not exclusively, via the institution of marriage. The case of sex work is thus much more than just an illustrative example of the economy/sexuality dichotomy in motion, for it is instead a central mechanism through which this dichotomy has been forged.

It is vital to stress, therefore, that the economy/sexuality dichotomy is not a simple one, for capitalism does not *either* deliver sexuality to the market *or* insist on a distance between them. Rather, the argument of this book is that this dichotomy obscures how the two are in fact entwined. Commercial sex may be condemned and often criminalized, but it also represents the logical extension of capitalist social relations in which all aspects of life are increasingly defined in terms of market rationalities. Accordingly, the book is less interested in the identification of a single systemic logic and more with the possibility of frictions, incongruities, and what Foucault calls "unstable mixtures."[21] Indeed, it is because of these deep ambiguities that sex work has become an object of such intense moral focus, for it has come to be constructed as neither "real" sex nor "real" work even as debates insist that it is either "really" sex or "really" work. Thus, the book seeks to overcome some of the dualisms that exist within feminism itself regarding the relationship between the economic and the sexual, and that continue to polarize debates about commercial sex. Rather than contending that the economic and sexual realms either comfortably coexist or must not adulterate each other, the book sets out to uncover and understand how sexuality is positioned within capitalism while simultaneously being positioned against it.

In so doing, the volume contributes both to IPE scholarship on capitalism and to queer and feminist scholarship on sexuality, first, by developing and advancing the still-burgeoning field of queer political economy; second, by demonstrating how capitalist social relations are always already sexual relations; and, third, by exploring how economy and sexuality have come to be constructed as not only different but opposite realms. As part of this agenda, the book also speaks directly to the field of sex work studies by placing sex work at the crux of its analysis. While there is a dearth of literature on queer theory and commercial sex, some scholars have begun to rectify this by asking, for instance, what it means to "be queer in" sex work in order to center non-normative sexualities in the contemporary sex industry, and by considering what it means to "do queer to" sex work in order to examine the interconnections between commercial sex and heteronormative power relations.[22] Yet queer accounts of sex work have, on the whole, treated commercial sex as a "merely cultural" issue rather than as a matter for the theory and practice of political economy.[23] The book thus aims to move this literature forward by highlighting the need for critical scholarship not only to think queerly about sex work but also to situate this within wider critiques of capitalism—including through mutually beneficial engagement with feminist political economy.[24] By investigating the constitution and effects of economy/sexuality and sex/work as interrelated dualisms, the book opens up new space for critical inquiry into the intersections, tensions, contradictions, and connections that characterize capitalism's relationship with sexuality.

HISTORICIZING CAPITALISM AND SEXUALITY

For the reasons outlined, capitalism's sexual relations are, above all, a question of power, and so this book is, above all, a political book. It is important to be upfront, therefore, that this study is not situated within the discipline of history, nor is it a history book. Nevertheless, the guiding methodology for the research is historical and, more precisely, genealogical in approach. Genealogy is not conventionally "political" in the sense that it does not routinely form part of the repertoire of those fields to claim political analysis as their domain (political science, international relations, and

IPE).[25] Yet, as Laura Jenkins compellingly argues, genealogy is, at heart, a politicizing endeavor that can be used to slacken, subvert, and sabotage perspectives and power relations that are otherwise taken for granted.[26] It is, then, a self-consciously political method of inquiry, even if it is not always acknowledged to be so.

In order to describe and reflect on the research undertaken for this book, it is helpful to set out what genealogy does and does not entail as a methodology. Specifically, genealogy is a mode of critique that charts the emergence of contemporary power relations to expose how they do not (and never did) rest on stable foundations but instead are (and always were) contingent. As such, genealogy is neither the history of politics nor the politics of history but instead seeks to historicize in order to politicize—that is, "to locate the historical conditions that allow us to think, speak, and act as we do now."[27] Most closely associated with Foucault, genealogical studies are "gray, meticulous, and patiently documentary"[28] but they are not "positivistic returns to a form of science that is more attentive and more accurate."[29] On the contrary, claims to objective truths—including appeals to scientific legitimacy—are exactly what genealogy sets out to investigate. Consequently, genealogy is not fastened to a specific set of procedures or techniques but is best understood as characterizing those forms of inquiry that use the past to critique the contemporary moment ("the history of the present"[30]).

In practicing historicization, genealogy resists rather than pursues the kind of all-embracing historical project where the identification of "root or singular causes"[31] is the stated or unstated goal. Accordingly, this book does not attempt to lay bare the causal processes through which history unfolds as a "unified developing totality"[32] or to offer a "linear narrative that reveals our progressive drive towards enlightenment."[33] Nor do I approach either capitalism or sexuality as a "pregiven, material reality"[34] that determines or causes the other. Instead, I am interested in the messy entanglements through which capitalism and sexuality constitute each other, and I do so by offering *a* history that is necessarily partial and specific. A key limitation of the research, therefore, is that it does not (intend to) provide *the* history of capitalism, sexuality, or sex work writ large. Here I draw inspiration from other genealogical studies such as Jemima Repo's *The Biopolitics of Gender*, which offers a highly specific account of the "birth" of gender identity in the clinic in postwar America rather than a history of gender in general.[35] Just as the titles of Foucault's *The History of Sexuality* and Repo's *The Biopolitics of Gender* rather teasingly imply all-encompassing histories and then go on to dismantle exactly this kind of agenda, the title of this book, *Capitalism's Sexual History,* is also meant in this spirit.[36] To openly acknowledge the incomplete and bounded nature of the research is not to abandon commitments to scholarly rigor but, quite the opposite, is to recognize—as both queer and feminist scholars urge us to do[37]—that being partial (in both senses of the word) is the "precondition of a politically engaged critique."[38] To embrace specificity can be an act of politicization, since it exposes not only how there is never just one perspective but also how the pretense of singularity is "always intensely political."[39]

The book therefore does not try to paint a general picture of capitalist development but instead chronicles a particular (and, perhaps, peculiar) sexual history: that of the British. I should immediately note that, in choosing a major European nation as the primary site of my study, I am keenly aware of the acute danger of further buttressing the systematic eurocentrism that bedevils both IPE and queer theory. It is for this reason that the feminist literature on global sexual economies has rightly concentrated on sex workers in and from the Global South so as to challenge the eurocentrism of Western colonial imaginaries.[40] Comparatively little attention has been devoted to the expansion and diversification of the sex trade in the postindustrial economies of the Global North,[41] and understandably so. Yet, at times, scholarship on gender and sexuality may reinforce such imaginaries even as it works to disrupt them.[42] The literature on sex tourism and sex trafficking, for instance, can sometimes construct women in the Global South as "people of the body,"[43] which perpetuates the mind/body dualism on which the "fantasy"[44] of white Western rationality is built. Seen in this light, it becomes important not only to recognize the agency of sex workers in and from postcolonial contexts[45] but also to critique the discourses that map sexual economies onto particular terrains (and bodies) and not others. Indeed, as the book will consider at various junctures, anti-immigration agendas are positively reliant on such discourses. Britain is a prime example of this, for the othering of migrant workers is caught up with the "fetishization"[46] of migrant women's bodies and this has, in turn, proved highly expedient for capitalism.

A further limitation of the book is that it tells the story of Britain through that of England specifically; it does so because, although "Britishness is not one thing and has never been one thing,"[47] it has nevertheless been historically constituted through conflations with both Englishness and whiteness.[48] There is some controversy as to whether England was the birthplace of capitalism: while some claim that "without English capitalism there would probably have been no capitalist system of any kind,"[49] others justifiably contest the eurocentrism of such accounts by tracing the ancestries of Western modernity (the supposed "European miracle") to non-European societies.[50] Yet there can be little doubt that England performed a leading part in establishing capitalism's dominance globally, not only because of the Industrial Revolution but also because of the sheer enormity of the British Empire (such that, at its height, the sun was said never to set upon it). The tale of England's political, economic, and cultural ascendancy and subsequent decline has been told any number of times before,[51] and so I will not re-rehearse that here. Instead, the book focuses on the very particular story of sexuality as one that, as discussed, has attracted a great deal of interest in queer theory but has largely been discounted in IPE, including vis-à-vis the British case.[52] By no stretch of the imagination is the economy/sexuality dichotomy quintessentially British—as illustrated by the open letter to Amnesty International mentioned earlier—but Britain's history is nevertheless implicated directly in its emergence, and it is this story that the book seeks to recount.

In keeping with the genealogical orientation of the research, I offer a "history of the discourses"[53] of sexuality in Britain to render visible how—as much as the economy/sexuality dichotomy might appear to be a natural fact and so beyond dispute—it has instead been carved out of history. It is worth reiterating that the research does not proceed from the positivist premise that the purpose and proper practice of social inquiry is to discover and record the nature of social reality by collecting data on, and reporting findings about, that nature ("The truth about sex work in Britain is . . . ").[54] Instead, I conceive of reality as constituted in and through discourses as "practices that systematically form the objects of which they speak."[55] I understand discourses not as neutral descriptors of exogenous forces that lie underneath social relations (e.g., objective interests) but as mutually constitutive of the power relations that govern what can and cannot be thought, said, and done in particular social contexts.[56] I therefore share Laura Shepherd's view that there is "nothing more fundamental to politics than the construction of the conceptual apparatus that structures knowledge in any given society"; indeed, by analyzing systems of truth and knowledge production, "we are essentially examining the production of possibility."[57]

The analysis that follows draws from extensive original research into a wide variety of primary sources, including policy, legal, medical, psychiatric, religious, literary, philosophical, and journalistic texts, as well as theoretical and historical studies by queer, feminist, and political economy scholars.[58] The primary sources were curated through a three-year process of in-depth archival research into multiple online repositories such as the National Archives, Hansard, and the British Newspaper Archive. I chose to consult a diverse range of sources (rather than, say, policy documents alone) as this approach was most consistent with my genealogical interest in the "massive, circulating, and discontinuous forms"[59] that meaning production can take. Indeed, I was surprised and fascinated by the sheer eccentricity of constructions of sex work that would, at times, appear in discursive sites that might otherwise seem completely unrelated. Yet, if discourses comprise "a series of discontinuous segments whose tactical function is neither uniform nor stable,"[60] then their articulation in divergent sites can itself be read as evidence that they are internal rather than incidental to the exercise of modern power under capitalism. Sadly, it is not feasible to reproduce text from the vast bulk of the materials consulted, so I have selected quotations that I believe best exemplify the multiform ways in which commercial sex has been discursively constructed in Britain over time. In quoting these documents, my intention is not to disregard the politico-economic context in which such texts are situated but, on the contrary, to bring together "text" and "context" through the analysis of discourse.[61] Thus, rather than conceiving of discourses in terms of individualistic intentionalism, I approach individuals, intentions, ideas, and institutions as co-constitutive of the "wider discursive terrain"[62] in which they are situated.

THE BOOK AHEAD

At the start of this Introduction, I asked what capitalism has to do with sexuality, and this is the central research question that animates the book as a whole. The first chapter addresses this question theoretically by developing a queer political economy lens to conceptualize capitalism's sexual relations. Arguing that queer political economy is best approached as a historicizing endeavor, the chapter combines insights from two historical projects that are seldom read alongside each other—Michel Foucault's *The History of Sexuality*[63] and Silvia Federici's *Caliban and the Witch*—to offer a new framework for the study of sexuality in/and political economy. By mapping the manifold and shifting ways in which sexuality has been produced and repressed, we can unearth how capitalism profits not only from the creation of the economy/sexuality dichotomy but also from its mystification.

The remaining four chapters attend to these themes empirically through analysis of the history of sex work in Britain, with the structure and argument of each chapter organized around the charting of multifarious historical threads in line with my genealogical approach. Chapter 2 begins this journey in medieval[64] England by showing how the sexual division of labor already rested on distinctions between legitimate and illegitimate sex. Charting the rise of capitalism in early modern England, the chapter explores how such distinctions were redefined by a new dichotomy—that between sex and work—that made possible the reconfiguration of the sexual division of labor into an instrument for capitalist appropriation. Chapter 3 turns to the Victorian period to consider the making of commercial sex into the "great social evil" of the modern age, and how the proliferation of discourses on sex work helped to naturalize the public/private split that underpinned the sexual division of labor. Chapter 4 examines how the economy/sexuality dichotomy was further normalized in the twentieth century—even as the private sphere was increasingly governed by market logics—and how sex work acted as the pivot on which this dichotomy hinged. Chapter 5 considers the evolutions and effects of these discursive legacies in the twenty-first century. It explores how the pathologization and criminalization of commercial sex is intertwined with the ongoing privatization of social reproduction and, with it, the privatization of wealth that continues apace under neoliberal capitalism.

The book concludes by reflecting on how queer, feminist, and leftist politics might oppose the economy/sexuality dichotomy in solidarity with the sex workers' movement, since sex workers' struggles cannot be detached from wider collective struggles against the extraction of unpaid sexual labor and the denigration of feminized work. Indeed, in refusing to accept that sex and work are innately antithetical, the sex workers' movement exposes how capitalism "makes use"[65] of sexuality not as an aberration or abomination but as a matter of course, just as it has done for centuries.

Before proceeding, I want to make a few final points. First, the book hopes to be of use and interest to other scholars seeking to develop the field of queer political economy but in no way does it claim or aspire to represent "the" queer political economy perspective or approach. Queer theory is a terrain, not a template, and so (to quote Jasbir Puar) "there is no exact recipe for a queer endeavor, no a priori system that taxonomizes the linkages, disruptions, and contradictions into a tidy vessel."[66] For example, my interest in "unstable mixtures" might be understood as compatible with Cynthia Weber's deployment of "queer logics" (i.e., plural logics of and/or) to expose and contest either/or dualisms such as order/anarchy and normal/perverse[67] (and to which we might add economy/sexuality and sex/work). Yet, as I will outline in due course, my analysis also differs from queer accounts such as Weber's in that it is not motivated by an ontological commitment to queerness as fluidity, whether or not this refers to fluid identities or the fluidity of identity *tout court*. This is not to discount the indispensable insights of such work but rather to recognize that queer theory's "celebrated energies of motility and resignification" can also be mobilized differently.[68] In particular, and following Lisa Downing and Robert Gillett, I approach queer inquiry not as the study of fluidity but as a historical project[69] and, as noted earlier, this takes the form of a "history of the discourses" of sexuality in this volume. As my historical framework is set out in the next chapter, suffice it to say that it is meant to contribute to the development of queer political economy as a field of *debate* rather than to provide a blueprint for a discrete position called "queer political economy."[70]

Second, the book does not conflate the history of sexuality with the history of homosexuality, although queer theory has centered stories of same-sex desire to counter how such desire has been discarded from and throughout history.[71] While not wishing to undermine this crucial project in any way, I agree with Cathy J. Cohen that it is also beneficial for queer (and feminist) scholarship to consider the "varying degrees and multiple sites of power distributed within all categories of sexuality, including the normative category of heterosexuality."[72] If homosexuality has been figured as both deviant and normal,[73] then so have particular configurations of heterosexuality been marked not only as natural and privileged but also as abnormal and immoral.[74] Nor should it be forgotten that the female reproductive body has long acted as an archetype for other constructions of the monstrous in Western discourse.[75] As will be discussed at various points in the book, the repression and production of homosexuality has been intimately connected to the repression and production of sex work, even if these linkages have been hidden from view. This discursive split between homosexuality and sex work continues today, hence why feminist theory often neglects the former and queer theory the latter.[76] The book seeks to remedy this by showing how the histories of sex work, sexuality, and the sexual division of labor are indivisibly entangled, and how this has involved *both* the specific targeting of women's bodies[77] for surveillance and control (which queer theory could do more to confront) *and* the multiplication of and differentiation between sexualities (which, likewise, feminist political economy could do more to confront). Indeed, the regulation of sex work has been integral to the naturalization of gender difference, to the normalization of particular expressions of heterosexual desire, and to the reproduction of the heteronormative family on which capitalism continues to depend.[78]

Lastly, a note on terminology. As Foucault was well aware, to write about discourses of sexuality is inevitably to participate in their production and not just their analysis. Choosing the "right" words can therefore be a fraught and, frankly, problematic process—especially when certain words are, to modern ears, downright offensive (e.g., "whore," "sodomite"). Yet the aim of this book is not to use modern-day morality to judge the past but, in contrast, to use the past to denaturalize modern-day morality. For example, medieval writers referred not to "sex workers" or "prostitutes" but to "whores" and "common women" and, while these older terms and concepts may seem distasteful today, I use them to demonstrate how the logics they represent cannot be assumed to have simply fallen away. Although the verb "prostitute" began to be used in English around 1530 and the label "sex worker" was coined in the 1980s,[79] this does not mean that the concept of whoredom vanished (and women can still find themselves being identified as "whores").[80] Thus, to insist on the exclusive use of contemporary, politically acceptable language runs the risk not only of anachronism but of losing sight of the very resonances and lineages that ought to be investigated.

Equally, though, to use only historically precise terms throws up problems of its own. This is not least because, by eschewing modern-day concepts, we can conjure up an image of the past that is entirely distant and unfamiliar—and yet the present has been forged out of the past. Sex was certainly sold in the Middle Ages, even if the people who did so were not called "sex workers," and even if whoredom included other forms of illicit sex.[81] To insist on purity of terminology (e.g., by refusing to refer to medieval sex workers as anything other than whores or, more accurately still, *meretrices*) can create the misleading impression of essential difference between then and now, thereby ascribing false unity and coherence to discourses that were (and are) contested. Moreover, the historian Ruth Mazo Karras cautions that "if we analyze all our modern categories out of existence, we are left without a language to talk about the past."[82] For example, Jemima Repo observes that it was not until the twentieth century that "gender" was habitually used to name "the sexual order of things," and so she recommends that feminists use terms such as "sex" and "sexual difference" instead.[83] Yet, given that the concept of sexual difference—as in two innately different, or opposite, sexes—can itself be read as a modern invention,[84] it is arguably no less of an instrument of modern power than is gender. In order to get around these issues—if somewhat imperfectly— I use a combination of contemporary terms and older ones (depending on the time period) throughout the book. When talking about medieval England, for instance, I refer to "sex workers" to describe people who sold sex while also discussing the concept of "whoredom"; likewise, I use both "sex worker" and "prostitute" when moving into the early modern period. This is consistent with my overall approach of tracing "the erratic and discontinuous process whereby the past became the present"[85] to politicize how capitalism's history is, at one and the same time, a history of sexuality.

CHAPTER 1

Queer Political Economy

Once again we get another postcard from the Topsy-Turvy land where current liberal intellectual life resides . . . Identity politics, fed with weak, nebulous ideas by the likes of Foucault and Butler, has killed opposition to real concentrated power—stone dead . . . I despair whenever I am reminded of the current direction intellectual life has taken.

This is an extract from a comment left by a fellow academic on a blog post I had written about queer theory. I get his point. It captures very well how queer theory is often treated as a frivolous indulgence rather than as relevant to "real" issues of capitalist power relations. And it is indeed the case that queer scholars have often remained silent on matters of political economy to the extent that, for some, it is high time to go post-queer. In this chapter I tackle such claims head on. Noting that the question of post-queer is an awkward one for international political economy (IPE) (since a field cannot move on from something that it never moved through), I argue that queer theory has much to offer the study of global capitalism. Yet queer scholars also need to engage more directly with feminist political economy so as to learn from, and contribute toward, this longstanding tradition. In order to draw out and build on these intersections, I turn to the work of Michel Foucault and Silvia Federici, whose projects are widely regarded as landmarks in queer theory and feminist political economy respectively. By bringing these projects together, we can assemble a queer political economy that interrogates both the linkages and the separations between the economic and sexual spheres, and that does so in explicitly historicizing and feminist terms.

Capitalism's Sexual History. Nicola J. Smith, Oxford University Press (2020). © Oxford University Press.
DOI: 10.1093/oso/9780197530276.001.0001.

Is queer history? For a number of commentators, it ought to be. In *After Queer Theory: The Limits of Sexual Politics*, James Penney contends that queer theory has "run its course, its project made obsolete by the full elaboration of its own logic." Queer approaches, he suggests, are "intellectually dead discourses" due to their failure to articulate "any program of thoroughgoing social change."[1] Similarly, in *Post-Queer Politics*, David V. Ruffolo argues that queer theory's "incessant investment in identity politics" means that it has "reached a political peak." He therefore highlights the need to move beyond queer in order to overcome its intellectual and political limitations.[2] Such claims are not new but form part of queer's own history. As Michael O'Rourke notes, queer studies has repeatedly been dismissed as "always already dead, buried, over, finished . . . Almost since it began we have been hearing about the death(s) of Queer Theory."[3]

In the field of IPE, the question of post-queer is especially pertinent for, as Sara Ahmed writes, proclamations that we are "over" certain forms of critique "create the impression that we are over what is being critiqued."[4] To go post-queer implies having first gone queer: it suggests that queer theory's key contributions have been recognized, responded to, and folded into a particular field of inquiry. Yet in IPE queer theory has been, and for the most part remains, conspicuous by its absence.[5] In part, this is because IPE has traditionally focused on the "upper circuits" of capitalist relations such as trade and investment flows rather than the "lower circuits" such as domestic labor and migration.[6] But, as discussed in the Introduction, it is also due to an ongoing tendency to position intimate and sexual relations on the outside rather than the inside of global capitalism and, hence, beyond the proper analysis of IPE. Queer theory is not the stuff of textbooks, core modules, and mainstream journals in IPE, and this both reflects and sustains a wider lack of interest in sexuality. It is not possible, then, for IPE to be over queer theory, as it has never been under it in the first place.

This oversight is problematic both intellectually and politically. Simply put, if IPE is to analyze and contest the structural hierarchies of global capitalism, then it cannot afford to overlook what Judith Butler has termed the "sexual order of political economy."[7] This means doing justice to—and not ignoring—the contributions of queer theory as the predominant (if not the only) field devoted to the study of sexuality.[8] Although queer theory is not exclusively concerned with sexuality—and it is by no means a synonym for lesbian and gay studies[9]—sexuality is nevertheless an enduring preoccupation. One of queer theory's major contributions has been to challenge dominant assumptions that sexuality is somehow natural, whether rooted in biology or individual psychology. Queer scholarship has highlighted that sexuality is not a "thing" that lies beyond or below social relations, quietly doing its work and untroubled by power. Instead, sexuality is deeply implicated in the constitution of modern power and warrants analysis accordingly.[10]

Nor, for that matter, can queer theory afford to neglect political economy. Indeed, a major charge made against queer theory in post-queer accounts is precisely that it fails to advance a political economy agenda. Penney, for instance, states that "sexual politics must be tied essentially and decisively to an analysis of basic economic conditions" and that queer studies, in contrast, has been "alarmingly distanced from the critique of capitalism." More than this, queer theory is a "symptom of capitalist social relations" due to its narrow focus on the subversion of identity.[11] Likewise, Ruffolo contends that queer theory's preoccupation with subjectivity and the queer/heteronormative dichotomy are "unproductive considering the contemporary complexities of neoliberal capitalism and globalization," hence the need for post-queer theorizing.[12]

Such critiques are not without foundation, for identity is indeed a central concern for many queer scholars. Among other agendas, they have explored how sexual and/or gender identities are constructed as monolithic and static rather than as multifaceted and fluid. In so doing, they have conceptualized queerness as "the messiness of identity, the fact that desire and thus desiring subjects cannot be placed into discrete identity categories."[13] Indeed, Cynthia Weber suggests that one "cannot claim to be doing queer work" if one has "no genuine interest in those who refuse/fail to signify monolithically in terms of sexes, genders, and sexualities."[14] Scholarship in this vein has been immensely valuable in challenging the fixity and duality of social categories, thereby disturbing the epistemological and methodological foundations of a great deal of social research.[15] Yet some have questioned whether, despite the explicit refusal of fixed identities, an implicit binary is reproduced in accounts that define "queer" subjectivities in opposition to "straight" ones, and that this may actually essentialize rather than destabilize difference.[16]

It is by no means the case, however, that queer is synonymous with the fluidity of identity.[17] On the contrary: what constitutes the proper domain of queer inquiry is itself highly fluid. Despite its name, queer theory is not a single theory or approach but rather represents an ever-shifting terrain of debate. It is significant that—when Eve Kosofsky Sedgwick famously described queer as an "open mesh of possibilities, overlaps, dissonances and resonances, lapses and excesses of meaning"—she added that this was only "one of the things" to which queer can refer and that some of the "most exciting" queer work was not pursuing this agenda.[18] Queerness has variously been read as performativity, anti-normativity, abjection, disability, death, unreason, failure, kinship, and futurity, to name just a few examples.[19] Queer theory, therefore, has no "fixed referent"[20] but rather comprises multitudinous (and sometimes conflicting) traditions. Indeed, as Kath Browne and Catherine J. Nash point out, the policing of queer boundaries is at odds with commitments to queerness as fluid and manifold.[21] It is for this reason that queer theory is best understood as a verb rather than a noun,[22] for queer *theorizing* can include "any form of research positioned within conceptual frameworks that highlight the instability of taken-for-granted meanings and resulting power relations."[23]

Nor is queer theory necessarily incompatible with political economy, especially given its multiple trajectories (it is, after all, a vast field that reaches across the humanities and social sciences). To be sure, the history of queer is not one in which debates about global capitalism have dominated. Yet, over recent years, queer scholars and activists have been taking up what Lisa Duggan and Richard Kim term a "new queer agenda." This places economic and social justice at the heart of the fight for sexual justice, so that sexual struggles are explicitly defined as socioeconomic struggles, and vice versa.[24] Such a project challenges the partitioning off of sexuality from so-called political economy issues such as low and unpaid labor, precarious employment, access to welfare services, homelessness, incarceration, and health care. Instead, sexuality is seen to intersect with other deep structural inequalities such as gender, race, class, dis/ability, and territory to produce poverty, violence, and discrimination worldwide.[25] For example, Duggan is strongly critical of the equal marriage agenda on the grounds that it reduces queer politics to the campaign for formal, legal rights rather than for economic and social justice. This diverts attention and resources away from struggles against poverty, inequality, and material oppression— issues that impact significantly on queer communities and yet have come to be defined as something other than "queer concerns."[26]

MATTERS OF LIFE AND DEATH

Increasingly, then, queer scholars are making connections between political economy and sexuality, arguing that just as global capitalism cannot be understood without reference to the sexual sphere, then so must sexuality be expanded to include the analysis of capitalist power relations. Such connections are often articulated in terms of a more open engagement with Marxist theory and even as marking the emergence of "queer

Marxism."[27] Yet they also owe a clear debt to long histories of scholarship in feminist political economy—a body of research that is ostensibly overlooked in queer theory, although queer/feminist intersections in political economy have long existed via the work of J. K. Gibson-Graham, V. Spike Peterson, and Rosemary Hennessy, among others.[28] For, although much leftist social theory has treated questions of sexuality as "footnotes" rather than "starting points,"[29] it is precisely the relations between gender, sexuality, and capitalism that, for decades, feminist political economists have taken as their point of departure. As Judith Butler acknowledges, socialist feminists of the 1970s and 1980s "sought to establish the sphere of sexual reproduction as part of the material conditions of life, a proper and constitutive feature of political economy." In so doing, they highlighted the importance of the regulation of sexuality in the reproduction of gender norms and the sexual division of labor, so that sexuality was understood as "systematically tied to the mode of production" rather than as somehow standing apart.[30]

Feminist political economists have taken this agenda forward by exploring how gender and sexuality are internal to the mechanics of global capitalism.[31] As part of this project, they have explored how capitalist relations are made possible by the sexual division of labor—a division that is reflected most transparently in persistent wage inequalities between women and men, and that is further exacerbated by the shift toward low-paid, temporary, part-time, and flexible work across the world due to processes of neoliberal capitalist restructuring.[32] Yet such developments in the public sphere of formal, paid work are only part of the story, for feminists also insist that the functioning of the "productive economy" is in itself dependent on that of the "reproductive economy."[33] By this they mean that systems of regulated production and exchange are sustained by unpaid and informal labor—such as domestic, caring, and sexual labor—so that economic production forms part of broader and deeper processes of social reproduction. Social reproduction refers to the practices and processes that are involved in the production of people and populations over time and that unfold at all levels of social existence, from the minutiae of everyday life to the large-scale structures of global political economy.[34] Important to this is an emphasis on sexual reproduction in (literally) re/making human life, but the term also encompasses the reproduction of the labor force and of the "institutions, processes, and social relations associated with the creation and maintenance of communities—and, upon which, ultimately all production and exchange rests."[35]

Although feminists contend that economic production is both part of, and contingent on, social reproduction, they also interrogate how the latter is treated as separable from the former in a move that enables it to be routinely devalued. Indeed, as Nancy Fraser puts it, this hierarchical split between the productive and reproductive economies is "a defining structure of capitalist society and a deep source of the gender asymmetries hard-wired in it."[36] A longstanding political project for feminist scholars and activists is therefore to reveal how reproductive labor is not counted as "labor" at all. As Silvia Federici has argued,

> We must admit that capital has been very successful in hiding our work . . . By denying housework a wage and transforming it into an act of love, capital has killed many birds with one stone . . . To say that we want wages for housework is to expose the fact that housework is already money for capital, that capital has made and makes money out of our cooking, smiling, fucking.[37]

A central element of this agenda has been to challenge how reproductive labor is devalued through its naturalization as "women's work"[38] and in its association with the private, domesticated sphere. Economic production, in contrast, is valorized as part of the public and masculine world of paid and "proper" work.[39] An important feminist priority, therefore, is to achieve recognition not only for the value of socially reproductive labor but also for its very existence—both as the precondition for human life and as the process through which such life is sustained. At the same time, however, feminists are highly critical of the symbolic and material harms that are associated with socially reproductive labor (or, more accurately, with the failure to count such labor as labor). For example, Shirin Rai, Catherine Hoskyns, and Dania Thomas employ the concept of depletion to describe the hidden costs of social reproduction for those who disproportionately shoulder its burden—that is, the deterioration that occurs when there is "a critical gap between the outflows—domestic, affective, and reproductive—and the inflows that sustain their health and wellbeing." This wearing down of embodied human lives is a gendered problem not only because women primarily bear the brunt of it but also because it arises directly out of the denigration of feminized labor.[40] Social reproduction is thus a question of sexual justice that is both material and discursive, with its erasure in discourse yielding substantive material effects. For, as Federici writes, one of the most powerful capitalist ruses is to render housework non-work and domestic laborers as non-laborers: "We are seen as nagging bitches, not workers in struggle."[41]

While the contributions of feminist political economy are, on the whole, ignored in queer accounts,[42] the question of reproduction has nevertheless been taken up as pivotal by queer scholars. The so-called anti-social turn[43] in queer theory might itself be described as an open challenge to capitalist demands for cooking and smiling, but it is not one that sits easily with feminist theories of social reproduction. Certainly both traditions regard reproduction as a site of oppression, but they nevertheless represent different (and, at times, opposing) intellectual and political agendas. For, while social reproduction denotes the maintenance and renewal of social relations, it is not life but death that acts as the key point of departure for queer anti-social thought. It is important to note here that same-sex sexuality has long been positioned in discourse as opposed to "natural" reproduction and thus to life itself,[44] the rectum of the homosexual a "grave," as Leo Bersani so viscerally puts it.[45] Particularly prominent in this vein is the work of Lee Edelman, who contends that it is precisely the unquestioning acceptance of the value of "reproductive futurism" that secures the "absolute privilege of heteronormativity." Instead, he advances a queer critique that actively opposes futurity by embracing the death drive: "what is queerest about us, queerest within us, and queerest despite us is this willingness to insist intransitively—to insist that the future stop here."[46] In contrast to calls from feminist political economists to recognize and redistribute reproduction, Edelman therefore calls for its rejection. This queer refusal is exemplified in his oft-cited call to arms to

> Fuck the social order and the Child in whose name we're collectively terrorized; fuck Annie; fuck the waif from *Les Mis*; fuck the poor, innocent kid on the Net; fuck Laws both with capital ls and with small; fuck the whole network of Symbolic relations and the future that serves as its prop.[47]

For Edelman, therefore, the problem is not one *for* reproduction but one *of* reproduction: it operates as the organizing principle of heteronormativity and, far from being undervalued, it is valued too much.

However, Edelman's work has rightly been criticized for its "curious feminist-citational vacuum"[48] and, as a consequence, for missing a fundamental point of feminist theories of social reproduction: that productive labor—including that of the professor of queer theory, "even within the horizon of the death-drive"[49]—cannot neatly be severed from reproductive labor. And so it carries with it the principal problem that feminist political economists have taken such pains to illuminate: that the erasure of social reproduction is in itself constitutive of power relations that are inextricably gendered, sexualized, racialized, classed, ableized, and territorialized. Put bluntly, Edelman's "stubborn refusal of futurity is structured by the privilege of having a guaranteed future,"[50] for the illusion of the autonomous masculine subject is exactly that: an illusion that functions by obfuscating the global political economies of socially reproductive labor that surround and sustain it.

That said, some queer scholars have sought to reclaim queer negativity by insisting that this need not equate to apolitical nihilism but can instead involve the very *political* rejection of systems of oppression that operate along axes of gender, race, class, dis/ability, and territory, as well as sexuality.[51] As Jack Halberstam writes, a "truly political negativity" must envisage refusal as a mode of imagining alternatives to dominant systems, including systems of gendered inequality:

> We need to craft a queer agenda that works cooperatively with the many other heads of the monstrous entity that opposes global capitalism, and to define queerness as a mode of crafting alternatives with others, alternatives which are not naively oriented to a liberal notion of progressive entitlement but a queer politics which is also not tied to a nihilism which always lines up against women, domesticity, and reproduction.[52]

Thus, although they undoubtedly begin from different starting points, it is not the case that queer theory is necessarily incompatible with feminist political economy. Rather, it is vital for scholarship on sexuality to interrogate how the "inequalities rooted in relations of production and reproduction shape the terrain of sexual politics in capitalist societies"[53]—a queer agenda, in other words, that is resolutely queer-feminist.[54]

Yet it is not simply that queer theory can learn lessons from feminist political economy, for it also makes distinctive contributions in its own right. Feminist scholars have laid much of the groundwork for queer theorists to understand sexuality as intimately related to global capitalism but, in so doing, they have often reproduced the "presumption of heterosexuality"[55] and so limited some of their own potential to contest the regulation of sexuality. For, although feminist political economists have illuminated the centrality of the family, household, and sexual division of labor in capitalist relations, conceptual frameworks and empirical analyses have frequently been based on assumptions that sexual relations equate to heterosexual relations, that the family comprises the nuclear family, and that the household consists of a husband, wife, and children.[56] One of the things that queer theory can bring to the table, therefore, is the opening up of sexuality as a category of analysis.[57] Queer scholars are particularly interested in how heterosexuality is not only privileged but is also depicted as natural and normal—indeed, it is constructed as so natural and normal that it no longer has to declare itself. One of queer theory's major projects, therefore, is to expose and oppose the ways in which the heteronorm is built into multiple scales of social existence.[58] Heteronormative power relations are both personal and political, built as they are on distinctions between the public/private and moral/immoral that prop up marriage and the nuclear family as economic, political, and cultural institutions.[59] Thus, queer theory draws attention to the need to interrogate how sexuality as a "normalizing regime"[60] is both produced by, and productive of, the politico-economic order.

Moreover, if feminist political economy casts vital light on the intersections between economic production and social reproduction, then queer theory can help to elucidate the status and significance of those deemed to be economically *un*productive and/or socially *un*reproductive.[61] What does it mean for practices, lives, and modes of being and working to be held not only to lack value but to be against value:[62] to be positioned in opposition to the economically productive and/or the socially reproductive? Roderick Ferguson, for instance, explores how the pathologization of some forms of labor as sexually non-normative helps to locate such labor—and the people who undertake it—as outside of the ideal of citizenship. Focusing on African American labor in the United States, he contends that the "construction of African American sexuality as wild, unstable, and undomesticated" places it "within the irrational, and therefore outside the bounds of the citizenship machinery." This exclusion from citizenship in turn enables African American labor to be produced as surplus labor.[63] Drawing on black feminist theorizing, James Bliss similarly argues that it is important to consider those modes of reproduction that are excluded from the symbolic order of futurity: the families and lives that are not counted as such. Specifically, he points to black reproduction as a mode of "reproduction without futurity" in the sense that black lives are racialized as unproductive.[64] In other contexts, queer scholars have taken up questions of gender, race, class, territory, and dis/ability to interrogate the multiple but nevertheless systemic cruelties of reproductive futurism. For example, Alison Kafer remarks wryly that there is "no future for crips," with the figure of the disabled person placed directly at odds with futurity. As she writes, "some populations are already marked as having no future, as destined for decay, as always already disabled."[65] Queer theory therefore opens up conceptual and political space to consider how the constitution of sexual and economic norms necessarily entails the "utter devaluation of poor, racialized, sexually and gender deviant populations,"[66] and how the very existence of such populations can be constructed as a threat to "normal" sexual and economic life.

So far this chapter has shown that closer engagements between IPE and queer theory are both possible and fruitful, especially when feminist political economy is brought into the mix. But it has only yet touched on an issue that is central to the book's queer political economy agenda, and that is the question of history. Indeed, queer theory has sometimes been criticized for prioritizing ontological questions over historical ones due to its interest in the instability of subjectivity.[67] For example, queer accounts of the (non)human—such as Butler's writings on vulnerable bodies—have been accused of diverting attention away from historical injustices by reifying abjection.[68] As Ida Danewid argues, such accounts critique the abstract universalism of the liberal subject but end up reproducing similar logics via appeals to the "generalized and anonymized suffering of a generic humanity." This enables the white, European subject to fashion itself as empathic and virtuous and so "innocent of its imperialist histories and present complicities," which "contribute[s] to an ideological formation that renders invisible the continuities between past and present forms of violence."[69] Queer anti-social theory has similarly been called out for its ahistoricism. Edelman's rejection of futurity, for instance, has been described as "another self-congratulatory, feel-good narrative of liberal humanism that celebrates homo-heroism" in ignoring how homosexual histories have, at times, involved complicity with both family and state as heteropatriarchal institutions.[70]

In order to counter such dynamics, this book takes up Lisa Downing and Robert Gillet's call to deploy queer not as fluidity but as history.[71] This is not to suggest that queer theory can/should only be understood as a historical project nor to imply that ahistorical scholarship cannot lay claim to the name "queer." It is, however, to highlight—as Heather Love does—that there is much to be learned from directing queer theory's gaze away from refusals of the future and "toward the past, toward the bad old days before Stonewall." It is through history, Love argues, that queer scholarship can expose how modern power relations are built as much on backwardness as on notions of progress, for modernity has been forged out of "excluded, denigrated, or superseded others" against which the modern queer subject becomes constituted as such.[72] Importantly, this desire to politicize (through) history is very much shared by many feminist political economists for whom contemporary sexual relations must be understood not as biologically given but as historically produced. The public/private split, for instance, is neither neutral nor inevitable but is enmeshed with the (re)making of a "historically specific gender order."[73] While the public boundary has come to circumscribe "the world of political and economic power, of decision-making and influence, to which masculine influence and identity are primarily attached," the private boundary has been defined as "the world of social reproduction, of home and family, to which feminine influence and identity are primarily attached."[74]

In fact, a formative part of queer's own history—and one that is often forgotten—is that queer theory emerged as a historical project.[75] The notion that the "truths" of sexuality are not biological or psychological but historical is most closely associated with the work of Michel Foucault.[76] Indeed, the first volume of *The History of Sexuality—The Will to Knowledge*—is often viewed as marking the birth of queer theory, if not uncontroversially so.[77] In this text, Foucault famously claims that what is distinctive about modern societies is "not that they consigned sex to a shadow existence, but that they dedicated themselves to speaking of it *ad infinitum*, while exploiting it as *the* secret."[78] He suggests that, from the eighteenth century onward, sex was neither repressed nor silenced but, quite the contrary, was "driven out of hiding" and compelled to "lead a discursive existence."[79] Rather than simply being a matter of private acts, sex instead became a public issue that involved a "whole web of discourses, special knowledges, analyses, and injunctions settled upon it."[80] Through the "endlessly proliferating economy of the discourse on sex,"[81] sexuality was not only produced as a category of knowledge in itself but also emerged as the central site on which the secrets of social reality could be uncovered. This burgeoning *scienta sexualis* ("science of sexuality") involved specifically individualizing discourses through which particular acts (e.g., sodomy) came to reveal the essential nature of particular persons (e.g., the homosexual); sex was no longer understood in terms of discrete practices that involved pleasure or sin but rather in terms of inner, fixed identities that, moreover, constituted the "kernel of the self" of individual subjects.[82] Foucault therefore points to the importance of confession, whether that be to a priest or to a psychiatrist, in extracting the truth of sex-as-self, for "it is in the confession that truth and sex are joined, through the obligatory and exhaustive expression of an individual secret."[83] Thus, our most intimate and apparently hidden identities are, for Foucault, in fact effects of power that function via "a regulated and polymorphous incitement to discourse" about sex, sexuality, and the sexual self.[84]

A great deal of ink has been spilled by queer scholars on *The Will to Knowledge*, but three points in particular are worth mentioning here. First, Foucault suggests that the discursive practices through which people become "known" through sexuality operate as political machineries through which not only individual subjects but also groups and populations can be governed. Indeed,

> One of the great innovations in the techniques of power in the eighteenth century was the emergence of "population" as an economic and political problem . . . Governments perceived that they were not dealing simply with subjects, or even with a "people," but with a "population" . . . At the heart of this economic and political problem of population was sex.[85]

Governments sought to analyze birth rates, legitimate and illegitimate births, fertility and sterility, the age of marriage, the frequency of sexual relations, and so on in order to govern sexual practices as well as to manage the nation's wealth and labor capacity.[86] The proliferation of discourses about sexuality thus served an important disciplinary function, for it was not only that unconventional practices could be identified, but that people and populations could be organized and categorized along axes of normal and perverse. The search for truth about sex thus served a distinctly "classificatory and normalizing purpose" through which individuals, groups, and populations could be divided into—and so managed as—normal and deviant forms.[87]

Second, Foucault points to the importance of reproduction. As he writes, "was this transformation of sex into discourse . . . not motivated by one basic concern: to ensure population, to reproduce labor capacity, to perpetuate the form of social relations: in short, to constitute a sexuality that is economically useful and politically conservative?" Although Foucault provides no definitive answer to this question, he nevertheless insists that "this much is certain: reduction has not been the means employed for trying to achieve it." Prior to the eighteenth century, sexual matters were governed via three main codes—canonical law, civil law, and the Christian pastoral—all of which were centered on matrimonial relations. Marriage "was the most intense focus of constraints; it was spoken of more than anything else." However, the "discursive explosion" of sex in the eighteenth and nineteenth centuries repositioned married monogamy as a norm that was "stricter, perhaps, but quieter" in the sense that the "legitimate couple . . . had a right to more discretion."[88] Instead, attention shifted to those figures that had been "scarcely noticed in the past" such as the juvenile, the criminal, and the insane, and these were now compelled "to step forward and speak, to make the difficult confession of what they were." And so there were "two great systems conceived by the West for governing sex: the law of marriage and the order of desires."[89] Whereas married monogamy became naturalized as an increasingly invisible and unspoken norm, the "world of perversion" became ever more marked out against the normal—a "natural order of disorder" to be disciplined precisely through its articulation and scrutiny.[90]

Third, Foucault contends that all of this was "indispensable" to capitalist development.[91] In order to thrive, capitalism not only required "the controlled insertion of bodies into the machinery of production and the adjustment of the phenomena of population to economic processes" but it also "had to have methods of power capable of optimizing forces, aptitudes, and life in general without at the same time making them more difficult to govern." The state's role in maintaining relations of production involved not only the expansion but also the proliferation of institutions across the social body, from the police to the medical profession to the family. These "techniques of power . . . operated in the sphere of economic processes, their development, and the forces working to sustain them."[92] This did not simply involve the dispersal of power, however, for it also facilitated and legitimated relations of domination by creating new social divisions, segregations, and hierarchies. Sex represented the linchpin of this:

> [Sex] was at the pivot of the two axes along which developed the entire political technology of life . . . Sex was a means of access both to the life of the body and the life of the species . . . Spread out from one pole to the other of this technology of sex was a whole series of different tactics that combined in varying proportions the objective of disciplining the body and that of regulating populations.[93]

This helped to maintain relations of domination and subjugation, but this was not just a story of repression. Although the disciplining of the proletarian body in order to exploit labor power for profit was certainly highly desirable, of principal concern was also "what the 'cultivation' of its own body could represent politically, economically, and historically for the present and the future of the bourgeoisie."[94]

In *The Will to Knowledge*, Foucault therefore advances the immensely significant thesis that sexuality possesses no essential meaning or truth to be located; rather, the "truths" that are assigned to sexuality are in themselves effects of power. He shows how sexuality is implicated not only in the production of individual subjectivities but also in the biopolitical management of groups and populations through disciplinary technologies that reach far into the intimate and reproductive spheres. In this way, Foucault expounds how specific constructions of sexuality, intimacy, and the family— including appeals to an innate biological "need" for procreation—are in fact historically contingent configurations that have played an integral part in the establishment of bourgeois hegemony under which capitalism rose to ascendancy.

Yet Foucault has also rightly been criticized for his own erasure of sexual histories, and especially of feminist ones. In *The Will to Knowledge* he makes no attempt to engage explicitly with his feminist contemporaries and so, consequently, he both neglects and appropriates key feminist insights.[95] That capitalism relied on the naturalization of marriage, the family, and sexuality was already a central theme in socialist feminist scholarship and activism, as was the desire to challenge appeals to innate characteristics such as the nurturing "instinct."[96] Certainly Foucault makes noteworthy contributions of his own, in particular by examining the "conditions of possibility—the rationalities, institutions, and practices—that enabled the emergence of the apparatus of sex."[97] Yet Foucault nevertheless seems to be "oblivious"[98] to the role of gender relations in producing sex as a historical formation; nor does he consider how this lacuna is, for feminists, itself a function of modern power.[99]

How then to address the "near-total absence of a gender analysis"[100] in Foucault's account, and the "will not to know" women in particular?[101] One need not conclude that Foucault simply "did not need" gender[102] or, alternatively, that his important project should be abandoned altogether.[103] In fact, Foucault did intend to compose a volume on women, maternity, and hysteria, but sadly died before he could undertake this work.[104] As it is, Foucault's failure to consider gender relations, and the position of women especially, means that he is unable fully to account for capitalism's connection to sex. How is it that women have come to be positioned as the chief (re)producers of people (and thus labor power) in service of capitalism, and why have the institutions of biopolitical governance often specifically targeted women?[105] This highlights the need to bring Foucault's agenda more closely into dialogue with feminist scholarship on the connections between sexuality and capitalism. Following Lynne Huffer, it is possible to forge a queer-feminist agenda that builds on (rather than disregards) Foucault's insights, while also recognizing how Foucault's work was made possible by feminist work, despite his apparent omission of it.[106]

A key text in feminist political economy to confront the above questions is Silvia Federici's *Caliban and the Witch,* which engages directly with Foucault's work if not queer theory more broadly. In this volume, Federici contends that the story of sexuality under capitalism "cannot be written from the viewpoint of a universal, abstract, asexual subject," as in Foucault's account. Instead, the category of "women" must be employed to refer not only to a "hidden history that needs to be made visible" but also to "a particular form of exploitation" under capitalism. Indeed, for Federici, women's bodies have been "the main targets, the privileged sites, for the deployment of power-techniques and power relations."[107]

Federici situates the development of capitalism in the context of the decline of feudalism in Europe in the Middle Ages. The feudal crisis, she argues, brought with it the first organized struggles against prevailing sexual norms, along with attempts to build more equal relations between men and women. Federici points to the signs of a bottom-up women's movement in opposition to dominant power structures, which pursued alternative modes of communal living. These efforts formed part of resistance to both bonded labor and commercial relations that offered a "powerful alternative" to feudalism. Capitalism, in turn, represented a "counter-revolution" forged by the ruling classes in response to these longstanding conflicts that threatened their power.[108]

Central here was the constitution of a new sexual division of labor through which women's reproductive labor could be harnessed to a broader capitalist project. Federici contends that this required the creation of a new patriarchal regime founded on the subjugation of women as well as their exclusion from waged work. Crucial to this (re)creation of patriarchal power relations was the "identification of women with a degraded conception of corporeal reality." Indeed,

> [T]he body has been for women in capitalist society what the factory has been for male waged workers: the primary ground of their exploitation and resistance, as the female body has been appropriated by the state and men and forced to function as a means for the reproduction and accumulation of labor.[109]

Of particular significance for Federici is "one of the most monstrous attacks on the body perpetrated in the modern era," the witch trials.[110] Prior to the fifteenth century, there had been no outbreaks of witch hunting in Europe, and witchcraft was not generally associated with evildoing. Yet the sixteenth and seventeenth centuries saw the torture and execution of thousands upon thousands of people, primarily women, for witchcraft.[111] As Federici demonstrates, it is no coincidence that the witch trials began during early modern times, for this was a period in which Europe was undergoing large-scale transformations due to the transition to capitalism. The ruling elite used the witch hunts to quash this opposition, as well as to destroy communal modes of living. Furthermore, the trials were designed to discipline women's bodies, and specifically to destroy women's control over their reproductive capacities. The consequence was the ushering in of a far more oppressive system of patriarchy under which the female body was transformed into the primary site on which power relations and techniques could be deployed. The witch embodied "a world of female subjects that capitalism had to destroy: the heretic, the healer, the disobedient wife, the woman who dared to live alone." For Federici, the decimation of the "witches" was therefore associated with the expansion of state control to cover all aspects of reproduction, and was a "cornerstone" of processes of primitive accumulation.[112]

Of critical importance for Federici, too, was the role of empire building in capitalist development. This stands in contrast to Foucault's inattention to colonialism as constitutive of biopolitics[113] and thus capitalism itself. In particular, Federici points to the importance of colonialism and imperialism in reproducing labor power, including through the systematic deployment of extreme violence and brutality in order to extract slave and other forced labor. Indeed, she contends that capitalism has been "necessarily committed to racism and sexism" since its inception. By essentializing and demeaning those it exploits—women, colonized peoples, migrants, and descendants of African slaves—capitalism could disguise and legitimize its intrinsic contradictions: "the promise of freedom vs. the reality of widespread coercion, and the promise of prosperity vs. the reality of widespread penury." That sexism and racism were intertwined could be seen, for instance, in the prohibition of intermarital relations in order to naturalize racial divisions through the enforcement of sexual norms.[114]

Thus, as valuable as Foucault's account of sexuality undoubtedly is, Federici teaches us that capitalism's history has involved the constitution not only of sexual identities but also of the sexual division of labor. In this way, gender and sexuality must be understood as "inextricably enmeshed," for conceptions of homosexual and heterosexual are themselves underpinned by the notion of gender difference.[115] More than this, the production of sex, sexuality, and gender has involved not only the "calculated management of life"[116] but also (to use Laura Shepherd's terminology) the "violent reproduction of gender."[117] As Federici writes, "torture and death can be placed at the service of 'life' or, better, at the service of the production of labor power, since the goal of capitalist society is to transform life into the capacity to work and 'dead labor.'"[118]

Federici's thesis—that capitalism has required the control and suppression of women's sexuality—therefore offers a helpful counterpoint to Foucault's emphasis on the productive nature of modern power. As noted, however, this does not mean that Foucault's agenda should be abandoned (although Federici sets up her own contribution as a refutation of Foucault's). This is not least because some of Federici's own claims may be overstated. For example, contemporary historians are by no means convinced that the witch trials were synonymous with a "war against women."[119]

Rather, they note that men were prosecuted in all regions that have been studied, and in some areas (such as Iceland, Normandy, and Estonia) men were predominantly targeted.[120] Research into judicial records has also challenged notions that accusations for witchcraft were primarily instigated by elites, as the impetus to prosecute tended to come from local communities (e.g., due to neighborly disputes).[121] Nevertheless, the effect of the trials was to establish the widely recognizable figure of the witch as a woman who was deviant, dangerous, and destructive of social and sexual norms. As the trials progressed, they often centered on the subversion of traditional female roles such as poisoning instead of feeding and infanticide instead of childrearing. This served to locate witchcraft more securely in the domestic domain, and to construct any woman who transgressed patriarchal expectations as a potential threat to the social order.[122]

As this example illuminates, there were multifarious forces at work that did not always flow in the same direction. Perhaps, then, the answer is neither to reject nor to reinstate what Foucault terms the "repressive hypothesis"[123]—although Foucault leans toward the former and Federici toward the latter. Indeed, while Foucault constructs something of a binary between "the production of sexuality" and "the repression of sex,"[124] there are times when he deliberately troubles his own distinction. As he writes, for instance: "Let there be no misunderstanding: I do not claim that sex has not been prohibited or barred or masked or misapprehended . . . nor do I even assert that it has suffered these things any less." Instead, sex entails "effects that may be those of refusal, blockage, and invalidation, but also incitement and intensification."[125] Likewise, Federici is highly critical of Foucault's emphasis on productive power but, on occasion, she also draws explicitly on it. For example, she charts the emergence of "a new bourgeois spirit that calculates, classifies, makes distinctions, and degrades the body only in order to rationalize its faculties, aiming not just at intensifying its subjection but at maximizing its social utility." As she explores, this bourgeois subjectivity of self-management became "an essential requirement in a capitalist socio-economic system in which self-ownership [was] assumed to be the fundamental social relation, and discipline no longer relie[d] purely on external coercion."[126]

It is helpful, then, to view Foucault's and Federici's projects as being not so much in opposition or collaboration as in generative tension. By reading these two historical accounts in conjunction, it becomes possible to offer a more nuanced understanding of the relationship between sexuality and capitalism. Foucault's insights can be mobilized to interrogate how capitalist power relations have not just involved the disciplining of "legal subjects over whom the ultimate dominion was death" (i.e., the "right to *take* life or *let* live") but also the management of "living beings" via techniques "applied at the level of life itself" (i.e., the "power to *foster* life or *disallow* it to the point of death").[127] Likewise, Federici's contributions encourage us to consider how the story of social reproduction under capitalism has not simply entailed the "calculated management of life," for capitalism has involved the "massive destruction of life"[128] from the outset. Nor have these genocidal tendencies declined with age, for death—including the "slow death"[129] of poverty and precarity—remains an ever-present feature of capitalism. If taken together, moreover, Foucault's and Federici's sexual histories can be used to explore how the circuits between life and death—and, hence, between economic production, social reproduction, and their opposites—must above all be understood as historically produced, not ontologically granted. As Jemima Repo suggests, "neither the functions of death nor life are historically stable"; for example, "both homosexuality and heterosexuality have been apparatuses of death and life, suggesting that the life and death functions of biopolitics manifest themselves through historically varying and specific discourses of difference."[130] Combining Foucault's and Federici's insights thus allows us to advance a queer political economy that is both historical and feminist (or, more specifically, queer-feminist) in its ethos and agenda.

In order to explain this framework in more detail, the next section takes up sex work as a particularly interesting case to analyze how the repressive and productive power relations associated with capitalist development have unfolded in historically contingent ways. While commercial sex is not the focus of either *The Will to Knowledge* or *Caliban and the Witch*,[131] it provides a unique vantage point from which to trace the linkages between capitalism and sexuality while also exploring how they have come to be separated. The remainder of this chapter therefore begins to unpick these complex and contradictory threads.

SEX, WORK, AND (RE)PRODUCTION

As noted in the Introduction, commercial sex is the subject of considerable feminist debate and yet it has received curiously little attention in queer theory.[132] Over recent years some scholars have sought to address this by shining a light on the diversity and flexibility of the identities, embodiments, and practices involved in the sex industry and by critically examining the relationship between heteronormativity and sex work (e.g., by challenging heterosexist assumptions that sex is invariably sold by women and bought by men).[133] Yet, in approaching queer as fluidity rather than history, queer accounts of sex work have largely left unexplored the historical mechanisms through which heteronormativity and sex work have come to constitute each other and, especially, how this relates to the sex/work split. For their part, feminist political economists have gone some way in connecting commercial sex to capitalism but they have similarly overlooked how the histories of sex, work, and heteronormativity coalesce.[134] More queer and feminist research is therefore needed on commercial sex—and not merely as an example of the work of sex and/or the sex of work but as a crucial instrument through which a series of interrelated and hierarchical separations (e.g., public/private, productive/reproductive) have been forged. As this book explicates, these divisions are neither incidental to, nor mere effects of, capitalist development but have instead been "indispensable" for it.

Controversies over commercial sex have a long and varied history that will be discussed in subsequent chapters, but a great deal of contemporary scholarship and activism centers on the issue of whether or not it can be counted as a mode of labor. One of the core tenets of radical feminist opposition to the legitimation and legalization of commercial sex is that

> Prostitution is not "work." It is violence against women and girls and a human rights violation. The term "sex work" completely masks the physical, psychological, and sexual violence inflicted on prostituted persons . . . Rather than refer to someone as a "sex worker," it is preferable to use "sexually exploited person," "prostituted woman," or "child used in prostitution." These terms do not pretend that a human rights abuse is "work."[135]

Conversely, the foundational premise for many sex worker activist organizations is that commercial sex should, more than anything else, be viewed as work ("sex work"). This most often involves appeals to commercial sex as a form of economically productive labor, with calls for sex workers to be "afforded the civil and labor rights and social protections that are the entitlement of all workers, regardless of occupation."[136] But it is sometimes also constructed as a mode of socially reproductive labor that holds social value accordingly. Wendy Chapkis, for instance, contends that sex work can take the form of caring labor that involves both nurturing and empathy, akin to childcare or therapy.[137]

Framings of commercial sex as labor are vitally important in contesting the cultural denigration, political silencing, and material subjugation of sex workers. They provide a language through which sex workers can demand recognition as individual and collective workers, and as comrades in broader struggles for economic and social justice.[138] At the same time, it is not quite the case that—as Heather Berg suggests—it becomes "impossible to exceptionalize sex work" once it is viewed as labor. For Berg, this is because all labor and all workers are exploited under capitalism.[139] Yet, clearly, labor takes many forms that involve divergent power dynamics, political effects, and modes of exploitation, and generic appeals to "work" flatten out the very specificities that need investigation.[140] Certain forms of labor are granted greater recognition, reward, and biopolitical power than others, and this is bound up with "particular and historical configurations" of gender, race, class, empire, and so on.[141] In order to take commercial sex seriously as labor, then, it is necessary to investigate how it becomes constituted in specific contexts and, especially, how it has come to be devalued (indeed, despised) as not really labor at all.

It is worth being upfront that, for some critics, the problem of commercial sex is not that it is denigrated but, on the contrary, that it is tolerated and even encouraged. For radical feminists, prostitution is the bedrock of patriarchal oppression, and the sexual exploitation of women now thrives on an unprecedented scale due to the expansion of global capitalism. Sheila Jeffreys, for instance, laments the transformation of the sex industry over recent decades from an "illegal, small-scale, largely local and socially despised" sector of the economy to one that is "large scale and concentrated, normalized and part of the mainstream corporate sphere." Indeed, "the vagina [is] the center of a business organized on an industrial scale."[142] Radical feminist opposition to commercial sex is thus frequently articulated as a mode of anti-capitalist critique to be contrasted with the "liberal determination to respect the free will of the individual and the market above all other values."[143] Others are supportive of decriminalization but nevertheless agree that the sex industry has gone mainstream, with sex worker rights organizing and rhetoric all too often "amalgamated with capitalist principles, processes, and structures" as a result.[144]

Yet, as Noah Zatz asks, if commercial sex is such a "seamless fit" with dominant power relations, then why is it "tolerated only as a marginal, degraded activity"; indeed, why is it not "legally sanctioned" and "culturally exalted"?[145] As this book examines with respect to the British case, the ascent of capitalism (including in its most extreme, neoliberal articulation) has not been accompanied by the normalization of sex work, let alone its valorization. On the contrary, commercial sex has been constituted as a highly contested, socially despised, and often criminalized site. It is not simply that commercial sex lies in the space between sex and work but, at different moments and in different ways, it has been positioned in opposition to both: to the sexually reproductive ("proper sex") and the economically productive ("proper work").

To be clear, this has sometimes involved the suppression of commercial sex so that it be "driven out, denied, and reduced to silence," to use Foucault's turn of phrase.[146] Yet this is only part of the story, for it is plainly not the case that the sex industry is dwindling over time. Indeed, it seems that commercial sex has never been so pervasive while simultaneously being so reviled. To tease out this puzzling paradox, this book draws on Foucault's thesis that modern power under capitalism has involved the "discursive production (which also administers silences, to be sure), of the production of power (which sometimes [has] the function of prohibiting)."[147] This has involved the proliferation of discourses of sex, and it is through this proliferation that deviance and perversity have been marked out from, and marked out against, the quiet normality of married monogamy in particular. In other words, the emergence of sexual diversity—including, and perhaps most especially, in the case of commercial sex—has not represented an equalizing move. Far from it: under modernity the "natural laws of matrimony and the immanent rules of sexuality" have been "recorded on two separate registers"—whereas for the married couple "nothing further was demanded of it than to define itself from day to day," the disordered world of perverse sexualities has been ever more spoken about in order to set it apart.[148]

This brings us to Federici's thesis for, although it has played out in complicated ways over time, a prime impetus for the delegitimation of sex work is that it confounds the division between the economically productive and socially reproductive spheres and, hence, the sexual division of labor. That is, the extraction of labor power that has been so integral to capitalist development has been made possible by the harnessing of women's socially reproductive labor, by the control of women's economically productive labor, and by the creation of clear boundaries around each. A recurring theme throughout the book is therefore how capitalism has required the disciplining of both sex and work or, more accurately, the disciplining of sex for and through work. As will be explored in depth, this has involved the construction of *both* the sexual division of labor (as the instrument through which women's and men's sexual and economic roles could be distinguished and naturalized) *and* sexual deviance (as the apparatus through which this separation could be policed and maintained). Sexuality, in other words, is both of the market and against the market, and commercial sex has played an important symbolic and material role in demarcating where, precisely, such boundaries begin and end.

To clarify, I do not mean to infer that the ontological condition of sex work should be reified as one of abjection, vulnerability, or marginalization.[149] This is not least because people's decisions to engage in sex work should be framed "not as aberrant or abject, but as a rational survival strategy in an often shitty world."[150] But it is also because this volume is less concerned with the ontological status of sexuality and more with its historical production. As will be explored throughout the chapters that follow, the constitution of commercial sex has transpired in historically contingent and sometimes quite tangled ways. Periodically, sex workers have been incriminated in "outbreaks of deviance, disease or deprivation," often involving moral panics and public debates.[151] Yet modern power under capitalism has also entailed the deployment of multifarious techniques—economic, juridical, scientific, medical, etc.—to fold sex workers "into life" (as Jasbir Puar might put it).[152] Indeed, sex work has offered something of a prototype for the biopolitical administration of life that Foucault considers while *also* operating as an instrument for the violent disciplining of women's bodies that Federici calls attention to. It has, moreover, repeatedly emerged as a specific target for the apparatuses of both life and death in ways that have directly enabled the construction of the economy/sexuality dichotomy. Commercial sex, then, has been vital to capitalism's wider project of making and breaking life—and it is this complex interplay between the production of sexuality and the repression of sex that will be examined in the empirical chapters to come.

CONCLUSION

To recap, in this chapter I have defended queer theory from charges that it is poorly equipped for political economic analysis, arguing instead that queer critiques are needed if we are to better comprehend the tensions and liaisons between capitalism and sexuality. To this end, I have utilized the contributions of Michel Foucault and Silvia Federici to invite closer conversation between queer theory and feminist political economy about the historical mechanisms through which capitalism and sexuality have made each other. Taking up sex work as an especially important site for this endeavor, I have begun to sketch out how capitalist development has been made possible by the appropriation of unpaid sexual labor that has rested, in turn, on the stimulation and suppression of paid sex. By tracing the historical construction of the sex/work split, we can begin to understand how sexuality has been constituted as uniquely private and intimate, and hence as something that can and should be protected from capitalism's adulterating influence. With these issues and themes in mind, the book now turns to the history of sex work in Britain.

CHAPTER 2

The Rise of a New Sexual Order

How has sex been taken out of work, and what work has this done for capitalism? This chapter anchors these questions in medieval and early modern England by investigating how the transition to capitalism was interwoven with the rise of a new sexual order. Using sex work as a vehicle, I explore how distinctions between married and illicit sex were central to England's political economy in the Middle Ages. Yet they did not map onto a dualism between economy and sexuality for, on the contrary, the institution of marriage placed the family at the center of economic and sexual life, and explicitly so. Nevertheless, marriage was itself made thinkable through its opposite—whoredom—such that the marking out of sexual vice was integral to the medieval sexual division of labor. Such distinctions, I argue, were to prove very handy indeed for capitalism, for they offered a logic through which the sexual division of labor could be remade into a tool for capitalist appropriation. In particular, capitalism's ascent in early modern England was tied to the creation of a new kind of division: that between sex and work. This was bound up with a discursive shift toward the economic aspects of sexual vice, so that sex work played a vital role in constituting the burgeoning split between the economically productive and socially reproductive spheres. The chapter also connects these developments to the rise of colonialism and imperialism as pivotal to capitalism's ascendancy.

SEX AND WORK IN MEDIEVAL ENGLAND

In the legal customs of the city of London, which were compiled in the *Liber Albus* of 1419, it was decreed that "if any woman shall be found

Capitalism's Sexual History. Nicola J. Smith, Oxford University Press (2020). © Oxford University Press.
DOI: 10.1093/oso/9780197530276.001.0001.

to be a common courtesan, and of the same shall be attainted, let her be taken from the prison unto Algate, with a hood of ray and a white wand in her hand." On a third offense, she should "let her hair be cut round about her head . . . and, after that, let her be taken to one of the City Gates, and let her forswear the City forever." Such measures, it was maintained, would ensure "the cleanness and honesty of the said city."[1] As this example illuminates, sex workers in the Middle Ages were—much like lepers—regarded as a source of contamination to be reviled and ostracized. Closely associated with sin, they were subjected to multiple degradations and punishments such as public humiliation, flogging, and incarceration.[2] Yet, although sex workers were socially despised, repression was sporadic rather than systematic. In England, as for elsewhere in medieval Europe, approaches varied greatly, but they were underpinned by the common desire to segregate sex workers both spatially and symbolically. As well as being required to wear distinctive clothing, sex workers were prohibited from working within the town walls, restricted to specific streets (such as Cock's Lane in London), or confined within brothels that were tolerated unofficially and, on occasion, formally sanctioned (as was the case in Southwark, Southampton, and Sandwich).[3] While sex workers were strongly identified with vice, however, this did not mean that they were viewed as a social problem or collective threat. Rather, their activities were, on the whole, tolerated as a necessary evil. Although laws to ban sex work and brothel keeping were commonplace, they were generally ignored and ineffective. The sale of sex was sinful, to be sure, but it represented a problem that could be quarantined rather than one that needed to be eradicated altogether.[4]

Nor was moral concern centered on the sale of sex specifically, for it was any sexual activity outside of marriage that was problematized. The concept of whoredom was particularly relevant for medieval understandings of sex: this referred to all forms of fornication and adultery rather than to the exchange of sex for money alone, and applied to women who were deemed to live sinful and disorderly lives regardless of whether they were paid for sex.[5] Thus, "common courtesans, common adulteresses, common bawds, and scolds"[6] were placed in the same category and penalized as such. Indeed, as Ruth Mazo Karras documents, none of the laws of the period articulated anxiety over the fact that money changed hands; instead, it was the sexual—rather than the commercial—nature of her activities that defined a whore. Common women were "common" in the sense that they did not belong to one man (whether that be a husband, father, or master), and any woman who was independent of a man could be accused of whoredom. Income earned from sexual relations outside of marriage was viewed as an "ill-gotten gain," certainly, but the exchange of sex for payment was not in itself viewed as a threat to the social body.[7]

The lack of interest in sex work as a commercial transaction was both constituted by, and constitutive of, England's politico-economic order of the time. In particular, economic relations were not yet commercialized but were organized around configurations of kinship and, especially, the family economy. During the Middle Ages Europe was, on the whole, a feudal system under which peasants worked the land in service of the landowning classes.[8] Although the peasants (or serfs) were legally and economically bound to the lords, they nevertheless had access to common rights and communal land, which meant that they "possessed, even if they did not own, the means of production of their own livelihood."[9] The locus of production was the family economy, which involved the labor of both women and men. Women not only performed a wide range of domestic activities (including childrearing) but they also worked in the fields and tended to livestock in the commons, and their domestic labor was exercised within the same social sphere as that of men.[10] Certainly, there was a clear sexual division of labor, with male-centered tasks including ploughing, reaping, and mowing, and female-centered tasks including planting, winnowing, and weeding. Yet "arrangements were generally flexible and sexually non-exclusive," and women had some involvement in most forms of labor.[11] Thus, although the family economy represented a specifically patriarchal setting that was "imagined—and largely functioned—as a male-headed enterprise,"[12] women were not yet relegated to the private sphere. Indeed, the very notion of private space was "all but absent" at this time.[13]

In medieval times, therefore, there was no sharp distinction between economy and sexuality and so they did not represent "hostile worlds"[14] to be kept apart. As the family was the central site of both economic production and social reproduction, there was no clear separation between the two spheres and, hence, between commercial and sexual transactions. This is not to suggest, however, that no concerns were raised if money changed hands for sex. In fact, there was considerable suspicion of anyone who was not deemed to produce value, and this applied not only to sex workers but also to merchants and others involved in commerce.[15] The pursuit of monetary profit was mistrusted and regarded as immoral—as could be seen, for instance, in the placing of usurers in Dante's seventh circle of hell, right below sodomites and blasphemers.[16] This distrust of money was also racialized,[17] for Jewish people were particularly despised for practicing usury (in fact one of the only trades that was not prohibited for them). Like the whore, the figure of the Jew was associated with "money, filth, and denigrated body parts," with the exchange of money between the whore/

merchant and their customers constructed as dirty and contaminating.[18] Bankruptcy, too, carried considerable stigma, associated as it was with a loss of control.[19] Nevertheless, if illicit sex and monetary profit were both condemned, then this was not primarily because boundaries between economy and sexuality were being transgressed.

The chief dividing line was instead between marital and extramarital sexual relations, which in turn reflected the centrality of marriage to the medieval social order. Marriage involved an "extraordinarily elaborate" system of rules and structures that reached into all aspects of life[20] and it was, in Foucault's words, "under constant surveillance."[21] Sex was understood as procreation, and no form of procreation could be legitimated outside of marriage; indeed, the religious ideal of marriage as "permanent, indissoluble, and created by publicly expressed consent" structured the "entire social scale."[22] Importantly, marriage produced the family not only as an economic and sexual unit but also as a spiritual one, and inseparably so. Religious principles sustained and legitimated hierarchies both within the family economy (i.e., between husbands and wives) and outside it (i.e., between lords and serfs): "The power and the glory of the heavenly father were metaphorically shared by the lord, and on a smaller scale, the male head of the household."[23] Sex was therefore organized around Christian morality, and the church profoundly influenced all aspects of life both in the formal legal sense (via the ecclesiastical courts) and at an individual level (via the practice of the confessional).[24] As Foucault writes, "more than any other relation, [marriage] was required to give a detailed accounting of itself."[25]

Marriage clearly positioned women as sexually and economically subordinate to men, even though married men were bound under the law to their wives for life.[26] Once wed, a married couple became one in both flesh and soul, and this did not mean equality but rather that a husband took over the legal rights of his wife. Yet at least a married woman could be recognized as a person, as she existed as an adjunct to her husband; the personhood of an unmarried woman, in contrast, was not acknowledged as she had no male body to join.[27] It was men rather than women, then, who were recognized as sovereign subjects, for women belonged to, and were possessed by, men in both the economic and sexual sense.

Although religious and legal discourses intersected with medical ones to construct women as inferior to men, womanhood and manhood were not conceptualized primarily as biological categories but were instead believed to reside in the soul. The principal division was not, therefore, between biological men and biological women but between the flesh and the soul, with sin located in the flesh and virtue in the soul.[28] Following the teachings of

Thomas Aquinas, many medieval scholars conceptualized men and women in terms of a one-sex model in which women were not fundamentally different from men but, on the contrary, were incomplete and imperfect men. The penis on women was simply inside out rather than lacking altogether. This notion that male and female bodies were "structurally homologous" meant that gender could be conceived as fairly pliable rather than as permanently fixed.[29] Manhood, for instance, was something to be achieved, and men who did not marry were often viewed as unmanly accordingly.[30]

Hence, gender and sexuality were intricately connected to personhood, but the self was understood not as innate to individuals but as inherently social. It was, in other words, both public and collective. A person's "repute" was essential in determining not just their societal status but also their economic prospects and life chances.[31] Sexual honor was important for all, but this was particularly the case for women. Virginity and chastity were held in the "highest regard"—as an expression of complete devotion to God in both flesh and soul—but marriage was nevertheless the "expected ideal."[32] A godly and honest woman was, therefore, a married one. Since a woman belonged to others (her husband, father, or master), then "any sexual relationship she took outside of marriage infringed on at least one other person's rights, and diminished someone else's honor."[33] Discourses of sexual morality had direct economic consequences as they made it extremely difficult for women to go it alone. Unmarried women could either work within another family economy or live by their own means and run the risk of being cast as a whore. Women who engaged in commercial activities in visible spaces (e.g., the street-based hawking of goods) were especially vulnerable to accusations of vulgarity. That women lacked economic independence was, moreover, actively imposed by the authorities, with unmarried women compelled to work as domestic servants or risk being fined or incarcerated.[34]

It was not only honor, then, but also shame that was fundamental to medieval conceptions of sex. Shame meant exclusion from the social body, as those who had lost their honor were to be openly avoided lest their dishonor "rub off." Indeed, honor and shame were "literally inscribed on the body" in that physical appearance operated as a key mechanism of social control[35]—hence the use of distinguishing clothing to mark and shame sex workers. This meant that, when the sale of sex was practiced "in secret,"[36] it could hold a rather ambivalent status. Although the church considered sex outside of marriage to be an egregious sin, the sale of sex was treated as something of a special case.[37] The brothel in particular was deemed to represent an important safety valve, and this related to medieval understandings of sexual desire. Women were believed to be closer to nature and more weak-minded than men, which made them both more lustful and more likely to succumb to the pleasures of the flesh. Men's sexual appetite, in contrast, was conceived in terms of a hydraulic model whereby, if left untended, it would build up and reach bursting point.[38] Notably, it was men's sexual urges rather than women's that were deemed to require an outlet. If common women were available, then this would divert male sexual attention away from honest women while minimizing the chance that honest women, for their part, could be tempted to act upon their lust. In this way, the sale of sex was understood as a supplement to marriage rather than a direct threat to it, so long as it was hidden from view.[39]

Although whoredom may have been tolerated, the whore herself was vilified.[40] As noted, the commercial aspect of sex work was not of great concern, but the shaming of sex workers related to economic logics nonetheless. As Karras highlights, the institution of marriage ensured that a woman remain the economic and sexual property of one man, and yet the whore belonged to no man and, at the same time, to all men. The whore thus both possessed and lacked economic and sexual independence.[41] Proper female sexuality was defined in opposition to whoredom, but whoredom was not placed on the outside of female sexuality. Indeed, what defined female sexuality—whether for the common woman or the married woman—was that it was commodified.[42] The sale of sex was therefore profoundly implicated in the constitution of sexual relations writ large, for the treatment of whores could be deployed as an instrument to control women generally. That no formal definition of whoredom existed in English legislation meant that the law could be used to discipline a wide variety of practices and, by implication, any woman could be punished as a whore if she contravened sexual norms.[43]

Yet not all women were recognized *as* women in medieval England, for gender identity was assumed to correspond directly with sex assignation in the Middle Ages, as was sexual orientation; indeed, distinctions between them were not only ill defined but were absent altogether.[44] This meant that medieval understandings left precious little space for transgender and gender nonconforming subjectivities to be thinkable. This could be seen most famously in the case of Eleanor Rykener, who was tried in London in 1394 for participating in "that detestable, unmentionable, and ignominious vice" with a man. Under questioning, Eleanor confessed to selling sex to men for payment (in her own words) "as a woman," as well as to having sex (in her own words) "as a man with many nuns."[45] It was not, however, Eleanor's admissions of either sodomy or sex working that most troubled the authorities but her subversion of gender norms and, not knowing how to conceptualize her, the court released her without penalty.[46]

Indeed, whoredom was not simply understood as a discrete set of practices but as a status, indeed a class of woman.[47] In 1344 in Bristol, for example, customs were recorded that banned lepers and common women from the town, and these referred to "categories of persons" rather than to specific behaviors. The regulation of the brothels in Southwark also exemplified this fact, for the women who worked within them were forbidden from having their own lovers: "If they were to be common, they must be entirely common."[48] Whoredom thus complicated Foucault's distinction between acts and individuals, for the whore possessed "an inherent, well-publicized, and permanent identity."[49] Yet this identity was not inborn, for it was itself the consequence of a whore's sinful behavior, and a sinner could always repent—hence why marriage for common women was not only accepted but even endorsed by the church on the grounds that it could mitigate sin.[50]

This is not to suggest, however, that men's sexuality was left untouched. The *Liber Albus*, for instance, ruled that "if any man shall be found to be a common whoremonger or bawd," he would be shaved and pilloried on the first offense, imprisoned on the second, and on the third offense "let him be taken to one of the City Gates, and there let him forswear the City for ever."[51] Men were, at times, charged with such offenses, as could be seen in the case of Peter Manyfield, who was tried in London in 1489. Manyfield confessed in court to being "a common procurer" who had "arranged lewdness" and "carried away, by stealth and violence and against her will, a certain Alice Burle from her parents' house and kept her in his room for a long time, committing with her the crime of fornication, and after he was tired of her, he sold her to a certain Easterling in the Steelyard." (As Manyfield failed to return to court, he escaped penalty except for a temporary ban on access to church services.)[52] Men who paid for sex, though, could generally expect to do so without sanction, and brothel keepers were also much less likely to be punished than whores. It is striking that the Bishop of Winchester himself felt fit to profit from brothels and this was, by all accounts, a highly lucrative endeavor.[53]

As whores were common women specifically, the notion of male sex work was largely unintelligible at this time. In the *Liber Albus*, women alone were recorded as being "common courtesans" and men alone were recorded as being "whoremongers."[54] This reflected not only the sexual double standard but also wider "silence and denial" about homosexuality in England.[55] This was in contrast to the continent, where sodomites were targeted as a threat to Christian society, and punished in a variety of novel and increasingly barbaric ways from the thirteenth century onward.[56] When sodomy was mentioned at all in England, it was described as a sin so grievous that it could not explicitly be named. While it may be that trials for sodomy or male prostitution did take place at this time, historians have yet to uncover the evidence for this.[57] Thus, it was not only men who bought sex but also men who sold sex who escaped the notice of the authorities. That feudal structures were built on the sexual subjugation of women meant that open expressions of same-sex desire among women also went unrecognized in medieval discourse.[58] Taken together, these variegated forces worked to constitute whoredom as a key instrument through which women's economic and sexual subordination—and therefore the sexual division of labor—could be legitimated and maintained.

THE TRANSITION TO CAPITALISM

While the sale of sex was broadly tolerated in medieval England, it became increasingly problematized from the turn of the sixteenth century onward. Whoredom had long been associated with disease and, when Europe was hit by a devastating outbreak of syphilis in the final few years of the fifteenth century, both lepers and sex workers were blamed for this.[59] Such discourses intersected with moral anxieties over carnality to heighten concerns that sex workers helped to spread pollution and disorder. Published works began to articulate moral condemnation more forcefully, and this focused not only on the whore's personal morality but also on her impact on society more broadly.[60] As the English cleric Thomas Becon wrote in his *Catechism*, "the curse and vengeance of God is upon the whore . . . she is despised of men, as dung in the street; and the best end of her is extreme beggary with shame . . . the whore causes strife and dissension, and sets men together by the ears."[61] There were also calls for harsher punishments to be imposed on sex workers and brothel keepers.[62] The *Anatomy of Abuses* by Philip Stubbes, for instance, declared that whores, adulterers, and fornicators should "drink a full draught of Moses' cup, that is, taste of present death" or else be "cauterized, and seared with a hot iron on the cheek, forehead, or some other part of their body that might be seen, to the end the honest and chaste Christians might be discerned from the adulterous Children of Satan."[63]

The censure of sex work was not, as it had been before, an ad hoc and localized matter, for it was instead formally legislated by the Tudor state. In 1546 Henry VIII announced that all brothels would henceforth be banned, including those that had been informally sanctioned.[64] As his proclamation put it, this was to put an end to the "toleration of such dissolute and miserable persons . . . [who] without punishment or correction exercise their abominable and detestable sin."[65] This formed part of a prolonged campaign to stamp out sexual vice. Under Edward VI, there was a "civic purge" of sexual offenders whereby local officials were obliged to locate and expose those who had been engaged in sexual transgressions, including sex workers, procurers, bawds, and whoremongers. Those found guilty by the authorities were punished via the pillory, ducking stool, flogging, imprisonment, or shaming.[66] By the reign of Elizabeth I, the toleration of sex work had largely come to an end. Many local governments, along with the church courts, sought to restrict or even eradicate sex work, and used a variety of progressively harsher measures to do so.[67]

How to account for this shift in approach to sex work? Where once its repression had been locally improvised and intermittent, now it was state-led and systematized. While the changes associated with Henry VIII's reign are popularly attributed to his personal marital problems,[68] Silvia Federici reminds us that such developments cannot be divorced from the broad-sweeping economic, political, and cultural transformations associated with the transition to capitalism. Central here was the crisis of feudalism and, especially, the social struggles that led from this. The Great Famine of 1315–1317 and the Black Death of 1346–1353 had decimated a large proportion of Europe's population, and "this unprecedented demographic collapse profoundly changed Europe's social and political life, practically inaugurating a new era."[69] The generalized reality of death, together with widespread labor shortages, weakened social control and threatened to upturn existing socioeconomic hierarchies.[70] In England, the lords sought to preserve the previous levels of rent and serfdom dues, and they were supported in this by royal statutes. This led to wide-reaching social unrest, with tensions reaching breaking point in the Great Revolt of 1381, when peasants managed to capture the Tower of London and to behead the King's Treasurer and the Lord Chancellor on Tower Hill.[71]

The peasants' revolt of 1381 was brutally crushed by the authorities, but the scale of social conflict was such that, by the sixteenth century, serfdom had all but vanished in England. Although the peasants were now ostensibly "free" laborers and so could demand better wages and working conditions, "a counter-revolution was already underway at every level of social and political life."[72] In particular, the locus of symbolic and material power began to shift away from the landed aristocracy and the church, on the one hand, to the state and the emergent bourgeoisie, on the other. The Reformation was a critical moment in which the new order began to take shape, as a great deal of the Catholic Church's wealth and property was seized by Henry VIII, and then sold off, in the most significant transfer in land since the Norman Conquest.[73] Many of the extant feudal regulations (such as those regarding copyhold tenure) were further dismantled during the English Revolution of 1640–1660, which helped to consolidate the economic and political power of the new bourgeoisie, and especially merchants and lawyers.[74]

Economic crisis brought on by the depletion of agrarian land, demographic pressure, and class strife upset traditional models of authority, and this radically altered kinship structures and sexual norms.[75] Particularly significant was the "crisis in social reproduction" brought on by the privatization of land (the so-called enclosures)[76]—a practice that saw many peasants forcibly removed from their communal land, laying waste to whole villages and stripping the very poor of their means of subsistence. The ability of local communities to sustain themselves was therefore put under tremendous strain. As a direct result of the mass expropriations, there was widespread food scarcity and famine, along with various forms of resistance from the poor, including protests, rioting, and theft.[77]

Having lost access to their land, large numbers of peasants were compelled to make a living as vagrants, and this led to moral panic about social disorder. The state's response was repression, with large numbers of people pauperized, criminalized, and incarcerated.[78] In 1556 an old palace, the Bridewell, was made into an institution for the poor who, notably, included sex workers and vagabonds. Here they were harshly disciplined and forced to undertake labor (often by making goods for the wealthy such as furniture and clothes) while also being positioned out of sight.[79]

However, such measures could not counter the surge of people without homes and livelihoods into urban areas. It was in this light that the state introduced the Poor Laws of 1597 and 1601, which sought to alleviate the effects of widespread impoverishment. The legislation moved responsibility for poor relief from the Catholic Church, which had been the principal custodian of the poor, to the state via local parishes.[80] It also involved a shift toward a more formalized categorization of the poor, in particular between the "impotent" poor (children, the elderly, the sick, and widowed families), the "able-bodied" poor (those who were able to work but were unemployed), and the "idle" poor (that is, beggars, vagrants, and sex workers). The Poor Laws cast the impotent poor as deserving of indoor or outdoor poor relief, whereas the able-bodied poor were forced to labor in workhouses.[81] The idle poor, however, were increasingly regarded as a threat to the social order: they were criminalized, branded, whipped, institutionalized, conscripted, or sent to a penal colony. The Poor Laws functioned alongside the Vagrancy Acts and other legislation to govern the growing underclass, and punishments for those who "refused" to work became more and more severe, including the death penalty for repeat offenders.[82]

The criminalization of sex work was therefore tightly bound up with the disciplining of the poor, for sex workers (or, more accurately, the poorest and most visible sex workers) were cast alongside the idle poor. Critically, state-led violence not only helped to impose labor discipline but, as Adrienne Roberts makes clear, it also had specifically gendered effects in fortifying patriarchal power relations and the sexual division of labor. In particular, the categorization of the poor into impotent, able-bodied, and idle was premised on the assumption that it was men's role to provide for themselves and their families; women, in contrast, were assumed to be provided for by men. The consequence was that women who adhered to sexual norms, especially regarding marriage, were treated rather more generously than women who broke them. Widows, for example, tended to be treated as the impotent poor and so given outdoor relief, whereas single women were defined as the idle poor and so offered indoor relief alone, justified on the grounds that they were fundamentally undeserving.[83] The cruel irony was that widespread poverty left many women—and especially unmarried mothers—so economically desperate that they had little choice but to engage in sex work: "most lived on the margins of respectable society, struggling to maintain themselves and their illegitimate children, moving frequently, and resorting to theft or other kinds of petty crime" at the risk of harsh punishment for doing so.[84]

Yet it was not just that sex workers were classified as the idle poor but that constructions of the poor as sinful, and especially sexually sinful, themselves functioned to demonize the poor. The repression of sex work must be understood in this context and, in particular, as part of a broader campaign to cleanse society of extramarital sex. This not only involved the imposition of cultural norms but—to draw on Federici's thesis—it also entailed the forging of a new politico-economic order. Pivotal here was the obscuring of women's status as workers, thus helping to usher in a sexual regime based on women's exclusion from the paid workforce. Indeed, while Federici focuses on the witch trials rather than prostitution in *Caliban and the Witch*, she nevertheless points to the criminalization of sex workers as a "drastic attack on female workers" that served to exclude women from the "sphere of socially recognized work and monetary relations."[85] In fact it is unclear if this was the deliberate intention, for moral discourses in England focused on the question of sexual depravity rather than the question of work. And yet sexual depravity was itself situated within wider discourses of economic and social disorder and, especially, the "corruption" of honest and decent citizens—or, as Henry VIII's proclamation described them, "the true laboring and well-disposed men."[86] Whether or not it was the stated objective, as Federici implies, the *effect* was certainly to forcibly impose sexual norms that meant, in turn, women's reproductive labor could more directly be controlled by the state. In this way, Federici is quite right to argue that the criminalization of sex workers was directly connected to "the expulsion of women from the organized workplace . . . and the reconstruction of the family as the locus for the production of labor power."[87]

It was, therefore, no accident that the criminalization of sex workers occurred at the same historical juncture as the witch trials. In 1542, Henry VIII introduced witchcraft legislation to England in the first of a series of acts that were finally repealed in 1736—but only after hundreds of people had been prosecuted for witchcraft, many of whom were executed.[88] Although sex workers were not routinely targeted as witches,[89] the figure of the witch was nevertheless shaped by preexisting discourses of whoredom, for the trials "drew on a long tradition of associating sexually promiscuous women with sin and forbidden acts."[90] They habitually focused on women's sexual crimes as the means to legitimate prosecution, with pamphlets of the time thick with detail on alleged sexual activity with the devil. Women accused of witchcraft were also explicitly depicted as whores (e.g., "old whore," "stinking whore," "common harlot," and "veiled strumpet").[91] Both witches and sex workers were thus positioned in opposition to honest women: like the common whore, the witch was the antithesis of the good wife and so represented "a warning to women" of the fate that could await them if they acted (or were seen to act) in noncompliant ways.[92]

The suppression of women's sexuality was, moreover, connected to insider/outsider logics, and especially to the fear of foreign bodies. Such fears were not in themselves new: for example, violent hatred of Flemish sex workers had motivated the destruction of a Flemish brothel in Southwark during the 1381 revolt.[93] Yet they were given new life as sex work was constructed as the corruption of the body politic from outside: syphilis in particular was blamed on sex workers from the continent and dubbed the "French disease."[94] The clampdown on sex workers and brothel owners was portrayed as a means of protecting the nation from vice that was distinctly un-English in character. This linked in turn to religion, for sex work was constructed as sinful precisely because it was un-Protestant.[95] Ongoing antisemitism meant that sex workers were sometimes described as Jews but, more often, they were labeled Catholics. For, if the figure of the whore could be depicted as Catholic, then so could the Catholic Church be condemned as a whore.[96] Such imagery featured prominently in political and religious commentary at the time, with Catholicism described as a "strumpet," "harlot," and "whorish mother."[97]

Notably, it was during this period that male sexuality, too, began to be more problematized, albeit to a far lesser extent than women's. On the continent, the treatment of sodomites bore much in common with that of witches: indeed, the *Malleus Maleficarum* of 1486 stated that "the power of the devil lies in the privy parts of men" and that "all devils equally, of whatever order, abominate" if they commit "vices against nature" such as sodomy.[98] In England, however, the disavowal of sodomy meant that there were not the executions by burning or hanging that proliferated in countries such as Italy and Spain. Indeed, in the thousands of trials in the church records in London in 1470–1516, there was just one case for sodomy (and the defendant missed his own trial and so was excommunicated).[99] Yet the Reformation brought with it a step up in the repression of sodomy in England. In 1533 Henry VIII introduced the Buggery Act, which transformed sodomy into an offense to be dealt with by the state rather than the church courts. As the Act stated, "there is not yet sufficient and condign punishment . . . for the detestable and abominable vice of buggery committed with mankind or beast," which would henceforth be punishable by "such pains of death."[100] As it was, the first execution was not carried out until nearly a century later, in 1631, and this involved an accusation of rape against a man who was in fact a political opponent of the king.[101] Nevertheless, the legislation was used as a means through which the wealth of the Catholic Church could be appropriated by the Tudor state. The 1533 Act meant that, along with death, offenders would suffer "losses, and penalties of their goods, cattle, debts, land, tenements, hereditaments" and that "no person offending in any such offence shall be admitted to his clergy."[102] Many monks were forced to confess to sodomy in their Disclosures, and within several years the monasteries had been disbanded and their wealth transferred to the crown.[103]

More broadly, the repression of sex formed an integral part of a politico-economic project through which the ideal of marriage that underpinned the sexual division of labor could be enforced and utilized. Of course, medieval relations had already been predicated on marital relations, but the Reformation nevertheless inscribed marriage with new meanings.[104] Under Catholicism, marriage was "ordained by God" but virginity and celibacy were nevertheless the most valorized modes of being. So long as it was properly contained within the marital unit, sexual desire could be channeled for procreative purposes, but procreation was not itself a moral duty.[105] Under Protestantism, the emphasis on virginity and chastity was replaced by an all-encompassing preoccupation with marriage and procreation. To reproduce the family unit through marriage was "not a poor substitute for celibacy" but was God's own institution.[106] From the creation of Adam and Eve onward, God had assigned men and women with specific roles: it was men's duty to provide for, and protect, the family unit;

and it was women's duty to serve their husbands, to bear children, and to nurture the family unit. The subordination of women to men was not only consistent with God's will but was a "divine injunction," and to deviate from this path was to disobey God himself.[107] The medical profession, too, espoused the view that those who transgressed patriarchal expectations were ungodly and unnatural, for they violated God's plan and hence the laws of nature. It was the role of the law, moreover, to ensure that God's will was realized on earth, and hence to punish those who departed from this path.[108]

At the same time—to draw on Foucault's thesis—the power relations at work did not only involve the exercise of repression. For, although the notion that women were naturally subservient to men was nothing new, Protestantism brought with it a subtle but salient shift in how this was conceived. In particular, while women must obey their husbands, this was not as a slave to a master but rather out of choosing[109]—as Becon wrote, "The faithful married woman delights in the presence of her husband . . . [and] has great joy when she beholds her true and natural children, being well assured that they are the blessings of God, forasmuch as they are the fruit of her matrimony to her lawful husband."[110] For bourgeois families in particular, kinship could be based not only on patriarchal male and religious authority but also on the concept of affection.[111] The idea of individual freedom was central here as marriage represented a "contractual union of individuals . . . bound together by mutual love."[112] A new moral discourse of the family could thus emerge that focused on the connections between body and soul and, hence, between sex and love. While sexual relations were still contained within marriage, they served the dual purpose of procreation and companionship. This did not undermine but further legitimated male authority, since wifely obedience was now a "choice," indeed an expression of love.[113]

The Reformation therefore formed part of a nascent shift in the relationship between family and economy in that they began to be constituted as separable, if not entirely separate, social spheres. Although economic production was already, to an extent, distinct from kinship relations, it began to be so to a much larger degree. There was not yet a sharp division between public and private, however.[114] As Patricia Crawford notes, the household did not so much represent the private sphere as the point of intersection between the public and the private, for the family remained a matter of public order that was subject to the authority of both church and state. As the head of the household, men were responsible for the conduct within it, and so wifely disobedience was still a matter of public shame for their husbands. Yet, if men were still tied to the domestic realm, they had nevertheless "claimed the public sphere, both secular and religious, as their domain."[115] Commercial endeavor could thus be staked out as men's own for (as Becon observed) godly and honest women did "not idly and wantonly to gad abroad, seeking new customers . . . [but] continually to remain at home in their house diligently and virtuously occupied" (although they could still attend church, tend to sick neighbors, and "go to the market to buy things necessary for her household, etc.").[116] This control of women's economic activities was in turn enforced by the regulation of their sexuality: indeed, following the closure of the brothels, any woman who allowed a man into her home—whether this be for business or trading purposes—could be deemed a whore.[117] It was through reference to whoredom, therefore, that domesticity could increasingly be constituted as women's natural, desirable, and expected state.

THE BIRTH OF COMMERCIAL SEX

While the Reformation laid the foundations for economy and sexuality to be understood as antithetical, it was not until the eighteenth century that this distinction became crystalized in and through understandings of sex work. Although the trope of the sexually voracious whore did not fall away, sex workers began to be constructed as driven not only by lust but also by money, with accounts explicitly emphasizing the commercial (as opposed to simply the sexual) nature of the transaction.[118] Reformers started to articulate prostitution as not just a moral danger but as an economic one that jeopardized the status of legitimate commerce by misdirecting the flow of capital to the illicit economy.[119] This meant that prostitution could "embody a new kind of commercial identity" for, if it represented an economic threat, then the implication was that it could represent an economic activity too. Prostitution, then, began to be cast as both sexual *and* commercial—indeed, as a site that transgressed the burgeoning (and still somewhat precarious) divide between the public and private spheres.[120]

This redefinition of commercial sex took place within the context of broad-sweeping transformations associated with the Industrial Revolution. Industrialization radically altered the shape of British society, entwined as it was with the emergence of new class configurations, population expansion, labor migrations, urbanization, and disturbances in the order of everyday life.[121] Structural economic changes affected the social status of men and women, the power relations between them, and the symbolic and material importance of the domestic sphere in which sex played a vital role.[122] Yet these shifts did not simply impact on sex, for they also required it. As

Imogen Tyler argues, the development of industrial capitalism needed a new set of state apparatus and, specifically, the patriarchal family and the separation of public and private spheres through which "the reproduction of labor power could be more effectively managed and controlled." Indeed, the "shift to biopolitical forms of governance required by capitalism inaugurated the mass securitization of reproduction."[123]

Integral to these developments was the whipping up of intense anxieties about the sexual—and thus the social—body. The seventeenth century had seen immense turmoil, including the civil wars of 1642–1651 that killed nearly 200,000 people and led to the execution of the king.[124] The state's reaction was to "control potential disorder by emphasizing the need to obey authority"[125]—an agenda in which the crusade against sexual vice played a principal role. Extramarital sex was cast as both a sin and a crime by the authorities, as exemplified by the Act for Suppressing the Detestable Sins of Incest, Adultery and Fornication of 1650. This marked a shift in approach whereby the punishment of sexual transgressions moved from the church to the secular authorities.[126] The Act stated, for instance, that "all and every person and persons" guilty of keeping a brothel or bawdy house should, on the first offense, be imprisoned for three years after having been "openly whipped and set on the Pillory, and there be marked with a hot Iron on the forehead with the letter B," and face death for a second offense.[127] The Restoration also birthed a series of social purity campaigns that sought to ensure that the legislation was properly enforced, as well as a number of riots against brothel keeping such as the Messenger Riots of 1668. In 1691, religious groups created the Society for the Reformation of Manners in London, which sought to track down and bring to justice those guilty of immorality, including sex workers and brothel keepers.[128]

By the mid-eighteenth century, there was growing anxiety over the deleterious effects of commercial sex, not only in terms of persistent worries over venereal disease but also in terms of its consequences for the national economy. Prostitution was constructed as a drain on the country's labor power specifically, for it not only robbed the workforce of wives and mothers but also depleted the supply of "plain, honest, industrious men" by transforming them into "dead weights to the nation" through debauchery and disease.[129] As the philanthropist Jonas Hanway wrote,

It ought to be constantly instilled as a ruling principle, in the minds of both sexes, and of all ranks; that man is an active being, and if he is not taught to do good, he will almost certainly do mischief. Idleness is very justly called the root of all evil in general, but it is particularly so in the case of prostitution.[130]

Yet it was women's sexuality in particular that was blamed for the "evil" of prostitution: indeed, "a corruption of manners in the women is the prelude to the fall of a nation. We have had mournful proofs of the increase in this disorder in our age."[131] The heightened sense of alarm about the economic aspects of sex work was also reflected in claims about its scale: mid-century, it was estimated that around 3,600 sex workers operated in London but, by the 1790s, this figure had risen to as high as 50,000.[132] The state responded by playing an increasingly important role in the creation and control of what was permitted and prohibited, moral and immoral.[133] This included new legislation to deal with commercial sex, most notably the Disorderly Houses Act of 1751, which encouraged the prosecution of "bawdy-houses, gaming-houses, or other disorderly houses" in order to "correct as far as may be the habit of idleness which is become too general over the whole kingdom, and is productive of much mischief and inconvenience."[134] Gendered expectations surrounding sexual conduct were again relevant here since it was poor women in particular who were associated with vulgarity and lewdness,[135] as personified by the figure of the prostitute.[136]

The disciplining of women's sexuality and, hence, their reproductive labor was epitomized by the repression of sex workers, but it could also be seen in the harsh treatment of reproductive offenses more generally. During the eighteenth century, punishments for infanticide were particularly prevalent and, as it was difficult to prove that a baby had been murdered, simply hiding the birth of a stillborn illegitimate child was classed as a capital offense.[137] The law functioned in such a way as to force women to assume full responsibility for parenthood since the bastardy laws particularly penalized women in comparison to men (i.e., they were more likely to be subjected to whippings, incarceration, or other harsh punishments).[138]

Yet this was by no means a single systemic logic, for the emphasis on the economic aspects of prostitution also opened up space for alternative discourses around women's sexuality to emerge. While the prostitute had been imagined as a "vicious and sexualized criminal" before, now there was space to imagine her as "a reluctant victim of commercial depravity."[139] In the second half of the eighteenth century, constructions of sex workers as pitiful victims of circumstance achieved growing prominence.[140] Reformers stressed the need for charitable endeavors to rehabilitate those who had entered into prostitution due to poverty, with the first Magdalene institution, the Magdalene Hospital for the Reception of Penitent Prostitutes, founded in London in 1758.[141] Its aim was to operate as "a means of employing the idle, of instructing them in, as well as habituating them to work; of reforming their morals; of rescuing their bodies from Disease and Death, and many souls from eternal Misery."[142]

Poetry devoted to the prostitute's fate began to appear in local newspapers, such as that by Thomas Lister, which declared: "Poor profligate! I will not chide thy sin."[143] Accounts of and by former sex workers were published, reveling in their tragedy, their salvation, or both (such as in *An Account of the Triumphant Death of F.S. A Converted Prostitute, Who Died April 1763, Aged Twenty-Six Years*).[144] In 1799 the letters of "the first penitent prostitute" of the Magdalene asylum were published, with the Reverend William Dodd calling for the "rescue such of their fellow creatures from a state so miserably dreadful . . . [to] render them not only happy in themselves, but make them, as members, again useful to society."[145]

This newfound emphasis on sex workers as individual victims of poverty bore the influence of Enlightenment rationality, which emphasized the value of the individual as well as the possibility of social progress.[146] The Reformation had seen the "birth of a new, individualized self," based on Protestant beliefs in personal responsibility and piety. By the eighteenth century, the "shame culture" that had prevailed during medieval times was supplanted by something rather different: "guilt culture."[147] As Foucault argues, the practice of penance had played a central role in governing erotic practices and preferences in the Middle Ages, but in early modern Europe there emerged a new kind of pastoral, one in which sex was simultaneously hidden and exposed. On the one hand, sex itself became less "visibly present" in language; it became more difficult (and dangerous) to speak of it by naming it explicitly.[148] On the other hand, it became ever more important to confess to the sins surrounding sex—the "thoughts, desires, voluptuous imaginings, delectations, combined movements of the body and the soul"—and so to declare the sexual without speaking openly of sex. By the eighteenth century, "this obligation was decreed, as an ideal at least, for every good Christian."[149] It brought with it a new emphasis on private space, with the private understood as personal in the sense that it represented an "externalization of the individualized 'self.' "[150] Conceived in this way, personal sin could be regarded as a private rather than public matter that need not necessarily threaten the entire community, thus laying the foundations for sex workers to be conceived more sympathetically.[151]

Discourses of commercial sex were, then, structured by notions of the deserving and undeserving poor—sex workers could be constructed not only as guilty/undeserving but also as pitiful/deserving. As Robbie Shilliam shows, the distinction between the deserving and undeserving poor was interlaced not only with class and gender but also with race. Of pivotal importance here was the development of mercantile capitalism and the advancement of colonialism and imperialism. By the time of the 1707 Act of Union with Scotland (which formed the Kingdom of Great Britain),

England had already established itself as an imperial power;[152] indeed, the Act in Restraint of Appeals under Henry VIII had declared that "by diverse sundry old authentic histories and chronicles it is manifestly declared and expressed that this realm of England is an empire, and so hath been accepted in the world, governed by one supreme head and king."[153] From the late sixteenth century onward, England forged a substantial empire overseas, for which "the true wealth was the labor accumulated through the slave trade, which made possible a mode of production that could not be imposed in Europe."[154]

As Shilliam writes, "the enslavement of Africans was a fundamental reference point for the initial racialization of deserving and undeserving characteristics, with the 'slave'—and thereby the condition of blackness—exemplifying the latter."[155] The jurist William Blackstone contended that "pure and proper slavery" was forbidden under English common law but possible, if not exactly desirable, in the Caribbean.[156] In fact, common law did demarcate between servitude (which was permitted) and enslavement (which was not), whereas commercial law included no concept of servitude and so justified the practice of enslavement abroad. As the Englishman could not be rendered a commodity but the African could, freedom was constituted as whiteness and unfreedom as blackness.[157] What this meant, too, was that other subjects could be constructed as neither truly white nor truly English and, hence, as undeserving.[158]

Such discourses were sexualized, for they increasingly connected whiteness to moral purity, and this both impacted on, and was articulated through, understandings of commercial sex. In the latter decades of the eighteenth century, social reformers began to use the language of slavery to highlight the plight of sex workers.[159] In the words of one anonymous author, "What are the sorrows of the enslaved negro from which the outcast prostitute of London is exempted? . . . Is the bosom of the unhappy girl less tender than that of the swarthy savage?"[160] Such concern did not extend to enslaved women in the colonies, who had almost no legal recourse if subjected to sexual assault by their masters or other white men.[161] On the contrary: the law helped to create and maintain racialized hierarchies that systematically privileged those of European descent and constructed them as naturally superior. This could be seen, for instance, in the introduction of anti-miscegenation laws in colonial America in the mid-seventeenth century—beginning in Virginia in 1662 and Maryland in 1663—that sought to protect whiteness from contamination.[162] Indeed, the attributes that had been associated with the witches—that they were "savage beings, mentally weak, insatiably lusty, rebellious, insubordinate, incapable of self-control"[163]—did not fall away but were instead attached to African slaves.

Commentators routinely ascribed promiscuity and depravity to blackness: according to the authors of *The Modern Part of a Universal History*, for instance, "Many of the negroes support themselves via the prostitution of their wives." Nor could the taint of blackness be purified with European blood, they argued, for it was the "Mulattoes, a mixed progeny" who were the "grossest" since "the greater part of their women prostitute their bodies publicly to Europeans, and privately to the Negroes."[164]

The essentialization of racial difference not only authorized the systematized oppressions of slavery, including the legalized institution of sexual violence by white Europeans (when black men, in contrast, faced the ongoing threat of accusations of rape such that even the suspicion of guilt could warrant a conviction).[165] It also provided a means to alleviate wider anxieties about the morality and legality of a colonial project that, at its heart, involved the violent extraction of land, labor, and resources on a massive scale. For example, the capture and cultivation of land in the Americas was explicitly justified on the grounds that it was necessary to "liberate" such land from indigenous peoples since they possessed lower mental, physical, and moral capacities than the English and so were naturally incapable of rendering it productive.[166]

But the racialization of sexuality had another side as well, for it meant that white femininity could itself be imagined as innocent and passive—indeed, as Kim F. Hall observes, white femininity could "exist only when posed next to blackness."[167] This represented a problem vis-à-vis the white sex worker, however, for her very existence unsettled the (still very tenuous) purity of whiteness itself. If the sexual immorality of the black slave could be attributed to her nature, then the sexual immorality of the white prostitute must entail the corruption of hers. As sex work was, at heart, an aberration in white femininity, then it was something that could also be viewed as temporary—and a woman's original state of moral goodness could be restored through repentance. Often, the "natural" passivity of the prostitute was achieved through her symbolic death. Narratives of dead and dying prostitutes became more commonplace toward the end of the eighteenth century. As one poem of 1785 (entitled "The Dying Prostitute") put it, "Spurn not my fainting body from your door . . . My sorrows soon shall lay me with the dead."[168]

To be sure, the passivity of white femininity had also been produced by a sustained campaign of "state terrorism" through which the ideal of women as "passive, asexual beings" had been violently enforced.[169] But it also bore the imprint of medical theories that destabilized longstanding associations between (white) female sexuality and carnality. Medieval medical theory had determined that conception required both men and women to ejaculate—meaning, in turn, that any woman who became pregnant through rape was assumed to have consented to her assault.[170] The assumption that conception could only take place through simultaneous ejaculation held fast during the Tudor period, but in the late seventeenth century it became challenged by the discovery of the egg and sperm. This led to the theory that children were pre-formed in the sperm or ova and "rendered female sexual pleasure irrelevant to the process of conception."[171]

While the creation of white femininity offered a new logic through which women's sexuality could be controlled and confined, it also brought more into focus how male sexuality, too, could be blameworthy. Stories of innocent women and girls being led into prostitution by debauched men featured with growing prominence in the late eighteenth century.[172] Although women were still held accountable for allowing themselves to become tempted by men, there was nevertheless some acceptance that, once corrupted, they had little option but to engage in prostitution. This did not dismantle the sexual double standard, however, for it was still the women who sold sex (rather than the men who bought it) who continued to bear the brunt of punitive treatment in Britain.[173] Nevertheless, male sexuality did become more subject to state control in the case of same-sex sexuality. The persecution of Catholic monks under Henry VIII notwithstanding, homosexuality had—for the most part—continued to be overlooked by the authorities and local communities alike.[174] Yet the destabilization of feudal kinship structures had created the conditions for same-sex subcultures to emerge, facilitated by processes of urbanization and the weakening of old social ties. During the seventeenth century, hundreds of coffeehouses were opened in the major cities, initially for those in the higher social classes but, subsequently, for a more diverse clientele. Increasingly, these were used by men who were interested in other men, often involving paid-for sexual exchange.[175] A "coherent social milieu" developed in the capital in particular, not only in the coffeehouses but also in taverns, public houses, and casual rendezvous locations outdoors, and commercial sexual transactions featured prominently in the social fabric of sex.[176]

By the eighteenth century, the emergence of a substantial sexual subculture in London—now the premier city in Europe—"could no longer be overlooked."[177] The Societies for the Reformation of Manners were particularly enthusiastic in tracking down both "lewd women" and "Gangs of detestable Sodomites" that, they argued, plagued London's streets.[178] By 1738, they claimed to have sent to trial over 100,000 people in the five decades previously. Most of these were for minor crimes that were punished via fines but, due to the Buggery Act, sodomy could be punished with death, and this sentence was indeed applied in several cases.[179] At times, sodomy was still articulated as "the heinous and detestable sin of Sodomy, not to be named among Christians"[180] or "that detestable crime, not fit to be named in a Christian country."[181] On other occasions, it was denounced more explicitly—in 1750, for instance, the editor of the journal *Old England* lamented that the death penalty was too good for sodomites, and that the appropriate penalty was disembowelment, as for High Treason.[182]

The repression of sodomy was closely connected to the imposition of norms regarding gender as well as sexuality. As one pamphlet declared, the "Gang of Sodomitical Wretches" that plagued London were "so far degenerated from all Masculine Deportment, or Manly Exercises, that they rather fancy themselves Women, imitating all the little Vanities, that Custom has reconciled to the Female Sex, affecting to speak, walk, tattle, curtsy, cry, scold, and mimic all manner of Effeminacy."[183] In 1726 police raided so-called molly houses in London, with scores of people arrested in one night alone. What particularly scandalized commentators was the mollies' unconcealed effeminacy and subversion of normative gender. Rather than performing femininity to valorize women, it was presumed, the mollies adopted women's speech and dress in order to mock them.[184] Frequently involving paid-for sexual exchange and marital ceremonies alike,[185] the mollies' relationships (and indeed their very existence) openly contravened the terms of the sexual division of labor. With this in mind, it is perhaps not surprising that gender transgressions began to be articulated more explicitly through the grammars of sexuality, family, nation, and race in the eighteenth century. According to one anonymous author, for example, any man displaying effeminacy would surely sire "a feeble unhealthy Infant, scarce worth the rearing; while the Father, instead of being the Head of the Family, makes it seem as if it were governed by two Women." This "enervated effeminate Animal" was thus "unfit to serve his King, his Country, or his Family . . . and leaves a Race as effeminate as himself."[186] And, as we shall see in the following chapter, it was through the proliferation of discourses of sexual and gender deviance that the notion of fundamentally *different* spheres for women and men could become more fully naturalized in the nineteenth century.

CONCLUSION

Given that the exchange of sex for money can be traced back to antiquity, if not further,[187] I have not meant to infer that capitalism either invented, or was invented by, sex work. Instead, I have sought to demonstrate that it is the concept of sex as *non*-work that is a fairly recent innovation, and one that is coeval with capitalism's rise to dominance. Beginning in the Middle Ages, I have explored how the dualism between proper and improper sexuality predates that between sex and work and, indeed, it was a condition of possibility for the economy/sexuality dichotomy to emerge. In particular, distinctions between marriage and whoredom provided the scaffolding around which a new sexual division of labor could be built— one that defined women's realm, status, and labor as "outside the sphere of market relations"[188] and thus beyond the economy itself. As Federici makes plain, the relegation of women to the sphere of non-work did not happen in an incremental or evolutionary manner, for it was instead enforced via an ongoing campaign of violence and repression.[189] Yet, as we have also seen, the reconfiguration of relations between economic production and social reproduction also created room for *some* deviant women to be viewed more sympathetically and, conversely, for male sexuality to become more contested. In the next chapter, I examine how these threads continued to pull alongside, and against, each other in the Victorian era.

CHAPTER 3

Sex, Work, and the Victorians

In this chapter I chart the transformation of commercial sex into "the most scandalous of our social evils"[1] in the Victorian period. While sex work had already come to be denigrated as non-work that depleted the economy of wealth and resources, it did not yet threaten the very viability of the social body. In the nineteenth century, however, the figure of the prostitute was increasingly constructed as a hazard not only to the moral integrity of the nation but also to its physical health. This was bound up with a shift from religious to scientific conceptions of sexuality so that sex workers were associated less with depravity and more with abnormality. The chapter thus considers how discourses of sex work plugged into "themes of health, progeny, race, the future of the species, the vitality of the social body."[2] The repression and production of commercial sex as deviant, I argue, did important politico-economic work in helping to constitute the domestic ideal of bourgeois sexuality as both desirable and necessary. Often couched in the language of rehabilitation, the pathologization of sex workers helped to naturalize the sexual division of labor that capitalism thrived on, so that the economy/sexuality dichotomy could begin to appear as more than just a moral good: it was the natural order of things on which the reproduction of individual, family, nation, and species was founded. In order to explore these themes, the chapter begins with the biopolitical regulation of female prostitution in Victorian Britain before examining its entanglements both with wider conceptions of sexual deviance and with biological logics of racial difference.

Capitalism's Sexual History. Nicola J. Smith, Oxford University Press (2020). © Oxford University Press.
DOI: 10.1093/oso/9780197530276.001.0001.

Prior to the nineteenth century, sex work was already aligned with disease and death and, at times, it had been constructed as a threat to the social order. But it was not until the Victorian era that sex work materialized as a problem that could not simply be suppressed or tolerated but that instead needed to be *governed*.[3] Efforts to censor and censure sex workers began to be "carefully supplanted by the administration of bodies and the calculated management of life"[4]—by efforts, in other words, to fold the prostitute into the social order rather than to expel her from it.[5]

At the turn of the century, it appeared that the regulation of commercial sex might take a different turn. In the wake of the French Revolution of 1789, there was considerable anxiety over economic and social stability, and this heightened contempt for the poor among the middle and upper classes. The Napoleonic Wars of 1803–1815 further exacerbated worries over attacks on the old order and, especially, the threat that the lower classes were thought to pose. This saw calls for harsher policing in order to discipline the poor, including sex workers.[6] Inspired by the earlier Societies for the Reformation of Manners, the Society for the Suppression of Vice was founded in 1802 in order to defend the public from the lower classes' criminality and immorality. Its focus was on those "pernicious" offenses that were "destructive, especially to the comforts and charities of social and domestic life," with sexual vice—including the keeping of disorderly houses and brothels—a key target.[7] The Society was joined by other organizations in this endeavor, including the Guardian Society for the Preservation of Public Morals, which spearheaded a campaign against "the injurious and ruinous effects of Female Prostitution" in London.[8] This concern with public order was also reflected in legislation. Prostitutes were situated among other "idle and disorderly Persons, Rogues and Vagabonds, incorrigible Rogues and other Vagrants" in the 1824 Vagrancy Act, which focused on nuisance behaviors and, specifically, "wandering in the public Streets or public Highways, or in any Place of public Resort, and behaving in a riotous or indecent Manner." The Act also made it an offense to "beg or gather Alms" in "any public Place, Street, Highway, Court, or Passage," on penalty of one month's hard labor.[9]

Yet, as the century progressed, constructions of prostitution as a "vehicle of sin" began to be superseded by constructions of prostitution as a "vector of disease."[10] It was not the first time, of course, that commercial sex had been framed as a health matter, for there had been persistent concerns over venereal disease from the late fifteenth century onward. However, what changed in the nineteenth century was that commercial sex became more closely affiliated with questions of public health.[11] Prominent studies of the time included *Prostitution, Considered in Its Moral, Social and Sanitary Aspects* by the medical doctor William Acton, which was first published in 1857. This influential and controversial volume sought to empirically map the social configuration of commercial sex in England in an explicitly moral scientific agenda that documented prostitution's "ravages, like those of disease and crime." Diagnosing a variety of diseases such as gonorrhea to be the direct consequence of prostitution, Acton noted that sex workers "almost inevitably" contracted infectious diseases and that, as such, they represented a "class of persons who ought . . . to become the objects of legislation."[12]

The Contagious Diseases Acts of the 1860s—which had in part been informed by public debates surrounding Acton's study—formed a key moment in which a certain conception of prostitution became crystalized and codified in the law.[13] The legislation decreed that—upon "information on oath" from the police that "a female therein named is a common prostitute"—a magistrate could "order that such female be subjected to a medical examination by the visiting surgeon" in order to ascertain "whether she is affected with a contagious disease." If a woman were to "neglect or refuse" to seek treatment at a designated hospital, then the police "may apprehend her and convey her with all practicable speed to that hospital and place her there for medical treatment."[14] Although the Contagious Diseases Acts were repealed by the end of the century, having only been enforced in a small number of districts, their purpose "was not simply to confer sovereign power but to facilitate a wider system of normative power."[15] To use Foucault's terminology, the prostitute was "now a species."[16]

Both the Acts themselves and the discourses surrounding them were profoundly gendered, for they perpetuated the double standard that danger and disease were to be found in female, not male, sexuality. Yet, in contrast to medieval discourses, female sexuality was no longer understood as more lustful than that of men. Instead, it was constructed as simultaneously moral and natural—that is, as tied both to notions of feminine virtue and to women's reproductive capacities.[17] Indeed, by the Victorian era, femininity was so closely associated with passivity that images of dead women in popular literature had become a cliché.[18] Nevertheless, as in the Middle Ages, women's sexuality continued to be understood through the lens of men's. Male sexuality was understood to be "instrumental, forceful and direct," whereas women were to be sexually receptive to men.[19] Viewed in these terms, proper female sexuality was defined against the very possibility of sexual pleasure and desire, which were instead contained within male sexuality. Whereas married monogamy was constructed as an essential marker of feminine virtue, commercial sex was—as it had long been—its opposite.[20]

This gendered division of sexuality was also deeply classed, for it was intimately connected to the production of bourgeois sexual morality. The nineteenth century saw the emergence of the bourgeoisie as a major politico-cultural force in the context of structural transformations associated with processes of industrialization and urbanization.[21] During the first half of the century, the bourgeoisie began to be constituted as a distinctive class identity that set itself apart from the immorality of both the aristocracy and the masses. It not only demanded economic, political, and social reforms in order to reduce aristocratic and landed privilege but sought to moralize the proletariat as well.[22] This led, for instance, to the introduction of the Act for the Amendment and Better Administration of the Laws Relating to the Poor in England and Wales of 1834, which included several (later repealed) "bastardy clauses" that aimed to discourage pregnancies outside of marriage by making mothers solely responsible for their illegitimate children.[23] As this example highlights, an important organizing principle for this new bourgeois morality was the ideal of the nuclear family. By the nineteenth century, there was general recognition—especially among the upper classes—of a single marital code.[24] Marriage was increasingly subject to state as opposed to religious control, with secular ceremonies formally recognized for the first time in the 1836 Act for Marriages. The consequence of the new legislation was to more clearly demarcate the unmarried from the married, thus ensuring that distinctions between legitimate and illicit sex could endure.[25]

As the treatment of sex workers under the Contagious Diseases Acts shows, the opposition between reproductive and anti-reproductive modes of female sexuality was violently enforced by the state through gratuitously cruel means. This does not sit well with Foucault's claim that sexuality was "not established as a principle of limitation of the pleasures of others" on the grounds that the bourgeoisie "first tried it on themselves."[26] If the bourgeois sexual ethic was organized around middle-class interests and values, then integral to this was the imposition of moral values on the working classes, and especially the poor, through the (literal) policing of their behavior.[27] Restrictions on sex work were implicated in a wider regime of state-sponsored violence, the effects of which were disproportionately borne by women. Crucially, the direct imposition of norms surrounding gendered behavior and sexual conduct had the consequence of excluding women from waged work, thus ensuring that they conformed to patriarchal expectations by providing unpaid labor in the home.[28]

This was only part of the story, however, for repression was by no means the only technique of modern power deployed. Rather, the nineteenth century also saw a different kind of apparatus feature more prominently: that which aimed to civilize the prostitute.[29] At once medical, religious, and criminal, scores of Magdalene hospitals, asylums, and voluntary bodies sprang up to provide "relief and reformation of wretched outcasts from society" by "restoring hundreds of unfortunate young women to industry."[30] The Magdalene hospitals professed to offer an alternative to prisons and workhouses by curing the mind and soul of the sex worker rather than by punishing her body. Corporal punishment and coercion were thus eschewed in favor of techniques to bolster dignity and self-worth,[31] or so it was claimed. If, in the Middle Ages, sex work had been placed within the confined space of the brothel, then social reformers increasingly tried to contain it within the individualized site of social care. The best way to address prostitution, they argued, was through reformative, not punitive, treatment.[32] The Magdalene asylums sought to offer social care to women to prevent them resorting/returning to sex work, with the overarching aim to eradicate commercial sex altogether.[33] In reality, however, they soon came to resemble workhouses in which women were forced to undertake manual labor, just as they had in the Bridewell Hospital.[34]

Nevertheless, as Annemieke van Drenth argues, this exercise in "caring power" did represent an important shift. Certainly, there was already a long tradition of church-based charitable interventions that had offered shelter and salvation for fallen women. What was new, however, was the focus of this mode of power: whereas the emphasis before had been on locating sin in order to prevent eternal damnation, attention now shifted to the self as a site of latent virtue. Although there was still an interest in matters of vice and sin, it was the self of the individual that now became the focus of efforts to preserve the wellbeing of both the person and society more widely. The inner self thus needed to be freed rather than quelled, with confessionals deemed to be an essential part of the rehabilitative process.[35] It was time for the prostitute to "step forward and speak, to make the difficult confession"[36] of what and who she was. Through this process, proper femininity could be restored to its natural state of virtue (at least in part), for the fallen woman "has still a woman's soul within her breast; and the remembrance of sober happiness stings the conscience oft and frequent."[37] The expansion of social care initiatives was intended to humanize and liberate sex workers by unlocking their individual potential, thereby creating the conditions for personal and social transformation. But, in so doing, such measures constituted sex workers as pathological subjects who, far from being just ordinary women, required therapeutic intervention in order to overcome their dysfunction.[38] It was thus in the name of women's individual "freedom" that sex workers were produced as deviant. Rather than being attributed to "the force of animal desire" in the prostitute herself, sex work was instead attributed to "the force of early habits and education—education, not in knowledge, but in vice and crime" so that re-education was both possible and desirable.[39]

The objective, therefore, was not to remove the prostitute from the social order[40] but to refashion the undeserving poor into the deserving poor. The prostitute may not have been reproductive (in that she violated the ideal of the bourgeois family), but she could nevertheless be made productive. "Two things," it was argued, were "indispensable for the prosperity of Magdalene Asylums—namely, liberal contributions, and a disposition on the part of private families to receive those females who have been reformed as servants."[41] The prostitute's threat to the bourgeois family could thus be overcome, for it was precisely in service of the bourgeois family that she could be put to work. Reproductive labor in her own household, however, could hinder her salvation: "How is her spiritual reformation to be carried on with any system amid all the domestic cares, the noise of children, the occupations, the common conversation and routine?"[42] Thus, the fallen woman could be "rescued from imminent danger, wretchedness, and suffering" by being "trained to new and industrious habits"[43] that would benefit the family—except the family in question did not, it seems, include her own.

The provision of charitable (as opposed to criminal) interventions meant that commercial sex could be conceived in different ways. The religious persecution of sex began to be supplanted with endeavors to exercise governance by the expanding state. This was inspired in part by religious reformers, but it was also rationalized on the basis of secular and scientific discourse.[44] The proliferation of new scientific techniques in the nineteenth century made it possible for sex workers to be studied as a population, as well as to investigate the most personal aspects of their lives as individuals, thus transforming them into "objectified subjects."[45] The budding fields of public health, hygiene, and sanitation, along with the rise of population statistics and social anthropology, both informed the legal regulation of prostitution and helped to produce the prostitute as a new social category—one that could be identified, classified, organized, and disciplined.[46]

As the nineteenth century progressed, the concept of sin began to intersect with, and then to be replaced by, that of abnormality.[47] In Foucault's words, this was a discourse that "spoke, not of sin and salvation, but of bodies and life processes—the discourse of science." Sex, in other words, could be understood not only in terms of morality but also in terms of rationality.[48] Although a more secular concern with sex had developed in the eighteenth century, what was novel in the nineteenth century was the attempt to transform this into a science. Through scientific pretensions toward objectivity, the budding field of sexology was able to lay claim to prestige and legitimacy.[49] By the end of the century, sexology had become established as a scientifically sanctioned field and its subject, sexuality, was now an area of scholarly inquiry, indeed a codified body of knowledge. It entailed a sustained endeavor to isolate, define, systematize, and catalogue the rich diversity in perverse sexualities; that is, to produce a taxonomy of sexuality.[50]

A critical moment in the development of these discourses was Charles Darwin's *On The Origin of Species by Means of Natural Selection*, which instigated a preoccupation with the sexual sources of behavior in the individual and the species in order to uncover the nature of nature itself.[51] In contrast to medieval understandings, this was not about the laws of nature as ordained by God but nature as biology, with "sex" now understood to reside in biology rather than the soul.[52] As nature was "infinitely complex and diversified,"[53] sexologists sought to uncover the secrets of sex through "analysis, stocktaking, classification, and specification."[54] In *Man and Woman*, for instance, Havelock Ellis interrogated the origins of sexuality through discussion of sexed difference.[55] This was significant because it explicitly connected the gender hierarchy, and thus the sexual division of labor, to the sexual instinct.[56] Ellis wrote,

> The female animal everywhere is more closely and for a longer period occupied with the process of reproduction which is Nature's main concern. This is, indeed, more than a zoological fact; it is a biological fact . . . The interests of women may therefore be said to be more closely identified with Nature's interests. Nature has made women more like children in order that they may better understand and care for children.[57]

Women's subjugation—and, especially, the burden of reproductive labor— could thus be attributed to biology and afforded the status of scientific truth. As Darwin put it, the biological facts of reproduction "cannot . . . be disputed."[58]

Discourses of proper female sexuality were therefore articulated through appeals to biological sex, and this served to further strengthen sexual hierarchies by subjugating women to their reproductive capacities. This is not to reduce material conditions to discursive norms but rather to highlight how these norms offered a framework of intelligibility through which such conditions could manifest. As Federici argues, the sexual division of labor required the (re)construction of masculine and feminine identities through which separate spheres could be configured for men and women along the public/private split, in turn meaning that women's work could be redefined as domestic (non)labor.[59] To be clear, working-class women were still expected to perform manual labor—but for bourgeois women (and, hence, the bourgeois ideal of femininity) it was their primary duty to perform reproductive labor in service of the family unit.[60] The ideology of respectability was pivotal here, for it sharply circumscribed what women could and could not do, both within and outside of the home.[61] The virtuous woman was devout, acquiescent, and, above all, a "humble housewife" characterized by her "love of home"—a love that was deemed to be "natural, and arises not so much from training as from constitution."[62] The respectable woman was, therefore, firmly located in the private realm in terms of both her sexuality and her labor. The prostitute, in contrast, represented all that was "dirty, repulsive, noisy, contaminating," and so was set against proper femininity and bourgeois identity itself.[63]

VISIBLE MEN, INVISIBLE WOMEN

While narratives continued to mark out the prostitute as a "distinct female body"[64] in the nineteenth century, moral panics over venereal disease also served to politicize male sexuality. Critiques of criminal justice interventions that had emerged in the eighteenth century increasingly drew on narratives of prostitutes as victims of male desire. The Contagious Diseases legislation was met with fierce opposition from abolitionist feminists such as Josephine Butler, who wrote (under the guise of "an English Mother"),

> The happiness and character of all virtuous women throughout the land must eventually suffer from the consequences of such measures, while upon the poor women, on whom the proposed Law takes immediate effect, there falls a blight and a destruction more complete than anything can in its absence experience.[65]

In particular, Butler sought to politicize how "large classes of men" were encouraged "to look upon fornication not as a sin and a shame, but as a necessity which the State takes care that they shall be able to practice with impunity."[66] Similarly, the socialist Annie Besant argued that venereal diseases "spring from sexual irregularities . . . these poor white slaves sold for man's use, these become their own avengers, repaying the degradation inflicted on them, and spreading ruin and disease among those for whose wants they exist as a class."[67] Such narratives confronted the hypocrisy of blaming women and not men for venereal disease, but they did so by reinforcing married monogamy as the privileged site for both female and male sexuality. In this vein, it was not only abolitionist feminists who articulated the purchase of sex as being at odds with men's "natural" status as husband and father. The medical profession, too, emphasized the indispensable role of marriage to men's physical and moral health. For example, the noted surgeon and medical author James Miller declared in *Prostitution Considered in Relation to its Cause and Cure* that prostitution would "wither and decay" if men were encouraged to marry early, for "the fire of this pure love will burn too hotly, to brook beside it another flame of mere animal lust." Marriage was not only "God's institution" but was the "normal state of the healthy adult man" that was vital for "domestic and social virtue" to flourish.[68]

Although men were still assumed to have a naturally active sex drive, the hydraulic model of male sexual energy—that release was natural and necessary—began to be replaced by the notion that men had a set quantity of energy that must not be wasted.[69] This was shaped by conceptions of the sovereign masculine subject as self-determined and autonomous. By the early nineteenth century, the need for self-control and restraint prevailed in laissez-faire doctrine, which emphasized individual competitiveness and self-assertion in economic affairs, and this was implicated in sexual imaginaries too.[70] If the Reformation had birthed the self as an "inner sanctum" for the individual to locate his moral worth, then the constitution of the private realm in the nineteenth century involved the drawing of "political, legal, and physical boundaries around that inner sanctum."[71] Increasingly, Victorian male sexuality was built around the notion that sexuality could be disciplined and mastered.[72] Bourgeois male sexuality in particular involved the "ideological rejection of sexual pleasure as valuable for its own sake," and thus the censuring of un(re)productive forms of sex.[73] That the public and the private should be properly separated was emphasized by social purity campaigners of the time, who appealed to discourses of public decency in order to justify this split.[74]

Imaginaries of male sexuality in turn connected to the ideology of the bourgeois family. In the words of Kevin Floyd, sexual pathology was located "both inside and outside the family cell, straddling its membrane, constantly struggling against the many temptations to waste that energy, temptations encountered everywhere in domesticity's sexually volatile outside."[75] This did not, however, translate into any kind of commitment to equality between men and women for, if the bourgeois sexual ethic sought to restrict intimate life to married life, then this was especially the case for women.[76] The church remained explicit in its insistence that "the world, with its activities, belongs to man," but the home was women's domain: "Home without woman can neither be made perfect nor happy. Can it be, without her, under any circumstances, in any sense, be called a home?"[77] Men were assumed to be naturally active and so best suited to productive labor in the public sphere, whereas women were inherently passive and so best suited to reproductive labor in the home.[78] Male dominance and female subordination were, quite literally, the natural order of things.

The most heinous way that men could violate the natural order of things, it was presumed, was to engage in sodomy.[79] In contrast to elsewhere in Europe where penalties were often being relaxed, the Buggery Act meant that the death penalty still applied and, by the Victorian era, scores of men had been executed for this "crime." (Indeed, in one year—1806—more men were put to death for sodomy than for murder.)[80] There had also been a rise in the number of prosecutions for attempted sodomy, the penalty for which was the pillory—a punishment so savage that it could lead to serious injury and even death.[81] It was not until 1861 that the death penalty was lifted, when the Offences Against the Person Act legislated that: "Whosoever shall be convicted of the abominable Crime of Buggery, committed either with Mankind or with any Animal, shall be liable, at the Discretion of the Court, to be kept in Penal Servitude for Life or for any Term not less than Ten Years."[82] Other sexual acts between men were brought under the banner of conspiracy to commit a major offense, although this was seldom enforced as proof was "notoriously difficult to obtain."[83]

This did not, however, signal the birth of a less oppressive regime, for the late nineteenth century witnessed a sustained campaign of brutality by the state. This came in the context of growing moral anxiety about female prostitution, and white slavery in particular. Public disquiet reached its height following a series of exposés in the *Pall Mall Gazette* by the editor, W.T. Stead, who wrote, "if the daughters of the people must be served up as dainty morsels to minister to the passions of the rich, let them at least attain an age when they can understand the nature of the sacrifice which they are asked to make."[84] To combat white slavery, the Criminal Law Amendment Act was introduced in 1885, which focused explicitly on "the Protection of Women and Girls" through the raising of the age of consent to sixteen years, the suppression of brothels, and other such measures.[85] Yet, this "attack on one form of sexual deviance" also "prepared the ground for attacking another."[86] During the closing stages of the bill, the Liberal politician Henry Labouchère proposed an amendment to include male prostitution and, in the wake of public furor over Stead's revelations, this was approved without debate in order to pass the bill.[87] The Labouchère Amendment stated that,

> Any male person who, in public or private, commits, or is a party to the commission of, or procures or attempts to procure the commission by any male person of, any act of gross indecency with another male person, shall be guilty of a misdemeanor, and being convicted thereof shall be liable at the discretion of the court to be imprisoned for any term not exceeding two years, with or without hard labor.[88]

In this one short, simple, and last-minute moment of male inclusion, all male sex work—and, with it, all male same-sex sexuality—was materially and symbolically placed outside of the bounds of legal and normative acceptability. The moral gaze of the law was now squarely focused not on men's public acts but on their private sexuality, and in so doing it positioned homosexuality itself as necessarily deviant and criminal.[89] The homosexual man was rendered a class of persons who was not just abnormal or perverse but who was literally against the law.

In this way, the regulation of prostitution was deeply implicated in the production and suppression of homosexuality more widely. This was evident, for example, in the high-profile trials and conviction of the celebrated Irish novelist, playwright, and author Oscar Wilde under the Criminal Law Amendment Act in 1895. Wilde's ordeal followed the Cleveland Street scandal of 1889, which involved a male brothel in London and "threatened to expose the homosexual activities of several high-ranking men."[90] The vile homophobia unleashed in public discourse often found its most intense expression in hatred and disgust for the "renters" whom Wilde paid for sex. As one tabloid put it at the time (in an article entitled "Male Prostitution"), the "male strumpets" who testified in Wilde's trial were the "putrid spawn of civilization" who "did not require Wilde to degrade them" as they were "loathsome creatures" already.[91] As Wilde's trial highlights, the legislation was not just used to penalize the poor, but it tied sexual deviance to poverty nonetheless. This could be seen most plainly in the 1898 Vagrancy Act, which legislated that any man who was found soliciting or importuning would be classed as a rogue and a vagabond—clauses that were repeatedly used against homosexual offenses. The legislation made public sex riskier—legally speaking—for male sex workers than for female ones, and this served to drive male prostitution further underground.[92]

While male sex work became visible in English law for the first time in 1885, the figure of the male prostitute had already emerged as both a discursive category and an object of social, scientific, and medical inquiry some years earlier.[93] By the mid-nineteenth century, moral concerns about male sex work were occasionally appearing in the press: as one newspaper proclaimed, for instance, "what term is there in the English language sufficiently expressive to characterize this monster?"[94] Indeed, the prevalence of commercial sexual transactions meant that any male same-sex sexual encounter had come to be labeled as "trade," even when no money changed hands. Nevertheless, official conceptions of male sex work in legal and medical discourse remained rudimentary to say the least.[95] In the 1860s, however, the male prostitute was formally constituted as an object of scientific knowledge, and this coincided directly with the discursive production of the homosexual as an identifiable category of persons.[96] It is notable that the first substantive quantitative research into homosexuality—undertaken by Félix Carlier in Paris in the 1860s—took the form of research into male sex work.[97]

Although theories of male prostitution were intertwined with those of homosexuality, medical discourses also allowed for their differentiation, with the production of new social classifications associated with the dissemination of scientific techniques allowing deviations from "normal" masculinity to be classified and ranked.[98] Rather than being a sinful choice of sexual practice, sexologists argued that homosexuality was a reversal of the normal sexual instinct ("inversion") and, as such, it was inborn rather than learned.[99] (To take just one example, an article in the journal *Nature* asked in 1869, "Is homosexuality hard-wired? A suggestion, based on measurements of post-mortem brains, that structures in the hypothalamus correlate with sexual behavior, should be taken seriously.")[100] If homosexuality was innate, however, then this raised the question of whether individuals could be blamed for something that was beyond their control. Indeed, most early sexologists, including Richard von Krafft-Ebing in Austria and Havelock Ellis in England, regarded the law as being gravely unenlightened regarding the "realities" of sex and so advocated the toleration, and indeed the decriminalization, of homosexuality. Rather than harsh corporal punishments, enforced surgical interventions such as castration and sterilization were recommended as (still undoubtedly horrific) interventions.[101]

The male prostitute presented something of a conundrum for sexologists, however, since his very existence challenged nascent understandings of who, and what, the homosexual was. Could a man who engaged in sexual activity with other men for payment rather than pleasure still be defined as "homosexual"?[102] The answer sexologists gave was to distinguish between the "sickly perversion" of true homosexuality and the "immoral perversity" of male prostitution—and, as Kerwin Kaye observes, these moral and medical distinctions were in reality classed ones. On the one hand, sexologists called for legal and social clemency for those afflicted with the disorder of genuine homosexuality (which in practice meant middle-class men); and, on the other hand, they advocated harsh punishment and moral reform for those who engaged in actual homosexual sex, especially for money (which in practice meant working-class men). A sharp divide was thus maintained between middle-class "inverts" and working-class "perverts"—the former were to be afforded compassion and leniency; the latter were to be disciplined and castigated. In this way, "class politics played a foundational role in the very inception of the invert/pervert distinction, and in opinions about those placed in each category."[103] Indeed, sexologists devoted much time and care to the task of identifying the precise forms of pathology and immorality that characterized male sex work. This focus on the male prostitute's inherent nature meant that he could be divorced from his politico-economic context, his activities explained by his inner predisposition toward delinquency and depravity.[104] Even his physical appearance was deemed to be an outward indicator of inward moral corruption: "congenital" inverts, for instance, were distinguished by their outward effeminacy, whereas "situational" perverts were characterized by their more masculine looks and manner.[105]

What this also meant was that homosexuality could be constituted as a discrete and somewhat exceptional identity to be differentiated not only from "normal" sexuality but from homosexual sex itself. Genuine homosexuality, sexologists suggested, was defined not by sexual activity but by sexual abstinence—this was sexuality, in other words, without the sex. The actual practice of same-sex sexual relations was therefore still condemned, with the sinful sodomite now demarcated from both the normal heterosexual and the asexual homosexual.[106] Indeed, the male prostitute was not only aberrant but abhorrent—as Krafft-Ebing wrote, male prostitution was "certainly more dangerous to society than that of females" and the "darkest stain" on human history.[107] Thus, rather than ushering in a new regime of sexual permissiveness, sexological understandings served to redraw existing boundaries and hierarchies. Homosexual acts—and especially paid ones—were rendered not only pathological but repugnant, meaning that married, monogamous procreation could remain untroubled as the natural and moral site for both sexual relations and relational sex.

Notably, and despite the preoccupation with questions of gender transgression in the nineteenth century, the lives of transgender sex workers were left unrecognized in dominant discourses. Medical theories subsumed gender nonconformity within understandings of the "homosexual," which was itself classified as a form of gender deviance,[108] and legal discourses rendered transgender personhood similarly unintelligible. A particularly prominent case to exemplify this unrecognizability was that of *The Queen v. Boulton and Others*, which took place in 1871. On the evening of April 28, 1870, Stella Boulton and Fanny Park were arrested outside the Strand Theatre on the grounds that they were "really" men dressed in women's clothes and so were guilty of indecent behavior. The police suspected that Stella and Fanny were also sex workers, and charged them with "conspiring and inciting persons to commit an unnatural offence" in a trial that made headlines across Europe and the United States.[109] As one pamphlet declared,

> Among the many extraordinary cases which are from time to time brought before the public, none have created more sensation, or a greater degree of dismay in the respectable portion of the community, than the astounding, and we fear, too-well founded charge against Boulton and Park, and the outrages of which they have been guilty; the social crime, for so it is, which they have openly perpetrated, cannot be too strongly condemned.[110]

The trial was conducted and reported as one involving two young "men," despite unambiguous evidence that Stella and Fanny were not just theatrical personas (as it was assumed, as they performed onstage) but also lived identities. Love letters between Stella and Lord Arthur Pelham-Clinton, who lived as Stella's husband and who died by possible suicide before the trial, attracted considerable intrigue, as did testimony from Stella's mother about her child's formative years.[111] The possibility that Stella Clinton and Fanny Winifred Park might actually exist as women was never countenanced and, significantly, this unintelligibility was framed in terms of anti-prostitution discourse. For example, the Lord Chief Justice argued that,

> [T]he defendants had the intention of inducing persons with whom they might be brought into contact to have an unnatural and detestable connection with them . . . [W]hat other inference can you draw if you find men painting and powdering themselves and tricking themselves out in a tawdry tinsel finery, assuming not only the appearance of women to whose sex they do not belong but of fallen women of the lowest description, what in euphemistic language are called gay women but what you and I should call prostitutes of the street?[112]

Charged with conspiracy to solicit "other" men and conspiracy to commit sodomy, the defendants were subjected to forensically detailed descriptions of the condition of their bodies from a succession of medical witnesses.[113] (This was despite the fact that, as the Attorney General claimed, English doctors knew hardly anything about such matters.)[114] In the end, "Boulton and Park" were acquitted, as a guilty verdict would have required the jury to have recognized the very possibility of Stella and Fanny. As Neil Bartlett writes, "You cannot legislate against a language simply by imprisoning two people who speak that language. Better to deny the existence of the language altogether."[115]

Commercial sex was therefore gendered very differently in discourse: "women and girls" were often cast as victims; male sex workers were defined as perverts; and transgender identities were rendered unintelligible. But what all of these figures shared was that they were placed in opposition to sexual norms and, especially, to the domestic ideal of marriage. In this way, it was not female prostitution alone but rather prostitution per se that was constructed as patriarchy's deviant other. As such, although they were positioned differently, all modes of prostitution were implicated in the production of normative sexuality and thus the sexual division of labor. For, as Kevin Floyd highlights, the gender hierarchy was, at heart, a sexual hierarchy: male bodies were cast as naturally active in both sexual and social terms and so biologically fitted for productive labor in the public realm; whereas female bodies were constructed as naturally passive and so biologically predisposed to reproductive labor in the private sphere.[116] This hierarchy was, moreover, founded as much on the exclusion of sexual excess as on the valorization of proper sexuality, with the married, procreative, monogamous, bourgeois couple made thinkable through the identification, specification, and persecution of those "peripheral sexualities" against which it was defined.[117]

As such, anti-prostitution discourses worked to naturalize and enforce the institution of marriage that had been so integral to the production of capitalist social relations. Marriage serviced capitalism not only by helping to protect private property by facilitating the transfer of land and inheritance but, as we have already seen, by securing women's unpaid labor in the household, thereby ensuring that the reproduction of labor power was positioned as women's domain.[118] While the family was no longer an economic site in the same way that it had been in medieval times, it was nevertheless transformed into an instrument through which women's labor could be disciplined, controlled, and harnessed. And all of this meant that there could be the "creation of a fully commodified labor market and the formal separation of the public (i.e., productive) and private (i.e., reproductive) spheres."[119] The ideals of bourgeois womanhood and manhood thus served to naturalize and authorize the sexual division of labor, and they did so through reference to their sexual others,[120] the prostitute and the homosexual alike.

As discussed, biological understandings of sexual normality and deviance rose to prominence in the Victorian era. Indeed, by the end of the century, the medical profession had taken on some of the characteristics that had been associated with the priesthood, not least in its claims to speak the truth about societal ills.[121] One effect of the medicalization of social problems was to offer a focal point for worries by the middle classes over social conflict and urbanization and, in so doing, it helped to naturalize economic inequalities. Poverty had become so omnipresent that it could no longer be attributed to individual sinfulness and immorality, and instead individual inferiorities—rooted in biology—became the principal discourse.[122] For example, the social reformer Henry Mayhew identified "two distinct races" of the "vagabond and the citizen" in his study *London Labour and the London Poor*. Characterized by physical differences, the former could be discerned by their "broad lozenge-shaped faces," and the latter by their "oval or elliptical" faces.[123] Criminality, too, was attributed to biology, as could be seen in Havelock Ellis's study *The Criminal*:

> Perhaps the most general statement to be made is that criminals present a far larger proportion of anatomical abnormalities than the ordinary European population. Now this is precisely the characteristic of the anatomy of the lower human races: they present a far larger proportion of anatomical abnormalities than the ordinary European population . . . Our survey of the psychical characteristics of criminals showed that they constantly reproduce the features of savage character—want of forethought, inaptitude for sustained labor, love of orgy, etc.[124]

As this quotation reflects, scientific discourse made it possible—or so it was believed—to explain differences not only within populations but also between them. Race was, moreover, enmeshed with sex since the survival of such populations was predicated on reproduction.[125] While Foucault traces the connections between sex and race to the European aristocracy's preoccupation with blood,[126] Ann Laura Stoler demonstrates that they were just as dependent on dynamics of imperial exclusion. That is to say, the European bourgeoisie was compared with, and constituted through, "the libidinal energies of the savage, the primitive, the colonized." The white European subject was constructed as not just racially different from colonized peoples but as racially superior, and this in turn linked to sex through the reproduction of the self, family, nation, and species.[127]

To be sure, Britain's abolition of slavery under the 1833 Slavery Abolition Act was conceived through humanitarian narratives that allowed the colonized to be imagined much more sympathetically than before.[128] Yet this legislation was introduced only after Britain had been able to siphon off vast resources—not least labor power—from the colonies. That empire was a condition of possibility for Britain's own economic, political, and military ascendancy was well recognized at the time, as could be seen in Patrick Colquhoun's *A Treatise on the Wealth, Power, and Resources of the British Empire in Every Quarter of the World*:

> An era has arrived in the affairs of the British Empire, discovering resources which have excited the wonder, the astonishment, and perhaps the envy of the civilized world. The accumulation of property, extensive beyond all credibility, and . . . rapid in its growth [is] beyond what the most sanguine mind could have conceived.[129]

The ongoing "right" of the British to extract wealth and labor from the colonies was embedded in the 1833 Act, which stipulated that it was "just and expedient" for slaves to be "manumitted and set free," but it was not they who should receive compensation. Instead, this should go to slaveowners as "the Persons hitherto entitled to the Services of such Slaves for the Loss which they will incur by being deprived of their Right to such Services."[130] With dire material conditions authorized for those "set free," the consequent social unrest—including the Morant Bay rebellion of 1865—troubled the benevolent universalism that had framed abolitionist rhetoric. As the nineteenth century progressed, narratives of racial equality gave way to eugenics, as Britishness—rooted in the English genus—was constituted as a distinct, and superior, civilization and race.[131]

Racial backwardness was already associated with sexual disorder, and sexuality became more and more significant in marking out the "civilized" from the "primitive." Vital here was the question of commercial sex and, especially, anxieties over the spread of venereal disease.[132] Within Britain, the Contagious Diseases Acts were implemented in just a few districts, but by the mid-1870s they had been introduced across the empire, and they remained in place long after their domestic repeal. In the colonies, the Acts were used as an apparatus through which the unruly sexuality of colonial subjects could be disciplined.[133] There was some recognition that it was in fact the Europeans who had introduced venereal disease to colonized peoples rather than vice versa[134]—a discourse that was made possible by prior understandings of *continental* Europeans as sexually disorderly.[135] Nevertheless, constructions of colonial societies as sexually dysfunctional were used to legitimate much more invasive interventions vis-à-vis these populations. Indeed, prostitution itself came to stand in for that which was backward and barbarous in societies where the body rather than the mind was believed to reign. Colonial officials habitually argued that commercial sex was an endemic feature of colonial societies, a sign of their primitive and disorderly nature.[136] Colonial intervention was sometimes articulated in terms of the need to save native women from native men,[137] but the emphasis was primarily on the need to protect European men from contamination from native women, and especially sex workers. It was assumed that contact with a prostitute could affect fertility or threaten the purity of the race through the birth of mixed-race offspring.[138] Thus, the problem of prostitution in the colonies was used to justify the desirability and necessity of imperial rule that, in reality, entailed ongoing violence, oppression, and the extraction of labor and resources.

It was also because of the question of race that male prostitution became more problematized at the very moment when homosexuality, at least for sexologists, was becoming more acceptable. To quote Cynthia Weber, the "racially whitened, Western European 'homosexual'" could be "put on a course of progressive correction so he could live within Victorian society" precisely through reference to figurations of the "sexualized and racially darkened degenerate and/or deviant 'perverse homosexuals.'"[139] The very existence of the male prostitute in colonized societies was testament to their general depravity and backwardness, or so it was claimed, with non-white masculinity constructed as both hypersexualized and effeminate in European discourse.[140] This related to economic logics for, as Grace Kyungwon Hong argues, the bourgeois subject was understood as a possessive individual: to possess property was not just an economic condition but a mode of subjectivity, and one that was both gendered and racialized since it was structured by masculinity and whiteness.[141] More than this, to possess property in one's own body was conceived as the supreme exercise of freedom. As sexuality was believed to reside in the body, and the body was itself owned by the individual subject, then it could be imagined as something to be mastered as an expression of individual freedom and, ultimately, self-ownership.[142] The figure of the colonized man—a figure who was always already possessed—thus stood in opposition to the rationality and self-restraint of the bourgeois man.[143] Of course, while the bourgeois masculine subject could conceive of himself as free from constraint, his ability to exercise autonomy in fact relied on the labor of others—both women's labor in the home, and the labor of colonial subjects abroad.[144] But since Britishness (in turn read as both whiteness and Englishness) was synonymous with freedom, then the truly British masculine subject could be neither enslaved nor commodified, sexually or otherwise.

What all of this meant was that prostitution could be constructed as a matter of distinctively *national* health. Venereal disease, it was suggested, did not simply infect individuals but could undermine the health and vitality of the English race and national genus.[145] The "old fears of venereal affliction" thus merged with "the great evolutionist myths" to "ensure the moral cleanliness of the social body."[146] In the second half of the nineteenth century, a full-blown moral panic materialized over the existence of "white slavery" in the capital. As a feature in the *Reynold's Newspaper* in 1870 declared,

> We have let loose our tongues and exercised our pens in denouncing slavery in America and Russia . . . But all this while we have never so much as dreamt that there exists white slavery at home—slavery which, in some of its features, is quite as iniquitous and intolerable as that we have so vigorously inveighed against abroad . . . Tens of thousands of women prostitute their bodies and pollute their souls for bread, which many can scarcely get even at this terrible price . . . "Britons shall never be slaves!" Would to God that such were the case![147]

It was not the colonies but rather the continent that was blamed here. As the physician and author Michael Ryan wrote of prostitution in London, "It is a historical fact, that soon after the French revolution of 1789, licentiousness spread throughout Europe."[148] Indeed, there were reported to be eighty thousand prostitutes in the capital alone—a number that had "swollen every succeeding year, for prostitution is an inevitable attendant upon extended civilization and increased population."[149] Whereas "wretched Frenchwomen" were said to "infest Regent-street,"[150] it was also claimed that English girls were being "decoyed and sold into the cruelest, most indecent, most revolting slavery that the world has ever known" in Belgium and elsewhere.[151] This represented a violation of the nation itself, for Britishness cherished individual liberty as inherent to its morality, greatness, and distinctiveness:[152] "To this glorious liberty England is travelling on; and at whatever distance, or however slowly, she is or will be followed by all the nations of the world."[153] And it was precisely in order to protect such liberty that prostitution must be dealt with. As an editorial in *The Times* put it,

> The Great Social Evil, as it is not unfairly called, will remain a problem in our time . . . We do not believe it is necessary to the preservation of our liberties that our most crowded thoroughfares should be daily and nightly paraded by scores

of gross foreign women, interspersed with a sprinkling of the most shameless among our own countrywomen.[154]

While the figure of the white slave was depicted as defilement of the English race and civilization, the cause of such defilement was not the empire (which, after all, symbolized Britain's greatness). Instead, it was to be found rather closer to home, within Europe's borders, for Britishness derived not only from whiteness but also from its "perceived distance from continental European mores,"[155] and the sexual mobility of women—from Europe, and to Europe—jeopardized freedom itself. The implications of these discourses were to be far-reaching—extending even into the present moment—as will be examined in the remaining chapters of this book.

CONCLUSION

If particular configurations of sexuality have "historically shifted from the realm of death to life,"[156] then prostitution in the Victorian era certainly seems to be a case in point. Before the nineteenth century, sex workers were discursively aligned with disorder, disease, and death both literally and figuratively. As this chapter has discussed, this changed markedly in the Victorian period as commercial sex was increasingly implicated in the "calculated management of life" so that sex workers' individual potential as productive subjects could be harnessed in service of the bourgeois family. Yet this should not be confused with the naturalization of prostitution for, at the same time, sex workers were increasingly identified as a source of infection that, if not governed appropriately, could pollute the entire body politic. The biopolitical governance of commercial sex was thus performed precisely in order to manage the threat to life that this "alien strain"[157] was believed to represent. More than this, the regulation of female prostitution was implicated in the cultivation and suppression of other "alien strains" including that of the homosexual, and the male prostitute in particular. As this chapter has also explored, it was through these medical, moral, and juridical diagnoses of prostitution's pathologies that the sex/work and public/private splits could be constituted not only as virtuous and necessary but as *healthy*. I shall pick up on these themes again at various junctures but, for now, I want to turn from the question of life to that of love in the next chapter.

CHAPTER 4

Buying Love in the Twentieth Century

Modern society is perverse, not in spite of its puritanism or as if from a backlash provoked
by its hypocrisy; it is in actual fact, and directly, perverse.
                              —Michel Foucault, *The Will to Knowledge*

I n the pages that follow, I explore how commercial sex was implicated
in the reconfiguration of relations between economy and sexuality in
the twentieth century. Specifically, I consider how the rise of consumer
culture meant that all aspects of life—including intimate and sexual
life—were increasingly governed by market rationalities. Since the purchase of commodities for the heteronormative family was understood
more and more as an expression of love, women's waged labor could
be reimagined as possible, even desirable, so long as it was in service
of the family. Yet I also interrogate how the twentieth century did not
see the normalization of commercial sex in Britain. On the contrary,
moral panics over sex work were the focus of wider anxieties about
transformations in the family, economy, nation, and empire. Indeed, it
was precisely through the marking out of sex work as aberrant that the
illusion of separate economic and sexual spheres could be maintained,
even as heteronormativity was itself organized around consumer logics.
The chapter proceeds as follows: the first section situates commercial
sex within wider consumerist shifts; the second section links these
developments to the labor of love; and the final section examines the
ongoing denigration of sex work in the twentieth century. Overall,
I contend that the fantasy of sex as something that could/should not
be commodified obscured how love, itself tied to sex, was already being

Capitalism's Sexual History. Nicola J. Smith, Oxford University Press (2020). © Oxford University Press.
DOI: 10.1093/oso/9780197530276.001.0001.

sold not only as a consumer product but as the ultimate mode of labor for women.

CONSUMING DESIRE

By the twentieth century, the public/private split had become firmly established in Britain, and yet women were by no means completely excluded from the formal economy. In part, this was because working-class women continued to perform waged labor outside of the home, but it was also because the economy was increasingly organized around consumption in which women played a leading role. The foundations for women to be positioned as consuming subjects had been laid some centuries earlier: we may recall that, as far back as the sixteenth century, Thomas Becon could remark that women may "go to the market to buy things necessary for her household, etc."[1] While it had long been unacceptable for women to *sell* wares in public (as exemplified by the figure of the street sex worker), the *purchase* of goods was permissible (so long as this was in service of women's proper function as housewife). It was in the eighteenth and nineteenth centuries, though, that the conditions for consumer culture were secured in place as the family, which had once been the locus of economic production, became a primary site of consumption.[2] By the late eighteenth century, consumption was regarded as a good in its own right such that the economist Adam Smith could describe it as "the sole end and purpose of all production."[3] And by the late nineteenth century, industrialization meant that a wider range of goods was more available and more affordable than ever before (for the middle classes, if not for the poor). Commodity consumption and consumer culture were in part driven by the confluence of technological developments, overproduction, and the rise of advertising.[4] But they were also bound up with empire, which made possible the supply of raw materials on which British manufacturing depended, along with inflows of increasingly exotic goods for direct consumption. Colonialism helped to create demand for such goods from bourgeois women in particular, for it "inscribed women as imperial subjects and created the conditions for specifically gendered desires for exotic goods."[5]

Of course, as for everything else she did, a woman's spending activities were expected to be in service of the family. And, in reality, women's consumer practices did involve considerable labor in and for the home, as Miranda Joseph highlights.[6] What was far less tolerable, however, was spending for its own sake. The rise of consumerism was, therefore, accompanied by the emergence of the profligate woman ("at once the most odious, mischievous, and hateful member of the community"[7]). Such discourses were sexualized in that they tapped into older narratives of the rapacious whore and the irresponsible prostitute, with "profligacy" denoting both sexually licentious and economically wasteful practices. By the early twentieth century, the figure of the sex worker had come to personify profligacy in both senses of the word. In his pioneering study of prostitution in Europe, for instance, Alexander Flexner wrote: "The London street-walker pays three guineas in rental where an honest family pays one . . . Her business interest and bad taste lead her to indulge in shoddy and relatively expensive luxuries, soon worn out or discarded."[8] Two decades later, George Ryley Scott's sweeping volume, *A History of Prostitution from Antiquity to the Present Day*, continued in this theme:

> No girl is driven into a life of prostitution through inability to secure a job. There is a bigger demand of domestic servants than there is a supply . . . She wants smart clothes, she wants gaiety, and when circumstances offer her a chance to secure fine clothes and to taste gaiety, she jumps at the opportunity with both feet. It is this dissatisfaction which impels servant girls, in such preponderating numbers, to become prostitutes . . . [The] main reasons which induce girls to take to the streets are love of luxury and idleness. Often the two are combined. The one breeds the other to such an extent that it becomes difficult to separate them.[9]

As these extracts illustrate, it was women's natural place to be tethered to the bourgeois family—even if, for working-class women, this was as domestic servants rather than as housewives. While economic independence for women was already associated with sexual deviance, the language of consumerism meant that such independence could be depicted as an indulgent luxury that society could ill afford. Sex workers had long been classed as the idle poor, and now they were simply portrayed as idle—as Flexner put it, "We may not overlook the loss involved in the unproductiveness of this army of women."[10] Rather than being driven by economic need (i.e., poverty), sex workers were thus perceived to be motivated by consumer desire (i.e., "to secure fine clothes and to taste gaiety"). The problem here was less consumerism per se and more consumerism by women (and, especially, working-class women) that was directed not toward the bourgeois family but, quite scandalously, toward themselves.

Yet, while the sex worker continued to be depicted as aberrant, such narratives were also made possible by consumerism itself, for here too the logic of economic need was increasingly being displaced by that of desire. By the twentieth century, the consumer economy was associated with a much broader openness to individual pleasure and gratification, the stimulation of which represented a key means through which capitalist production could be organized.[11] For the working classes, leisure was becoming more important as a means of compensation for "ever more routinized, tedious, deskilled work environments";[12] and for the middle classes, consumption could be channeled into the cultivation of self and family.[13] The development of the mass media and expansion of the advertising industry further facilitated the creation and direction of new "economies of pleasure" via commodity consumption. In this way, material processes of capitalist production and consumption were embroiled in the development of new modes of consciousness and lived realities.[14]

Crucially, the logic of desire connected not only to consumerism but also to sexuality. As Kevin Floyd contends, from the early twentieth century onward, bodies were "increasingly, if quite unevenly, normalized" as *both* consuming subjects *and* hetero/homosexual subjects.[15] While the concept of inversion had emerged in the late nineteenth century out of scientific attempts to define, explain, and discipline deviations, this began to fall away as sexual identity was understood more and more in terms of a desiring subject's object choice.[16] Sigmund Freud's contributions were especially influential here: in *Three Essays on the Theory of Sex*, first published in 1905, Freud argued that the conflation of human sexuality with human needs akin to hunger (the "sexual instinct") gave "a very false picture of the true situation." Rather, sexuality should first and foremost be understood in terms of "the person from whom sexual attraction proceeds" ("the sexual object") and "the act towards which the instinct tends" ("the sexual aim"), within which there could be "numerous deviations." The task of scientific inquiry, Freud posited, was to uncover the "relation between these deviations and what is assumed to be normal."[17] The concept of sexual object choice opened up space for sexuality to be conceptualized in terms of a multiplicity of subjects and objects of desire along a variety of axes of difference (e.g., masculine male desire for a masculine male object; feminine male desire for a masculine male object; masculine female desire for a masculine female object; and so on).[18]

The identification of heterosexual and homosexual desire represented an important change in prevailing understandings of sexuality, for it entailed a move from questions of gender congruence to an understanding of sexual desire as the foundation for identity.[19] While "heterosexuality" as a specific term had been coined in the late nineteenth century to diagnose pathology,[20] it began to be used to denote the "common, default, and reference sexuality—the 'true' sexuality at the top of the hierarchy."[21] More than this, sexuality itself could be located in, and conducted through, desire. Indeed, as Foucault writes, desire was one of the "most essential internal operating principles" of sexuality: "the desire for sex—the desire to have it, to have access to it, to discover it, to liberate it, to articulate it in discourse, to formulate it in truth."[22] The emergence of sexual object choice as the dominant paradigm thus differed from prior understandings of sex as predicated on reproduction (whether of the individual, family, nation, or species). It meant that pleasure and sensation could be detached from family need as the organizing principle of sexuality,[23] thus constituting "'sex' itself as something desirable."[24]

Yet, as Rosemary Hennessy outlines, this does not mean that the importance of reproduction began to dwindle. On the contrary, the constitution of the new desiring subject created opportunities for reproduction—and women's reproductive capacities in particular—to be harnessed in new ways. As we have seen, the Victorian sexual division of labor had been framed around a dualism—assumed to be biologically given—between active male sexuality and passive female sexuality. Now the question of sexual object choice became the focus, but this reinvigorated rather than dismantled the oppositional gender binary. Not only were male/female bodies assumed to naturally correspond with masculine/feminine attributes, but desire could also be disciplined in accordance with a hierarchy between sexual subject (male/masculine) and object choice (female/feminine). Just as it had in Victorian times, active sexuality remained associated with masculinity, and passive asexuality with femininity. Men (or, more accurately, heterosexual men) were still assumed to be fundamentally different from/ superior to women via their physical strength, their rationality, and their sexual virility.[25] The heterosexual man was "sexually assertive, emotionally detached, with a voracious sexual desire and a body that guaranteed [him] satisfaction." The heterosexual woman, in contrast, continued to be associated with weakness, irrationality, and sexual passivity: she was more emotional, more caring, more vulnerable, and less connected to erotic desire/ pleasure than men.[26] Proper femininity therefore remained rooted in the notion that women must, above all, be desired objects rather than desiring subjects. Hence, the notion of *opposite* sexes remained very much in force, except now it was articulated via the dichotomy between heterosexuality and homosexuality.[27]

The creation of the new normal of heterosexuality—heteronormativity— authorized the continued "patriarchal regulation of women's bodies, labor, and desires," thus legitimating the prevailing sexual and economic order.[28] Through the "reification of sexual desire"[29] as discrete and bounded identities that mapped, in turn, onto preexisting sexual hierarchies, the sexual division of labor could be maintained, thereby enabling the continued extraction of women's socially reproductive labor in and for the family/household.[30] While the unfastening of sexuality from reproduction might have posed a threat to the patriarchal sexual order, the hetero/homosexual binary meant that this danger could, for the most part, be contained.[31] Moreover, while homosexuality could be brought more out into the open, it too was assumed to adhere to the heteronorm, albeit in an inverted fashion. Thus, the new discourse of desire helped to control the "unruly possibilit[ies] posed by the new desiring subject"—that is, the potential for all manner of sexual identities, expressions, and relations to erupt into being.[32]

A particularly unruly possibility was that of the prostitute, since her existence both confirmed and confused heteronormative logics. On the one hand, heterosexual male desire for female sex workers traced fairly neatly onto the desiring subject/desired object dualism, especially since male sexual pleasure "does not necessarily imply love," as George Ryley Scott put it. So too could the female sex worker be identified by her lack of desire, for "she goes through the sexual act and its concomitants devoid of any pleasurable feelings whatever."[33] On the other hand, the hetero/homosexual binary recognized some potential for female sexual desire, including between women.[34] Perhaps, then, the female sex worker might herself experience some pleasure, even if this was not for her male clients. Havelock Ellis, for instance, suggested that homosexuality was "frequently found among prostitutes"; indeed, they presented with congenital sexual inversion "in a considerable proportion of cases" and this (along with "an accompanying indifference to intercourse with men") was a "predisposing cause of the adoption of a prostitute's career."[35] As I shall tease out later in this chapter, such deviance was believed to be distinctively foreign in provenance. Homosexuality, Ellis proposed, was far more prevalent in French sex workers than English ones, as was the tendency to engage in irregular sexual practices: "The difference evidently is that the British women, when they seek gratification, find it in normal coitus, while the foreign women prefer more abnormal methods."[36]

What commercial sex illuminated, too, was how male and female bodies could become objects of sexual *and* consumer desire. To quote Peter Drucker, heteronormativity meant that male and female bodies could be "reduced to things that can and must be obtained, notably by acquiring all sorts of other things."[37] The opening up and expansion of consumer markets and the development of mass-scale consumer culture not only entailed the creation of new identities, including sexual ones, but commodity was itself reflected in sexuality. As the individual was, above all else, a free consumer of desire, then pleasure could be conceived as the consumption of commodities.[38]

Important here was the expansion of romance industries throughout the twentieth century, which monetized heteronormative narratives that heterosexual intercourse simultaneously embodied the supreme mode of intimacy (heterosexual love) and the supreme mode of physical pleasure (the orgasm).[39] Lauren Berlant illuminates how romance constituted heterosexuality both as the ultimate fantasy in its own right and as the ordinary site in which the fantasy of intimate life could be lived. Heteronormative imaginaries were, moreover, generic in their individualism, for they reflected "subjects who believe that their love story expresses their true, nuanced, and unique feelings, their own personal destiny."[40] Although the concept of romantic love had constituted the individual liberal subject for centuries, what was distinctive about the twentieth century was the intensification of its connections with consumerism. Both love and consumerism involved the exercise of individual choice, the pursuit of personal autonomy, and the chance for self-fulfillment.[41] What they offered, in other words, was the "promise of happiness."[42]

The concurrence of heteronormativity and consumerism did not just mean that heterosexual desire could become more explicitly commodified, though, for the uncoupling of sexuality from reproduction also created opportunities for the commercialization of sex itself. In Foucault's words, "the truth and the sovereignty of sex"[43] was becoming an object of desire in its own right. It is no coincidence that the sex industry expanded under late capitalism, for it was able to utilize strategies for profit generation that had proved effective elsewhere (e.g., mass marketing), and that helped to insert "the commodification of sexual functions and the integrity of sexuality into a capitalist market system."[44] In the latter decades of the twentieth century, the mainstreaming of the industry could be seen both within the adult entertainment sector itself (in the incorporation of conventional advertising strategies and corporate structures, and in closer interactions with traditional businesses) and outside of it (in the spread of erotic services and products to business that did not otherwise specialize in sex, such as pay-per-view in hotels).[45] At the same time, there was considerable market specialization and diversification in the adult industry, including the development of niche markets that required specialist products, skills, and forms of knowledge around sexual diversity and erotic practice, as well as the constitution of new identities and communities to service them.[46] Thus, even as sexual experimentation and heterogeneity were cast as modes of cultural transgression, so too the melding together of sexual and consumer culture in the creation of niche markets and subcultures could represent "another great opportunity for sales."[47]

Yet, while the production and proliferation of sexual commodities was not at all incongruous with the development of late capitalism, this was also contradictory and contested. For, although consumerism allowed the "perverse implantation"[48] of capitalist markets into the realms of sex, fantasy, and fetish, on the one hand, heteronormativity was also busy in the business of making love, on the other. In the next section I discuss how—although women had long been expected to perform the labor of love—the nature, and significance, of love as a justification for the sexual division of labor nevertheless altered in important ways in the twentieth century.

MAKING LOVE

As we saw in the previous chapter, the truth of sex had come to be located in the self of individual persons in the Victorian era, and predominant understandings in the twentieth century continued to conceive of sexuality in these terms. Quite *how* it related to selfhood did, however, change shape, for explanations of sexuality as acquired/psychological began to supplant understandings that it was innate/biological.[49] Certainly, eugenicist ideas of inborn normality/abnormality remained profoundly influential, especially in the first half of the century. Sexual deviance, including prostitution, was still frequently blamed on inherited traits—as the acclaimed socialists Sidney Webb and Beatrice Webb suggested, the solution was "to search out and permanently segregate, under reasonably comfortable conditions and firm but kindly control, all the congenitally feeble-minded."[50] Nevertheless, social and scientific discourses began to entertain more seriously the possibility that aberrant behavior might be learned, not inbred. According to the noted surgeon C. F. Marshall, it was indeed the case that prostitution could denote "the presence of an innate immorality due to bad heredity." But, since "the conditions leading to prostitution may be inherited or acquired," the prostitute herself "may be born or made," and interventions should take account of this.[51]

Of particular significance was the notion that the secrets of an individual's sexuality lay not in their heredity but in their formative experiences. Prior theories of sexuality, Freud wrote, had focused on "the primeval period which is comprised in the life of the individual's ancestors" (i.e., heredity) rather than "the other primeval period, which falls within the lifetime of the individual himself" (i.e., childhood).[52] While Freud did not deny that "the germs of sexual impulses are already present in the newborn child," he suggested that it was in childhood that sexuality started to take shape, and in puberty that "changes set in which are destined to give infantile sexual life its final, normal shape."[53] But it was not until after the Second World War, when the genocidal logics of eugenics had been starkly exposed by the death camps,[54] that psychological theories could prevail over biological ones. The development of new scientific knowledge in the fields of psychiatry, clinical psychology, and medical theory more broadly brought "a new kind of attention" to the behavioral mechanisms through which individuals adhered to, or diverged from, societal norms.[55] In particular, the relations between mother and child were viewed as critical for an individual's mental, moral, and physical health. Medical theories of transsexualism, for instance, diagnosed the "problem" as lying with the mother rather than the child—and it was in the mother's own troubled childhood that, in turn, such pathologies originated.[56] Prostitution, too, was increasingly explained in psychological terms, if not exclusively so. Women who committed the "sexual offences" of sex work were "depraved and alcoholic; others are mentally defective or psychotic; some are constitutional psychic inferiors; many are temperamentally unstable, hysterical and suggestible; others are idle, vicious, deceitful and unscrupulous."[57]

As Jemima Repo explores, these new forms of scientific knowledge enabled the infiltration of the state into the bourgeois family by institutionalizing conceptions of normal/healthy minds and bodies. Since it was mothers who nurtured the individuals who represented the heart of society in liberal discourse, motherhood was constituted as essential for the health of the family, economy, and nation under capitalism.[58] Central here was the concept of love. Love was nothing new to sexuality, grounded as it was in the notions of individuality, autonomy, consent, and privacy that had emerged during the Reformation and that constituted bourgeois sexuality ("Love is the fulfilling of every law, and the perfection of the highest state"[59]). But what changed in the twentieth century was that "love was no longer just a moral duty or romantic ideal" but rather "an affective technology that shaped normal and abnormal children." Freedom was, moreover, no longer simply about being liberated from sin but rather involved the "imperative for subjects to be free and happy"—free and happy, that was, for white, middle-class subjects within the confines of the heteronormative nuclear family. And yet the figure of the wife/mother remained at the very center of affective technologies, just as she had been in Victorian times.[60]

That the sexual division of labor needed to be rejuvenated through the logic of love is, perhaps, no surprise. During the Second World War, the need to shackle women's economically productive labor to the war effort—including through the widespread use of manual labor—confounded discourses that tied normative femininity to natural passivity and physical weakness. This led to considerable anxiety about the longer-term impact of women undertaking "men's work" (especially given calls for them to be paid men's wages). The *Sunday Mirror* captured these fears beautifully:

> At the moment—we all realize—it is essential for women to do men's work. Production demands this extra labor, and the demand must swiftly be met. But what is going to happen when the war is over? For several years, women will have enjoyed an extra independence of their menfolk, and many people are troubled lest the women might not return to their homes with such glee as hitherto. Here we have the nucleus of a monumental social upheaval . . . Let the homes be real homes. It will be discovered, then, that a baby, like the man she loves, means more to any woman than a packet of pound notes every Friday.[61]

For women to earn a packet of pound notes every Friday to enable their own basic subsistence was clearly not thinkable here. Still, the *Sunday Mirror* need not have worried. Despite women's participation in the formal workforce, their socially reproductive labor was still required throughout the war to service the home—both the home of domestic life and the home of national economy. Following the war, state provisions to support women in the workforce were rapidly withdrawn, including the strict limiting of childcare places, and a "cultural offensive was launched to return women to domesticity."[62] By the 1950s, the ideal of marriage-with-children was no longer just an ideal but also a norm that everyone was expected to adhere to, and in Britain (as for elsewhere in Western Europe) this was organized around the model of the male breadwinner and female homemaker.[63] The notion that unmarried women were surplus to requirements was articulated quite literally in official understandings—The *Registrar-General's Statistical Review of England and Wales* noted approvingly in 1954 that the "surplus of women" was "now largely confined, in this country, to the higher ages" due to the high marriage rates.[64]

That said, while women were expected (and often made) to forfeit men's "rightful" jobs, it was also the case that the number of women working outside the home actually increased after the war. If the archetypal working woman was young and single prior to 1939, then this changed markedly during the 1950s and 1960s, as married women—many with dependent children—entered the workforce at an unprecedented rate.[65] In these two decades, the number of part-time workers increased over fourfold, most of whom were married women. In fact, this did not seriously challenge the male breadwinner model, for women's participation in the formal labor market was explained by their desire to undertake paid employment in order to purchase "extras" for the family.[66] Men's waged labor, in other words, was constructed as necessary for the very survival of the family: it was husbands who put food on tables and roofs over heads. Women's waged labor, in contrast, was something of a luxury—indeed, it was performed precisely in order to pay for luxuries. It was, moreover, undertaken in order to nurture the family, so that women's economically productive labor outside of the home was, in effect, an extension of their socially reproductive labor within it. Women's paid work, in other words, could itself be conceptualized as a mode of consumption.

Nevertheless, the lines between the public sphere of waged labor and the private sphere of domestic labor were becoming more noticeably blurred. In reality, of course, the lines were *already* blurred given that many women (primarily single, working-class women) had long done paid work outside of their own homes, often in service of the bourgeois family. In the 1950s and 1960s, however, this changed markedly: by 1971, half of married women of working age were employed in paid jobs, compared to just one in ten in 1911.[67] This unsettled the distinction between working "girls" (for whom paid work had been conceptualized as a "temporary aberration"[68]) and married women (for whom non-work had been conceptualized as a natural state of being). The answer was to imagine *all* of women's economically productive labor as a temporary aberration: it was an extravagance that could be indulged, for sure, but only on the condition that it formed part of a wider repertoire of socially reproductive duties. In this sense, women's waged labor could be refigured as reproductive rather than antireproductive, for it serviced rather than threatened the family and, hence, the social order. At the same time, as women's work *outside* of the home could be labeled as work *for* the home, then it could also be denigrated as nonproductive labor (i.e., not "real" work).

All of this allowed the sexual division of labor to be constituted in subtly different ways from before. The fact that marriage became so thoroughly normalized in the 1950s meant that it no longer needed to be defended so overtly, although in the 1960s divorce rates did begin to rise.[69] Proper sexuality was, by now, less associated with active restraint (i.e., something to be achieved) than the realm of quiet conventionality (i.e., something that could be "spoken of less and less"[70]). Even so, although married life was unmarked in this way, then its normality still needed to be defined against any deviations. In particular, if women's economically productive labor must be performed for the family, then it must be done "out of love"—it was, in other words, an extension of wifely and motherly duties. It could not be defined as necessary labor; nor could it be performed for its own sake, or for women's own sake. Rather, "women's work" could be refashioned to include waged labor so long as it kept its place as supplementary labor—supplementary, that was, to men's paid labor in the workplace and to women's unpaid labor in the home. Adjunct labor, then, was the very definition of women's work.

Thus, although women were entering the waged workforce in greater numbers than ever before, the new cult of motherhood ("a mother's love") meant that their socially reproductive labor in the home could still be secured. This is not to suggest, however, that other forces were not in play in enabling women's economically productive labor to be mobilized more easily. Particularly important here was the expansion of welfare and social interventions, especially in the postwar decades. The experience of the Great Depression and the advent of two world wars, the consolidation of power within industry, and the growing organization of labor, all helped to restructure relations between state, society, and economy.[71] While social policies were often predicated on a male breadwinner model and so exacerbated rather than alleviated women's dependence on men, welfarism did mean that some of the burden of socially reproductive labor (e.g., health care, care for the elderly) could move from the household to the state.[72] Postwar immigration also meant that migrant workers could shoulder an ever greater load of socially reproductive labor. As Drucilla Barker contends, the paradox was that migrant populations were "often cast as dangerous, disenfranchised, disposable, and undeserving of the rights and privileges of human dignity" and yet it was they who increasingly, and disproportionately, performed the caring and domestic labor on which the affluent family depended. The valuing of socially reproductive labor thus took on specifically racialized connotations, for the woman who worked full time in the home could be held up as an exemplar of loving motherhood if she was white and wealthy but depicted as a "lazy parasite on the social body" if she was a poor woman of color.[73]

So too the prostitute continued to represent the antithesis of the nurturing mother. It was not simply that "prostitution is itself a rejection of maternity," as the social hygienist, Eleanor French, wrote in 1955. It was that "she has become a prostitute because she is a misfit and is maladjusted to society," which could in turn be attributed to her upbringing: "overcrowding, with the whole family sleeping together in one room, cannot afford a good start in life . . . she acquires a precocious knowledge of sex in the worst possible way, which makes it all the easier for her to take to the game." Nor was the prostitute deemed to be capable of mothering children of her own: the "fate of the prostitute's child as it grows up hardly bears thinking about."[74] But it was not only the prostitute and prostitute's mother who could be blamed for commercial sex, for the mother of the male client was also brought under scrutiny. In the postwar decades, a scientific literature on male clients developed in psychology, medicine, sociology, and law, which framed men who bought sex as psychologically disturbed.[75] And the mother of the male sex worker did not escape attention either, for male prostitution was similarly conceptualized as psychopathological.[76] Whereas congenital homosexuality "could not be rooted out," it was claimed, acquired homosexuality "may be prevented by a decent moral upbringing."[77] The roots of pathology could, therefore, still be traced back to the mother—although fathers also appeared, at times, as either absent or abusive: "Parental squabbling, desertions, drunkenness, emotional coldness or violence meant that few had received consistent and stable parenting during their formative years," as Donald J. West wrote of those interviewed for his study of male prostitution in London in the 1980s.[78] It was, then, not only the bodies but also the minds of sex workers and their clients that were increasingly subjected to medical and scientific intrusion, with the "causes" of commercial sex often located in the childhood and/or adolescence of individuals rather than in the politico-economic context in which it was practiced.

Still, while biological explanations for sexual deviance were often supplanted by psychological ones, this did not mean that they disappeared altogether. Transgender sex workers were frequently lumped into the category of male prostitution in both medical and legal discourses, and this was on the basis of their presumed biology. In the case of *R v. Tan* in 1983, for instance, the Court of Appeal ruled that a transgender woman, who was working as a sex worker alongside another woman, could rightfully be convicted as a "man" on the grounds that her identity as a prostitute was unalterably determined by her biological sex (which was in turn assumed to correspond to the gender she had been assigned at birth).[79] Even so, biological framings intersected with psychological ones, as medical theories had already traced noncompliance with gender norms back to childhood, and especially to the role of the mother. Interestingly, it was not the absence of motherly love that was necessarily blamed, for sexology had also allowed for the possibility that transsexuality, transvestism, and male homosexuality were "all caused by an excessively intimate and loving relationship" between mother and child.[80] Whether biological or psychological, what discourses of sexual and gender deviance did was to constitute the heteronormative family as "the source of love, affection, and emotional security, the place where our need for stable, intimate human relationships is satisfied."[81] Prostitution, in contrast, was constructed as all that was insecure, unstable, unintimate and, above all, as the "distortion of love."[82]

Commercial sex, then, was constructed as anything but normal in the twentieth century. Yet I have also argued that the intensification of capitalist social relations facilitated the expansion of markets into the sexual sphere, and that this involved the commodification and commercialization of not only love but sex itself. Here it is helpful to return to Foucault's core point that deviant sexualities "did not multiply apart from or against power, but in the very space and as the means of its exercise."[83] The proliferation of sexual commerce, in other words, was not the same thing as its normalization. In the rest of this chapter I explore how, from the outset, sex work was the focal point of wider controversies about the morality and health of the family, economy, and nation in the twentieth century, and how this had significant effects for the regulation of sexuality more broadly.

The birth of the century came in the midst of a moral panic about white slavery. Commercial sex had already come to be constructed as a problem that was distinctly *foreign* in origin and, as the first few years of the century unfolded, moral concern focused even more closely on the penetration of the national body by foreign sex workers (who were believed to corrupt English men) and foreign procurers (who were believed to corrupt English women). Considerable media attention was devoted to the "open parade of vice in our streets,"[84] with estimates of the "tremendous size of the evil to be dealt with" reaching eighty thousand "poor lost sisters" in London alone.[85] Animated by claims that London was the epicenter of the white slave trade, moral reform and anti-vice organizations paid growing attention to commercial sex as an international phenomenon that required international intervention.[86] Following the first International Congress on the White Slave Trade in London in 1899, which was spearheaded by the National Vigilance Association, a series of international conventions were held to consider the "preventive measures which might be taken . . . to deprive this trade of its vigor and profit."[87]

It was in this light that the Royal Commission on Alien Immigration launched an inquiry into the "character and the extent of the evils which are attributed to the unrestricted immigration of Aliens, especially in the Metropolis," and identified prostitution to be a major cause of the influx of "undesirables" into the country.[88] The commission's recommendations were incorporated into the Aliens Act of 1905, which introduced powers to expel, or prevent the landing of, "undesirable immigrants" (defined as those without the means of "decently supporting" themselves).[89] Although part of the justification for these measures was to protect women and girls from exploitation, they were used in practice to control female migration by targeting foreign sex workers for punishment and deportation.[90] But it was foreign procurers who were the focus of the Criminal Law Amendment (White Slavery) Bill, which was passed in 1912. This centered on the racialized threat of "scoundrels who by fraud and false pretenses decoy English girls away to foreign countries for immoral purposes."[91] There were, however, some critical voices: indeed, the Conservative politician Frederick Banbury argued that there was "no proof" that white slavery even existed.[92] Nevertheless, the House voted in vigorous support of a flogging clause for procuring, and this applied to any male person convicted of the offense.[93]

Narratives of innocent girls and predatory men were troubled, however, by the advent of the First World War. Fears over the spread of venereal disease rekindled the sexual double standard, as sex workers were blamed both for the spread of disease and for damaging soldiers' marital ties.[94] The state's response was to renew the contagious diseases legislation via emergency powers granted under the 1914 Defence of the Realm Act, with the fingerprinting of sex workers also introduced in 1917. By 1918, any woman found guilty of soliciting, or having sexual relations with, a British soldier was criminalized if she had a venereal disease, irrespective of whether he had actually infected her rather than vice versa. As such, the legislation sought to contain the sexuality of all women.[95] Yet it was foreign sex workers in particular who were deemed to jeopardize the physical and moral health of the nation.[96] A "considerable number of foreign prostitutes," it was suggested to the Royal Commission on Venereal Diseases in 1916, were unable to "ply their trade" in their own countries due to infection, and so they "take a ticket to London, and spread syphilis in this country."[97] So too foreign sex workers were believed to risk the nation's safety and security—as the Liberal Unionist politician Rowland Hunt told the Commons in February 1917, there were "40,000 prostitutes of alien birth in the county of London . . . Are they not very likely to be spies if they are left in this country?"[98] Far from seeking to absorb foreign sex workers into the social body by redeeming and rehabilitating them, the solution was instead to identify, criminalize, and deport them. After the war, the 1919 Aliens Restriction (Amendment) Act extended the powers of incarceration and expulsion that had been introduced under the 1914 Aliens Restriction Act, and these measures continued to be used to deport non-British sex workers.[99] While moral and feminist organizations did campaign for changes in the law, this was often on the grounds that it was ineffective. The celebrated feminist magazine *The Women's Leader*, for instance, decried the singling out of foreign sex workers because "straightaway the brothel becomes a legal institution, and by implication it is legal for native prostitutes to practice there."[100]

The real push to tackle commercial sex came after the Second World War, however. It is telling that this came at a time when the sexual division of labor had been destabilized, but moral panics over prostitution also coalesced with the question of migration. Following the war, the government rapidly realized that the reconstruction of the postwar economy would require substantial labor from abroad; the "broad general policy" was thus "to admit immigrants who can make a positive contribution to the national economy."[101] Yet, while some foreign bodies could be regarded as productive, this was also contested. Postwar patriotism powerfully shaped national imaginaries, but this was accompanied by growing anxieties over national identity, race, and the decline of empire. As Britain's imperial order began to fracture, fears over migration increased, except this time it was not migration from the continent but rather from the Caribbean, South Africa, and Asia that caused particular concern.[102] The press frequently ran features on the arrival of migrant workers, with the number of "colored immigrant living and working in this country" reported as rising from 50,000 in October 1954[103] to 190,000 in May 1958 ("And there is no sign of the flow slowing up"[104]). Migration was depicted as both a cause of domestic instability and a symptom of imperial decline. Had Britain not neglected the colonies, it was argued, "the necessity for colored immigration would never have arisen."[105]

It was against this backdrop that commercial sex once again materialized as a powerful symbol of economic and social disorder. And, once again, narratives honed in on commercial sex in the metropolis: the *Daily Mail*, for instance, announced its "great campaign" as one that would "end the vice parade which makes foreigners call London 'The Shocking City.'"[106] Commercial sex in the capital was depicted as a cause for national shame, an emblem of Britain's decline, and one that "nightly affronts the decent Londoner and sickens foreign visitors."[107] This was, in the words of the *Daily Mirror*, "a disgrace to the Commonwealth."[108] There was nothing in itself new about this agitation over sex work, for the figures of the white slave and the foreign procurer remained prominent ("Maltese, Cypriots and West Indians are numerous among the ponces and managers of the girls"[109]). But what was distinctive was the sheer fervor by which such narratives were articulated, with stories featured in nearly all the major newspapers.[110] What was needed, it was claimed, was a "great clean up" to rid London of the "vice racketeers"[111]—and it was to address this task that a new committee was formed in 1954 under the chairmanship of John Wolfenden.

Ostensibly founded in order to find ways to remove women from the streets,[112] the Wolfenden Committee focused on "those activities which offend against public order and decency or expose the ordinary citizen to what is offensive or injurious."[113] While the Committee was clear in its assessment of prostitution as a moral problem ("an evil of which any society which claims to be civilised should seek to rid itself"), it noted that "the great majority of prostitutes are women whose psychological make-up is such that they choose this life because they find in it a style of living which is to them easier, freer and more profitable than would be provided by any other occupation."[114] Its explicit concern, therefore, was not with prostitution per se but rather the visible face of prostitution, and on-street prostitution in particular. The Committee not only endorsed the retention of existing solicitation laws but also advocated that they further be strengthened, first, by bringing together existing law in order to ensure consistency across the country and, second, by removing the need to prove annoyance in order to prosecute or convict for soliciting. It also argued that repeat offenders should be subject to increasingly severe punishments, beginning with a fine, and culminating in three months' imprisonment.[115] These recommendations were put into force under the Street Offences Act of 1959. As existing legislation had recently been consolidated under the 1956 Sexual Offences Act, there was finally a "uniform, universal approach and philosophy to the regulation, policing and punishment of prostitution," at least in principle.[116]

The Wolfenden report and subsequent legislation did not usher in a whole new regulatory regime so much as to formalize the system of liberal governance that was already de facto in place.[117] Solicitation laws had long been integral to the state's approach—although, admittedly, these were rather convoluted and only sporadically applied. In London, for instance, a system had been established between magistrates and the police that meant there was seldom need for proof that a sex worker (if female) was causing a nuisance; rather, it was adequate simply to demonstrate that she was a "common prostitute" who was inhabiting public space (i.e., that she was on the street).[118] Nevertheless, by strengthening the state's ability to intervene in public transgressions, the Wolfenden report fortified the division between public and private space that had become established in the nineteenth century. This fastened sexuality even more firmly into place within the private realm, with the purpose of the law to, in effect, ensure that it remained so.[119] In so doing, the report reflected and reinforced gendered expectations that women's bodies—and especially their sexuality—should be situated within the private (and hence the domestic) realm rather than in the public realm of society and economy. In the words of the Labour Party politician Frank Pakenham, "We must attach the label of 'grievous sin' to all sexual intercourse outside marriage"—and this was in support of, not opposition to, the Committee's recommendations.[120]

Where the Wolfenden report did mark a major rupture, however, was with respect to homosexuality. Initially set up to tackle on-street prostitution, the Committee also included homosexuality in its remit in response to a recent surge in arrests for related offenses.[121] Under the Criminal Law Amendment Act of 1912, any person found guilty of offenses that breached the 1885 Act could be imprisoned for up to two years, with or without hard labor, and in the case of a second conviction, the court could "sentence the offender if a male to be once privately whipped."[122] While the legislation had been framed as an intervention against the exploitation of women, the most punitive measures were often borne by homosexual men. The new clauses were certainly less severe than previous sentences for buggery (death; life imprisonment), but they were implemented much more rigorously—and it was men soliciting other men (rather than men soliciting women) to whom they were enthusiastically applied.[123]

Initially, the Committee did not set out to decriminalize homosexuality, and Wolfenden himself was in favor of retaining sodomy as a crime.[124] However, after hearing evidence from a number of witnesses—including Peter Wildeblood, who had been imprisoned for eighteen months for homosexual offenses—the Committee made the striking claim that "It is not, in our view, the function of the law to intervene in the private lives of citizens, or to seek to enforce any particular pattern of behavior."[125] The report advocated the decriminalization of homosexual acts between consenting adults, and it did so by defining homosexuality as a matter of private identity as opposed to public morality: "Homosexuality . . . is a state or condition, and as such does not, and cannot, come within the purview of the criminal law."[126] Although it took a decade, the Committee's recommendations were brought into force under the Sexual Offences Act of 1967, which made legal consensual homosexual acts between men over the age of twenty-one.[127]

Yet, while the adult homosexual man was finally afforded some degree of sexual citizenship in Britain, this represented a very particular vision of citizenship. It was, to borrow from David Bell and Jon Binnie, "confined in all senses of the word: kept in place, policed, limited."[128] The homosexual subject was first and foremost a private individual, and this was achieved in part by formally breaking off homosexuality from its longstanding, if ambiguous, association with male sex work. The Committee explicitly noted that "for the most part, those convicted of importuning are in no sense male prostitutes; they are simply homosexuals seeking a partner for subsequent homosexual behavior." It suggested that, although private homosexual acts should be tolerated, the penalties attached to importuning should not be reduced "in any way" as this could be taken as a "general license to adult homosexuals to behave as they please."[129] Accordingly, the Sexual Offences Act of 1967 actually increased the maximum penalty for gross indecency or procurement from two years' imprisonment to a period of five years.[130] The separation between (private) homosexual identity and (public) homosexual practices was thus finally enshrined in the law, and it was the commercialized body of the male sex worker that marked this boundary between legitimate sexuality and illegitimate sex.

In the latter decades of the twentieth century, the ascendancy of the neoliberal state, with its attendant mechanics of privatization, further individualized sexual citizenship. The neoconservative political agenda was particularly aggressive in constructing the individual sphere of private/domestic life as "the site of civic virtue,"[131] as could be seen in Margaret Thatcher's oft-cited description of society: "There is no such thing! There are individual men and women and there are families."[132] Same-sex sexuality, too, was restricted to the private sphere under Section 28 of the 1988 Local Government Act, which banned "promoting homosexuality by teaching or by publishing material."[133] And yet other forces were at work too for, as John D'Emilio contends, commodity production and the spread of wage labor had also eroded the family as an economic unit and, with it, the material basis for family life. This had disruptive effects, as it meant that it was increasingly possible for men and, to a lesser extent, women to pursue a personal (and thus sexual) life outside of the family. Indeed, it was becoming viable for people not only to identify as gay and lesbian individuals, but also to organize as gay and lesbian political communities.[134] As noted, the terms of the sexual order were also disrupted by the Second World War and, although the domestic ideal of the housewife was quickly reinstated, the notion that women were physically or mentally incapable of performing "men's work" had been profoundly destabilized. Critiques of the traditional sexual order gathered momentum from the 1960s onward as sexuality became constituted as a major terrain on which both heterosexuality and patriarchy could be resisted.[135] As the Gay Liberation Front declared in its manifesto,

> The oppression of gay people starts in the most basic unit of society, the family . . . Freedom for gay people will never be permanently won until everyone is freed from sexist role-playing and the straightjacket of sexist rules about our sexuality. And we will not be freed from these so long as each succeeding generation is brought up in the same old sexist way in the Patriarchal family.[136]

It was in this context that controversies over commercial sex yet again came to the fore. Particularly prominent were the feminist "sex wars" of the 1970s and 1980s, which took the form of a series of sustained and often heated[137] contestations over the true nature of commercial sex. Victorian narratives of prostitutes as victims of male desire were reignited in radical feminist accounts, which identified commercial sex as the keystone of the patriarchal oppression of women that must be eradicated accordingly (as the American feminist Kathleen Barry put it, "sexual slavery lurks at the corner of every woman's life" but it was prostitutes who were "alienated from their sexual being"[138]). Other feminists drew on Marxist theorizing to argue that prostitution reduced women to commodities. For Carole Pateman, for instance, what made prostitution such a powerful instrument of male domination—and indeed what distinguished it from other forms of labor—was that it involved the sexual use of women's bodies. Since womanhood was "confirmed in sexual activity," a woman who sold her body was "thus selling herself in a very real sense."[139] Such accounts broke new ground in highlighting the structural sources of women's subordination, but they did so by drawing on longstanding constructions of sexuality as uniquely connected to the self—a self that was, in turn, predicated on the very liberal individualism that anti-prostitution feminists sought to eschew.[140]

Yet mounting opposition to such accounts also came from sex-radical and sex-positive feminists, who suggested that commercial sex was not the epitome of women's sexual subordination but a manifestation of their sexual emancipation. Feminist activist organizations such as Feminists Against Censorship, which was founded in London in 1989, emphasized the right to freedom of sexual expression: "Those of us who still want liberation for women are not interested in having the government snoop into our bedrooms."[141] Like anti-prostitution discourse, pro-sex work accounts sometimes constructed the sexual self as natural, innate, and fixed, even if that sexual self was to be freed through (rather than protected from) commercial sex.[142] But the sex workers' rights movement also sought to politicize the deployment of sexuality under capitalism. Calling for commercial sex to be recognized as a form of work, they insisted that it was through the decriminalization of commercial sex that collective working and organizing could become possible, thus "putting control with the workers" themselves.[143] More than this, sex worker activists argued that the key distinction between wives and sex workers was simply that sex workers refused to go unpaid for their sexual labor.[144] In so doing, they threatened to expose how the sexual division of labor was not a natural fact, nor did it rest on steadfast foundations. Instead, it was enshrined and defended through that most powerful of capitalist instruments—what Silvia Federici has termed the "fraud that goes under the name of love and marriage."[145]

CONCLUSION

[F]rom the earliest days of life you are trained to be docile, subservient, dependent and most important *to sacrifice yourself* and even to get pleasure from it. If you don't like it, it is your problem, your failure, your guilt, and your abnormality.
                    —Silvia Federici, *Wages Against Housework*

In this chapter I have interrogated how the sexual division of labor was normalized in the twentieth century to the extent that women were expected to "get pleasure from it": pleasure from buying commodities for the family, pleasure from undertaking paid labor to pay for those commodities, pleasure from performing unpaid domestic chores, pleasure from heterosexual intercourse, and, most of all, pleasure from bearing and caring for children. Indeed, the very possibility of true and authentic pleasure for women was predicated on the economy/sexuality dichotomy, for sex workers were believed to personify the "problem," "failure," "guilt," and "abnormality" that womanhood could represent. Yet such characteristics were not reserved for female sex workers alone, for the regulation of prostitution meant that male sexuality—and especially male same-sex sexuality—was increasingly defined against the abnormality of commercial sex. What this meant, in turn, was that the conditions were put into place for homosexuality to become more aligned with the private realm of domesticity and consumption.[146] Thus, even though the hetero/homosexual binary came to define sexuality in the twentieth century, it did not replace the sex/work binary but instead coexisted with, and was articulated through, this preexisting dualism. This was to have unpredictable effects in the twenty-first century, for the inherent contradictions of heteronormativity meant that heterosexuality could itself be cast as deviant—the subject of the final chapter.

CHAPTER 5

Deviant Heterosexuality in Austere Times

How does the separation of sex and work play out in the contemporary moment? My aim in this chapter is to analyze how commercial sex continues to be constructed as a violation of, and threat to, "normal" economic, political, and cultural life. More precisely, I contend that sex work is assumed (and, indeed, insisted) to be a mode of deviant heterosexuality that is simultaneously sexualized, gendered, racialized, and territorialized. Yet I also explore how discourses of commercial sex—and especially those regarding anti-trafficking and modern slavery—divert attention away from the constitutive role of heteronormativity in producing economic injustice. Turning first to the austerity agenda that has defined Britain's political economy over the past decade, I argue that its curious disappearance in official discourses of commercial sex reveals the economy/sexuality dichotomy to be alive and well in the twenty-first century. The absenting of austerity allows sexual injustice to be attributed to pathology rather than to poverty and, in so doing, it facilitates the ongoing privatization of social reproduction on which welfare retrenchment depends. The chapter then considers how the grammars of race and nationality have been used to construct commercial sex as a mode of criminally perverse heterosexuality that jeopardizes not just "the physical vigor and the moral cleanliness of the social body"[1] but the reproduction of the nation itself. The repression and production of sex work has therefore played a central role in advancing the great capitalist ruse that immigration, not neoliberalism, is to blame for the intensification of economic and social depletion that, in Britain at least, governments have actively chosen to engender.

Capitalism's Sexual History. Nicola J. Smith, Oxford University Press (2020). © Oxford University Press.
DOI: 10.1093/oso/9780197530276.001.0001.

In the early twenty-first century, Britain has earned the dubious distinction of being one of the most economically unequal of the world's wealthy nations.[2] Since the 1970s, neoliberal modes of governance have increasingly supplanted postwar commitments to state interventionism and social protectionism, with governments on both sides of the political spectrum actively promoting the commodification and marketization of publicly owned goods and the restructuring and corrosion of welfare provision.[3] But it is since 2010 that the privatization of collective wealth and resources has really gathered pace under an aggressive program of austerity that has been pursued under successive Conservative governments, and which has left 14.3 million people in poverty, including 4.6 million in persistent poverty and 1.5 million in destitution.[4] Indeed, the scale and intensity of poverty in the United Kingdom is such that the United Nations (UN) has been prompted to conduct an investigation into it. The assessment offered by the UN's Special Rapporteur on Extreme Poverty and Human Rights, Philip Alston, is damning: "great misery has . . . been inflicted unnecessarily, especially on the working poor, on single mothers struggling against mighty odds, on people with disabilities who are already marginalized, and on millions of children who are being locked into a cycle of poverty from which most will have great difficulty escaping." Pointing to the massive rise in food-bank use and homelessness under nearly a decade of austerity, Alston explicitly notes that he has spoken to people who have "sold sex for money or shelter"; indeed, the extremity of poverty in the United Kingdom is "obvious to anyone who opens their eyes."[5]

The UN's statement was released just a few months after the findings of another report—*Behind Closed Doors: Organized Sexual Exploitation in England and Wales* by the All-Party Parliamentary Group (APPG) on Prostitution and the Global Sex Trade—were debated in the House of Commons.[6] Strikingly, despite Alston's remark that the effects of austerity are "obvious to anyone who opens their eyes," the intersections between austerity and sex work are noticeable only by their absence in both the APPG's report and the Parliamentary debate about its recommendations. There is occasional recognition of the existence of homelessness—the report, for instance, makes no reference to poverty but uses the term "homelessness" (twice) in the form of the following quote from a representative of Hope for Justice (a charity that helps to identify trafficked women): "[Traffickers are] very, very clever on who they are targeting. In our experience victims are targeted due to a variety of vulnerabilities which can include but are not limited to childhood trauma, unemployment, homelessness, drug or alcohol issues, homelessness, mental health issues and learning disabilities."[7] Other vulnerabilities to be identified, this time by an Expert Witness, include "a prior history of abuse (including child abuse), violence and/or exploitation; a prior history of neglect (physical, emotional and/or psychological) and/or of parental mental health problems or parents with substance misuse problems and chaotic lifestyles that may result from this."[8] As these quotations reveal, homelessness is discursively framed in the report as just one of a long list of individual pathologies— and not those of the government ministers who have, in Alston's words, quite deliberately sought to achieve "radical social re-engineering" through austerity.[9] Rather, the sources of destitution are to be found in the faulty psyches of sex workers themselves, or so the report appears to suggest.

While the APPG's calls for the purchase of sex to be criminalized have not (yet) been enacted in legislation, understandings of sex workers as psychologically vulnerable have nevertheless been utilized over recent years to justify heightened intervention by the state. Under New Labour,[10] the release of a consultation paper by the Home Office in 2004—the first wide-ranging review of prostitution policy since Wolfenden—signaled an important change in official conceptions of sex work.[11] Entitled *Paying the Price*, the paper argued that "[s]ystematic abuse, violence and exploitation are endemic" and that "some of the most serious exploitation" was taking place in off-street premises.[12] In a separate document, *A Coordinated Prostitution Strategy*, the Home Office stated that "no form of commercial sexual exploitation" could be tolerated, "whether it takes place on the street, behind the doors of a massage parlor or in a private residence."[13] This marked a shift in which commercial sex began to be conceptualized not as private immorality versus public criminality but as violence versus vulnerability. While the governance of sex work had been predicated on the public/private split since Wolfenden, it was now the clandestine as well as the visible aspects of prostitution that required direct action by the state.[14]

Purporting to safeguard women from exploitation (the "mark of any civilized society is how it protects the most vulnerable"[15]), the new paradigm functioned instead to further pathologize sex workers. Understandings of prostitutes as victims of psychic harm had emerged during the twentieth century (see Chapter 4), and this provided a language through which increased state intervention could be authorized. The Labour politician Fiona McTaggart elaborated on this theme in support of the Policing and Crime Bill in 2009:

> Sex workers, as they are called by many people—I do not like to think of it as a job, as it is so exploitative—are often vulnerable young women with disturbed

backgrounds, who have never known a stable relationship or respect from others and are therefore prey to pimps. It is all too easy for such a person to fall under the influence of a dominant male, who exploits the vulnerability for financial gain.[16]

Although sex workers were no longer depicted as sinful in such accounts, the figure of the disorderly woman continued to loom large. Framed in terms of "social inclusion," the vulnerability paradigm sought to responsibilize prostitutes in a manner similar to the disciplinary technologies employed in the Magdalene asylums in the nineteenth century, which had alleged to "save" them from sin but operated as a means through which social control could be exercised over the poor.[17] The answer for debt, for instance, was not to address its socioeconomic causes but rather to "help" individuals to overcome the effects of poverty with "support" such as debt counseling.[18] And yet the logic of vulnerability did more than simply reduce sex workers to their own (presumed) psychological dysfunction, for it encompassed both the sex worker herself and those around her: "her pimp, her trafficker, or the person maintaining her addiction," in McTaggart's words.[19] *Paying the Price*, for example, conflated "partners" with "pimps" ("pimps/partners"), thus collapsing a whole diversity of intimate relationships into the category of exploitation. This meant that any situation where a partner gained financially from a sex worker's earnings—and, hence, domestic arrangements that were not predicated on the male breadwinner model—could be rendered deviant and subject to state regulation.[20]

Thus, although the vulnerability paradigm troubled the public/private split, it did not work against the sexual division of labor but, on the contrary, sought to directly impose it on sex workers. Clearly, while it was acceptable for "ordinary" women to engage in economically productive labor as part of their socially reproductive duties, this was a privilege that could not be extended to sex workers. Already marked out as a temporary aberration, women's paid labor was still expected to serve the normative family that was made intelligible through the heteronormative ideals of married, monogamous, romantic love, and against which commercial sex was defined. This meant that official understandings could excise sex workers from their wider politico-economic context while rendering them individually culpable for the material conditions in which they lived. It is revealing, for instance, that during the second reading of the Policing and Crime Bill the term "poverty" was mentioned just once.[21] By this token, the state's own part in sustaining structural exclusion could be obscured by the purportedly "progressive governance" of commercial sex.[22]

By positioning commercial sex as an issue not of economic inequality but of criminality, the vulnerability paradigm helped to legitimate a more punitive approach by the state.[23] The 2009 Policing and Crime Act, for instance, introduced closure orders for premises in which prostitution-related offenses took place, and it streamlined kerb-crawling offenses so that it was no longer necessary to demonstrate that clients soliciting in public were doing so persistently in order to prosecute.[24] On-street sex workers continued to be framed as a public nuisance (i.e., as "anti-social"), with heightened surveillance of these populations and a comprehensive arsenal of measures including (but not limited to) arrest, anti-social behavior orders, drug testing, curfews, and compliance agreements, as well as the use of closed-circuit cameras, street lighting projects, traffic management plans, and neighborhood watch initiatives to deter kerb-crawling and soliciting.[25] Especially important was the requirement to exit the sex industry: those found guilty of loitering or soliciting for the purposes of prostitution must attend three compulsory meetings with a supervisor to "assist the offender" in identifying, and overcoming, the "causes of conduct" but, "[i]f the supervisor is of the opinion that the offender has failed without reasonable excuse to comply with the order," then criminal proceedings could be instigated.[26] As Jane Scoular and Maggie O'Neill observe, the idea that individuals should exit prostitution was not unique to the twenty-first century, but what *was* distinctive was the making of exit into the bedrock of a wider regime of governance. The consequence was that the reforms further marginalized and criminalized those sex workers who would/could not leave the industry and so "entrenched the ongoing hegemonic moral and political regulation of sex workers by continuing to privilege certain forms of citizenship."[27]

While the policy reforms proclaimed in principle to protect the "victims" of commercial sex, their effect in practice has been quite the opposite. This is not just because criminal justice measures actively discourage sex workers from reporting violent assaults to the police.[28] Rather, what they both foster and mask is violence by the state itself. In stark contrast to the professed "shift away from a system that punishes women towards a more supportive framework that helps people that end up in prostitution,"[29] the English Collective of Prostitutes documents case after case in which sex workers have been targeted by the police under the legislation.[30] To take just one example, in 2010 a woman was charged with keeping a brothel after working in the same premises as other women for safety purposes. She pleaded guilty on the grounds that it would minimize the possibility of a prison sentence but, despite being the caregiver for her disabled son, she was given a nine-month custodial sentence and her life savings were confiscated.[31] As this disgraceful example illustrates, the state has perpetuated violence against women in the name of combating violence against women. As sex workers themselves report, this includes direct physical violence and sexual assault under threat of arrest by police officers,[32] as well as structural violence in the form of regimes of criminalization, stigmatization, and material exclusion.[33] Efforts to "end demand" via criminalization have, moreover, only compounded the specific forms of violence, discrimination, and marginalization that LGBTQ sex workers face, with trans women, migrants, and/or people of color especially likely to come up against structural obstacles such as poverty, unemployment, and homelessness; to be subjected to over-policing, arrest, and abuse; and to be ignored by the police when sexually and/or violently assaulted.[34]

It is within this context that the APPG's report of 2018 must be viewed, and especially its conceptualization of commercial sex as a question of criminal justice rather than of economic justice. The report makes no mention, for instance, of the fact that four fifths of the combined expenditure saved and revenue raised through the changes to social security and personal taxation have come from women,[35] or that the effects of austerity are worse still for single mothers, women with disabilities, migrant women, women of color, and trans women.[36] Nor is there reference to the gendered impact of the shift toward part-time, temporary, and low-paid labor that has accompanied the austerity agenda, entailing economic precarity that relates not only to the work itself but also to the context in which it is performed, including with respect to childcare, family leave, sick leave, health care, and pensions.[37] The evasion of such questions might appear odd given that, in other contexts, APPG representatives such as the Labour politician Jess Phillips have missed few opportunities to point to austerity's multiple harms.[38] Yet, in the case of commercial sex, to recognize that economic and sexual inequality are co-constitutive would lead to a rather different outcome from that being proposed. It is not just that criminal justice interventions do precious little to tackle economic injustice but, as has been discussed in earlier chapters, the repression of sex work forms an integral part of the machinery through which such injustice is produced to start with. At the very least, to conceive of sex work in economic terms means acknowledging how it is, for many, a survival strategy and that "[w]hen you enact a policy that makes a survival behavior 'not work any more,' some of the people using it to attempt to survive may no longer survive."[39]

To be fair, the Commons debate did include some mention of "inequality," even if the report did not. As the APPG's Vice Chair, Gavin Shuker, told the Commons, "by failing to tackle demand we perpetuate the inequality of focusing on the most visible part of the transaction, rather than on those who create the demand in the first place."[40] In a similar vein, the Scottish National Party (SNP) politician Angela Crawley described prostitution as "a form of gendered violence" that is "both a cause and a consequence of sexual inequality." As she continued, "Without the demand from sex buyers, there would be no need for a supply. We are therefore looking at tackling the root cause of that form of sexual inequality, rather than a symptom."[41] Yet, while these narratives employ the economic language of supply and demand as a metaphor for sexual inequality, they should not be confused with discourses about the economic sources of sexual inequality. On the contrary, they can be understood to be "non-performative"—a term used by Sara Ahmed to capture how "naming can be a way of not bringing something into effect."[42] It is by employing the rhetoric of supply and demand that the impression can be created of a discourse centered on the relationship between commercial sex, on the one hand, and the economy, on the other. Meanwhile, actual questions about economic injustice—such as the social devastation being wrought by years of austerity—can be sidestepped altogether.

It is important to note, however, that it is not simply the APPG's report and Commons debate that have separated sexuality from economy, for the intersections between sexual and economic justice in austerity Britain have been met with silence in other contexts too. The issue of sexuality received little attention in public debates about the Housing Benefit social sector size limit, for instance, which formed part of the Welfare Reform Act of 2012 and entailed restrictions on the size of accommodation for working-age people in receipt of state support for social housing.[43] Indeed, the only reference made to sexuality in the equality impact assessment document by the Department of Work and Pensions was to note that "[t]he Department does not have information on its administrative systems on the sexual orientation of its claimants. The Government does not envisage an adverse impact on these grounds."[44] The deep irony here is that the appropriately nicknamed "bedroom tax" could scarcely be more sexualized in its unambiguous delineation of the boundaries of a properly gendered sexuality as tied to the social and economic domain of the household. Simply put, the tax does not just reflect a cultural privileging of the heterosexual ideal of married monogamy but represents the forcible and state-sanctioned imposition of that ideal. Those who fall outside of the norm of the nuclear family—such as single parents whose children live with them over the weekend but not during the week—are not only explicitly placed on the outside of social acceptability in terms of the configuration of their home/family/caring arrangements but are, quite literally, penalized by the state for this.

And yet, from the outset, heteronormativity has provided a language and logic through which austerity could be made thinkable and therefore politically possible. As Tracey Jensen persuasively argues, it was not only the public indebtedness and "extravagant waste" of previous governments that were used to justify the need for austerity in the wake of the financial crisis, but the austerity imperative was also expressed through a series of metaphors surrounding the family: the "hardworking" family, the "solvent family," and, most of all, the "responsible family."[45] Important here was the linking of economic crisis to social decline through the drawing of explicit parallels between the profligacy, greed, and wastefulness of both the state and the household.[46] Public and private debt were coupled together as "fundamental problems" of the British economy, with Britain itself likened to a "hardworking family" that was not "owed a living in the modern, global economy" but had to "earn it—and earn it the hard way."[47] This need for national recovery in turn relied on a conflation of what it was to be economically "broke"[48] and socially "broken,"[49] with economic and social problems both attributed to the failure of individuals. Crucially, it was not (just) individuals per se but (also) individual families that were constructed of lying at the heart of this such that "Broken Britain" *was* the "broken family."[50] In his speech on "Troubled Families" in December 2011, for instance, David Cameron, then the prime minister, argued:

> [W]e need a social recovery in Britain every bit as much as we need an economic one. So while the government's immediate duty is to deal with the budget deficit, my mission in politics—the thing I am really passionate about—is fixing the responsibility deficit . . . Whatever you call them, we've known for years that a relatively small number of families are the source of a large proportion of the problems in society. Drug addiction. Alcohol abuse. Crime. A culture of disruption and irresponsibility that cascades through generations.[51]

Family crisis was identified as more than just a symptom or symbol of economic and social crisis but as its root cause—as Cameron put it, "if we want to have any hope of mending our broken society, family and parenting is where we've got to start."[52]

Let us not forget that the advent of austerity marked the same historical moment that Britain became hailed as the billionaire capital of the world,[53] with the richest thousand people in the United Kingdom increasing their wealth by £274 billion in the space of just five years, their combined wealth far exceeding that of the poorest 40 percent of households (£724 billion compared to £567 billion).[54] Intriguingly, while socioeconomic disadvantage was consistently attributed to "family breakdown," no mention was made of the logical corollary of this: that the wealth of Britain's billionaires must therefore be due to some exceptionally strong marriages.

Put another way, appeals to family values are no "merely cultural"[55] matter when viewed in the light of the dismemberment of the welfare state and the privatization of economic and social provision.[56] As Wendy Brown contends, neoliberalism is often understood to be a discrete package of free-market policies, yet it also represents a governing rationality that is at once economic, political, and cultural, and that constitutes people as individual entrepreneurs whose "moral autonomy is measured by their capacity for 'self-care.'"[57] As the welfare state is rolled back, citizens are rendered ever more responsible for their own welfare as individuals and, since individuals are increasingly situated within market forces, the market becomes *the* place to enhance welfare.[58] The burden of caring labor for children, the elderly, the sick, and those with disabilities is thus increasingly situated within the private realm of domesticity and consumption, with kinship relations often the only available resource for the sustenance of life itself.[59] By "shifting the burden of caretaking onto kin as if this caretaking were a natural expression of pre-existing biological ties,"[60] married monogamy and the sexual division of labor come to appear as the only viable choices available.[61]

With all of this in mind, it is no puzzle that the advent of austerity coincided with the achievement of same-sex marriage in the United Kingdom nor that Cameron proudly proclaimed his personal support for this ("It's something I feel passionately about"[62]). Although this welcoming of gay and lesbian couples into the Conservative Party fold might seem a somewhat socially and sexually progressive move in the wake of the party's long history of homophobic discourse and policy practice,[63] it also represents a very particular vision of what constitutes social and sexual "progress." Both under Cameron's leadership and since, the government has done little to situate equal marriage within a wider discourse of material justice, nor has it offered any kind of substantive commitment to ending material *in*justice for LGBTQ communities. And yet research commissioned by the public service union UNISON finds that the austerity measures have had a significant and disproportionate impact on LGBTQ people in the United Kingdom, including in terms of a sharp reduction in specialist services (e.g., information, advice, and support services; health services such as sexual health, mental health, drugs and alcohol, and gender confirmation services; youth and community services; specialist forums and networks; and social cohesion projects) as a direct consequence of the spending cuts and of the instability in statutory and other funding sources.[64] Similarly, Stonewall reports that two thirds of people who approach the organization for advice and help identify their sexual orientation or gender identity as directly related to their housing problem; that four fifths of the organization's advice clients are out of work; that two fifths are experiencing harassment; and that hate crimes and incidents against LGBTQ people have risen, not fallen, over recent years.[65]

Thus, in contrast to the advancement of a collectivist program for economic justice that, in the British context, would entail a critique of, and resistance to, austerity politics, the equal marriage agenda has instead articulated the privatized, domestic sphere as the central locus of sexual rights. As Rosemary Hennessy argues, the construction of the normative family may have relied on homophobia historically, but this does not mean that capitalism is always and essentially homophobic. Indeed, if gay and lesbian couples are willing and/or able to participate in the very institution that props up the sexual division of labor—marriage—then it makes sense for capitalism to begin to tolerate, and even embrace, homosexuality.[66] Likewise, Lauren Berlant and Michael Warner contend that by limiting (homo)sexuality to the private realm, heteronormativity can constitute the domestic sphere as the privileged site of both social reproduction and capitalist accumulation. This, moreover, has depoliticizing effects, for it not only obstructs the formation of non-normative, visible, and politicized sexual cultures but also constitutes sexuality itself as non-political:

> Intimate life is the endlessly cited elsewhere of political public discourse, a promised haven that distracts citizens from the unequal conditions of their political and economic lives, consoles them for the damaged humanity of mass society, and shames them for any divergence between their lives and the intimate sphere that is alleged to be simple personhood.[67]

Yet, while access to the normative family may offer a way for *some* lesbian and gay subjects to become recognized as responsible and deserving citizens, this involves the redrawing of heteronormative boundaries to exclude those populations that are unwilling or unable to conform to such expectations[68]—the focus of the following section.

ATTACK OF THE HETEROS

At the same time as identities that had once been vilified and outlawed are being rewritten as "virtually"[69]—if tenuously—normal, others are being marked out as aberrant in new ways. One notable appearance is that of the male client—although I should quickly add that, in practice, it is not clients but sex workers who continue to be the main targets of repression by the state. Nevertheless, recent decades have seen a step up in the pathologization of male clients: a key impetus here has been the reinvigoration of prostitution as a public health issue due to the HIV/AIDS pandemic in the 1980s and 1990s.[70] The spread of the virus was blamed on both homosexuality (in which male prostitution was categorized) and female prostitution, with the figure of the male client forming the common thread between these two modes of deviance.[71] While public debates were preoccupied with the "nuisance" of on-street sex work in the late twentieth century, there was also growing interest in male clients: indeed, the introduction of kerb-crawling as an offense under the 1985 Sexual Offences Act "created a new category of offender."[72] As the state sanctioning of the hidden aspects of commercial sex became more contested, older discourses of sex workers as innocent victims of predatory men were reinvigorated.[73] By the turn of the century, the purchase of sex had come to be associated not with a "politically unenlightened male" but with what Don Kulick calls a "disturbed male, a deviant male, an unintelligible male."[74]

While male clients have been problematized for centuries, the emphasis on tackling male demand does represent a twenty-first-century innovation in Britain. A Coordinated Prostitution Strategy stated that the "solution must not only provide routes out for those providing sexual services but also deter those who create the demand for them."[75] It was by placing "an onus on those whose demand actually creates the exploitation in the first place," Home Secretary Jacqui Smith argued to Parliament, that the "misery of prostitution and human exploitation" could best be countered.[76] The 2008 Criminal Justice and Immigration Act, for instance, criminalizes those who consume (rather than simply produce) sexual services, including by introducing the offense of owning "extreme" pornography (defined as images that have been produced with the sole or primary aim of instigating sexual arousal). Prior to this legislation, it had only been an offense to produce or distribute materials that could "deprave or corrupt the viewer."[77] The Policing and Crime Act of 2009 also makes it a strict liability offense to pay for the services of a prostitute who has been subject to coercion, making it "irrelevant" if a client had no knowledge of coercion having taken place.[78]

Admittedly, the specific wording of the Policing and Crime Act is not openly gendered in the sense that a "person" can be convicted of this offense.[79] Nevertheless, the legislation bears a clear heteronormative imprint in that its rationale was consistently articulated through appeals to the male demand/female supply dualism (i.e., that it is "men who choose to pay to have sex with women who have been exploited" and "women in this country who do not make a free choice to engage in prostitution"[80]). It is therefore framed around prevailing gendered logics that tie sexual objectification to female bodies and sexual subjectivity to male ones.[81] While *A Coordinated Prostitution Strategy*, for instance, did acknowledge that men could sell sex, it nevertheless explicitly restricted its focus to the "needs of women in prostitution" on the grounds that men were unlikely to be subject to coercion,[82] so deftly ascribing vulnerability to women alone. It is, of course, not accidental that the image of the "injured prostitute"[83] is that of a female sex worker, for it relies on an oppositional gender binary that would lose its political purchase (and indeed its intelligibility) if framed in terms of the "sexually exploited men" and "sexually predatory women."[84] While the problem of prostitution has thus become more closely aligned with the male client, on the one hand, this has buttressed rather than unsettled the active male/passive female dualism on which heteronormativity depends, on the other. This does not just foreclose the possibility of queer desire in the sex industry,[85] but, as Anna Carline observes, it also augments cultural expectations that "appropriate expressions of female sexuality are those that are not only heterosexual but also passive, receptive, and non-threatening."[86]

Such discourses are specifically racialized, even if they do not openly declare themselves to be so. Albeit a prominent concern in the past, trafficking did not used to be the defining issue around which prostitution itself was conceptually organized. At the turn of the millennium, however, trafficking began to be constructed not only as a "horrific crime" that was "directly linked to the demand for prostitution in this country"[87] but as *the* central problem of commercial sex.[88] As the sex industry expanded as an economic sector and became more visible in political and cultural terms, so too the late twentieth century had seen the ascendancy of a powerful abolitionist lobby that proved remarkably effective in advancing what can only be described as a "moral crusade" against commercial sex globally.[89] This lobby spearheaded a global anti-trafficking agenda that led most prominently to the UN's *Protocol to Prevent, Suppress and Punish Trafficking in Persons, Especially Women and Children* of 2000, which was signed by 117 countries, as well as to a flurry of anti-trafficking declarations, policies, and measures at both international and national levels, including in the United Kingdom.[90]

The anti-trafficking agenda has drawn on longstanding narratives of female sexual passivity to portray migrant women as "suffering bodies" who possess no agency of their own.[91] As outlined in Chapter 2, depictions of prostitutes as so passive that they were dead or dying had proliferated from the eighteenth century onward, performing the discursive function of restoring white femininity to its "natural" state of docility. (We should re-call that this was a "natural" state that had been forged through the horror and brutality of the witch trials and colonialism alike.) Yet the emergence of heteronormativity in the twentieth century also unsettled gendered ex-pectations for, although this relied on the active male/passive female du-alism, it also opened up possibilities for some women to be imagined as desiring subjects. This has allowed white femininity to develop a rather ambiguous relationship to sexuality. On the one hand, whiteness is associ-ated with what Gargi Bhattacharyya calls an "absence of sexuality":[92] it is not only that whiteness is passionless but that innocence itself is racialized as white.[93] On the other hand, it is sexual freedom that constitutes the modern subject *as* a subject, so that liberal subjectivity—itself codified as whiteness—is defined against, and defined through, the sexual *un*freedom of racialized others.[94]

Past discourses of white slavery—now defined as "this modern-day form of slavery"[95]—have thus been harnessed to attach new meanings to foreign bodies. If innocence and purity were once understood as the natural state of the white, English woman, then it is migrant sex workers who have been figured as the prototypical victims in twenty-first-century Britain, albeit in highly uneven, stratified, and contradictory ways. It is significant, in par-ticular, that anti-trafficking discourses have routinely depicted trafficked women as eastern European,[96] since this means that they can be associated with white innocence (and so constructed as pitiable subjects) while also being associated with unfreedom (and so excluded from citizenship). These racialized logics reveal what Claudia Aradau terms a "perverse continuity" between humanitarian and security discourses of trafficking. Rather than being at odds with each other, the "politics of pity" inherent in humani-tarianism is interlaced with the "politics of risk" that associates migrant women with insecurity and threat.[97] For example, *A Coordinated Prostitution Strategy* emphasized the need for supportive interventions: "Victims of trafficking are often highly traumatised by their experiences and will often need specialist care and protection." Yet "[s]helter and basic care" were to be provided for only "up to four weeks" unless "a woman decides to stay to help provide evidence against her exploiters."[98] The provision of support has, therefore, been contingent on the self-identification of migrant sex workers as "victims," as well as their willingness to testify against their "abusers," ultimately leading to their "rescue" (i.e., deportation). It involves a complex repertoire of techniques, including psychological profiling to identify and classify trafficked women, and therapeutic interventions to rehabilitate them through confessionals and testimonials.[99] ("Psychological indicators of modern slavery," for instance, are deemed to include "expression of fear or anxiety," "depression," "isolation," "hostility," "aggression," "self-harm," and "difficulty recalling details or entire episodes"[100]—reactions that might otherwise be explained by the stress and fear induced by the threat of deportation). If a migrant sex worker is to re-offend, moreover, then she is no longer a victim of trafficking but instead becomes guilty of immigration, thus transforming her into a threat; to be disassociated from danger, then, she must identify as, and behave as, a victim.[101] Jo Doezema shows us that the "myth of the unwilling slave" has always depended on a "counter-myth," that of the willing prostitute—a "guilty whore" who, in consenting to sex, becomes culpable for her own fate.[102] Racialized assumptions that non-white and non-European women are always already guilty/willing can be seen, for instance, in their relative invisibility in humanitarian discourses of trafficking, combined with their relative visibility in terms of actual prosecutions and deportations.[103]

Yet, while techniques of responsibilization have been employed to demarcate innocent slaves from guilty prostitutes, their underlying rationality remains the same.[104] Much like the quarantining of sex workers during medieval times, the aim is not to fold foreign bodies into the social order but to expunge them from it. White innocence is not enough, in other words, to secure literal or metaphorical citizenship; nor is non-British Europeanness. Why might this be so? Here it is instructive to consider Imogen Tyler's argument that the securitization of migration in Britain has intersected with the securitization of reproduction. More specifically, the trinity of state–nation–territory has been underpinned by another trinity, that of citizen–nation–biological kinship. As Tyler explores, the unwanted immigrant has been constructed as a threat not only to territorial borders but also to the "species life" (i.e., biological kinship) of the British nation. Under the 1981 Nationality Act, for example, the British-born children of non-citizen mothers have been formally excluded from British citizenship, in turn reflecting fears that foreign women will populate the country with non-native children. The targeting of migrant women for surveillance and deportation has therefore mirrored anxieties that the very lifeblood of the nation could be jeopardized by the "wrong" kind of reproduction.[105] Indeed, the reproductive energies of the migrant woman have been positioned as a threat to the reproduction of the nation itself, her own body symbolizing how the body of the nation could become implanted with "alien seed."[106] The violation and ruin of the migrant sex worker thus stands in for the violation and ruin of the body politic.[107] Put another way, it is not deviant homosexuality but deviant heterosexuality that threatens to adulterate the purity of the English genus. Just as Roderick Ferguson points to straight African Americans as "reproductive rather than productive, heterosexual but never heteronormative,"[108] the migrant sex worker is similarly figured as dangerous not despite, but because of, her association with heterosexuality.

Anti-trafficking campaigns have thus required and reinforced patriarchal assumptions that women's sexuality must be constrained and contained. In so doing, they have utilized historic fears over women's mobility and bolstered longstanding notions that women should remain within the home of both household and nation.[109] By symbolically "fixing" women into place, these discourses create the impression of order and control while also feeding anxieties about the instability of the body politic.[110] Figurations of bodies as sexually perverse allow such bodies to be cast as dangerously mobile—as transgressing their "assigned spaces"—so that the sexual regulation of such bodies can, in turn, secure the stability of both nation and family.[111] It is thus the migrant sex worker's mobility as well as her sexuality—indeed, the mobility of her sexuality[112]—that risks the viability not only of the home as nation, but also of the home as domestic and intimate life.

That migrant sex workers embody a specifically heterosexual threat is not tacitly assumed; it is openly insisted. As noted, twenty-first-century policy interventions have consistently been justified through heteronormative appeals to an oppositional gender binary (e.g., to "make sure that we do not have the demand that leads to the exploitation of vulnerable women who are trafficked in to be used for sexual purposes by British men"[113]). Writing about the Swedish case, Don Kulick highlights that the purchase of sex is not just counterposed against "healthy, natural, good sex" but authorizes heteronormativity as both morally good and distinctly Swedish; it is constitutive of "national sexuality" as *the* official and legitimate sexuality to which all must conform. Conversely, sexual offenses (e.g., rape) when committed by migrant men are attributed to immigrant sexuality writ large, whereas the same crimes when committed by Swedish men are exceptionalized through appeals to individual psychopathology.[114] Public discourse in Britain has similarly reproduced these logics: several high-profile cases involving politically influential white men (such as *Operation Yewtree* and *Operation Fernbridge*) have been articulated in terms of the individual criminality and psychological dysfunction of the perpetrators; whereas cases involving men of Pakistani heritage have entailed representations of racialized others as the archetypal perpetrators and white girls as the archetypal victims.[115] The *Times*, for instance, ran a feature on the domestic trafficking of British girls in 2011 and noted that the girls' home town "could be almost anywhere in northern England with a sizeable South Asian community"[116]—the implication being that sexual exploitation could occur in any such location. Thus, even when trafficking has been reported as a "domestic" issue, it has still been characterized as a problem of immigration.

TROUBLING UNFREE LABOR

With prostitution equated with trafficking, and trafficking equated with immigration, commercial sex has functioned as a conduit for disquiet about larger economic, political, and cultural transformations.[117] Stories of a sudden and most unprecedented flood of foreign sex workers—which have in fact circulated since at least medieval times—have been given renewed vigor in the twenty-first century and, interestingly, the figure of 80,000 has made a new appearance. While it was claimed just over a century ago that 80,000 "white slaves" could be found in London (a figure that also cropped up in the 1850s), now it is up and down the country that "80,000 women work in the vice trade, most foreign nationals—and the numbers are thought to be growing."[118] The presence of foreign prostitution has also been used as a powerful metaphor for Britain's international standing. Considerable concern was expressed, for example, over the potential for a major influx of trafficked women during the 2012 Olympics. As the Minister for the Olympics, Tessa Jowell, advised the House of Commons in 2009, the government was "absolutely determined to take every pre-emptive action that we can" to ensure that the Olympics "do not become a target for that vile trade and are not tainted as a result."[119]

Fueled by exaggerated statistics and "anecdotal horror stories," moral panics have been shored up by claims that sex trafficking is a global epidemic.[120] *Paying the Price*, for instance, argued that sex trafficking must be understood as "both a global and a local trade" that is "highly lucrative" and "often linked to other forms of organized crime."[121] More recently, *Behind Closed Doors* has painted trafficking as a "global human rights crisis" that is explicitly gendered ("the people who are exploited are overwhelmingly women and the people who pay to sexually abuse them are overwhelmingly men") and non-British ("85% of potential victims are non-UK nationals" and "Romanian suspects constitute the largest nationality group among individuals under investigation").[122] In so doing, the report utilizes historical narratives of foreign bodies as polluting, but it also weaponizes such narratives through appeals to a new kind of danger: that of the "pop-up brothel." Threatening to strike the nation in any place and at any time, the pop-up brothel is "changing migration patterns with huge numbers of women, particularly from Eastern Europe, being brought in by these groups to service British men who have an expectation of an absolute right to buy sex . . . The result is a trade that is organized, industrialized and highly damaging for those whose consent is purchased."[123] In order to maximize the sense of an intangible, generalized, and existential threat, the AAPG's report points to a plethora of operations (e.g., *Operation Ludlow* and *Operation Greengrass*) and proposes a "holistic approach" that involves "mobilizing all available measures to disrupt and robustly respond to sexual exploitation happening now."[124] The National Crime Agency, too, emphasizes the pervasive risk of sexual exploitation: "This is a crime which affects all types of communities across every part of the United Kingdom. It is difficult to spot because often victims don't even know they are being exploited." Encouraging responsible citizens to telephone the Modern Slavery Helpline, the Agency urges that "we need those communities to be our eyes and ears."[125]

Sex trafficking discourses thus feed into, and feed from, broader concerns surrounding globalization as "a corroding force that creeps in uninvited, contaminating the affluent with the diseases of the poor world."[126] In reality, neoliberal globalization has indeed fostered conditions of extreme insecurity for whole populations over recent decades, as precarity and debility are "endemic rather than epidemic or exceptional" to global capitalism.[127] And such developments have indeed been interwoven with the growth and diversification of the sex industry worldwide, especially in tourism-dependent countries in the Global South as well as postindustrial cities of the Global North.[128] Indeed, Silvia Federici argues that commercial sex must be understood as "an essential part of the global restructuring of the sexual division of labor and of the reproduction of labor power, of which sex work is one of the pillars."[129] Central to this is the creation of mass pauperization and unemployment that have led directly to migration from poorer to wealthier countries, and that allow more and more labor in imperialist nations—including domestic, caring, and sexual labor—to be offloaded on to people from postcolonial and postcommunist contexts.[130]

Yet, even as commercial sex is depicted as a flourishing, organized, and globalized mode of criminality,[131] it is reduced to violence by individual men against individual women in anti-trafficking discourses, thus neatly obscuring the global political economies of poverty and inequality that structure the conditions under which sex workers labor.[132] It is precisely because of the dearth of "livable"[133] alternatives, together with the lack of labor and civil rights for sex workers (and especially migrant sex workers), that commercial sex has been described as "the ultimate precarious labor."[134] It is truly perverse that, as a direct consequence of the very anti-trafficking policies that proclaim to protect them, migrant sex workers' mobility and ability to work under decent and fair conditions are even more tightly restricted, thus increasing their reliance on third parties and limiting their capacity to seek protection from the state when abused.[135] As such, the anti-trafficking agenda overlooks how trafficking and labor exploitation are themselves exacerbated by strict labor market and immigration controls, which have made it enormously difficult for non-European Union (EU) nationals to gain access to working visas unless they have significant financial support.[136] Moral discourses therefore conveniently mask Britain's own morally dubious approach to labor mobility and the regulation of markets while eliding the historically specific conditions under which labor exploitation takes place.[137] In so doing, they help to construct slavery as something that originates from less "advanced" societies and free labor as something that is natural to "developed" nations,[138] conveniently ignoring Britain's colonial legacies in the process. Thus, even though such discourses do not map onto "familiar patterns of racial stratification," they nevertheless reflect and sustain what are distinctively racialized hierarchies of inclusion and exclusion.[139] Britain's pending withdrawal from the EU is further redrawing these divisions, with an increase in arrests and deportations of EU sex workers residing in the United Kingdom as a direct consequence of the lack of legal recognition for sex work, since many do not possess the required documentation (e.g., a record of waged work) to remain.[140]

Ironically, the language of sex has paved the way for the language of work in official discourse. Under successive Conservative governments from 2010 onward (including in coalition with the Liberal Democrats in 2010–2015), there has been a shift in focus from sexual exploitation to slavery, human trafficking, and the abuse of labor for profit in all sectors.[141] The much-lauded Modern Slavery Act of 2015—which seeks to "make provision about slavery, servitude and forced or compulsory labor and about human trafficking"[142]—has amalgamated existing legislation regarding forced labor and trafficking, established an Independent Anti-Slavery Commissioner, raised the maximum sentence to life imprisonment, and enhanced the powers of the authorities to seize assets and enforce reparations.[143] Evoking the antislavery crusade of the eighteenth century, the modern slavery agenda problematizes slavery as a mode of unfree labor rather than as a mode of unfree sex. In the words of the home secretary and subsequently prime minister, Theresa May, it is "nearly two hundred years after the slave trade was abolished in this country" that modern slavery has become "the great human rights issue of our time . . . I am determined that we will make it a national and international mission to rid the world of this barbaric evil."[144]

At first sight, this represents a fissure in discourses that conflate sexual exploitation with trafficking. Yet the modern slavery agenda should not be misconstrued as desexualized, for preexisting campaigns against sex trafficking have already profoundly shaped the contours of political debate and policy practice. For example, the Nationality, Immigration and Asylum Act of 2002 prohibited a "person" from arranging or facilitating another individual's travel in/to/from the United Kingdom with the *intention* of exercising control over prostitution;[145] and the Sexual Offences Act of 2003, again, framed trafficking as the *intention* to transport another for the purposes of prostitution, even if there were no coercion, deception, threat, or lack of consent involved.[146] It is this notion that consent is "irrelevant to exploitation" that is pivotal to the modern slavery agenda: indeed, it is not just that "a person cannot consent to their own exploitation" but that exploitation "need not have taken place yet to constitute slavery or human trafficking."[147] By this sleight of hand, labor mobility for undocumented workers can be classified as modern slavery whether or not any actual exploitation has taken place.

Nor has the question of prostitution disappeared from official discourse: for instance, the term "sexual exploitation" appears twenty-six times in the Home Office's sixty-two-page advisory document on modern slavery.[148] Nevertheless, unfree sex is being reframed as one facet—if still a very important one—of a much bigger problem: that of unfree labor. Thus, Theresa May can point to "the horrendous existence of exploitation, forced prostitution, and inhumane labor" as part of the same overarching issue.[149] Significantly, the language of modern slavery is ascribing new meanings to old discourses of commercial sex as non-work since unfree labor, as a mode of slavery, is unrecognizable as "labor" just as unfree sex had been before it. Indeed, anti-prostitution discourses must be seen as integral to wider antislavery discourses given that commercial sex has historically been constructed as *the* exemplar of the unfreedom of slavery. To be sure, the sexual politics of the modern slavery agenda are not declared so openly as they had been when the principal focus was on sex trafficking (and the political economy literature has shifted its gaze accordingly[150]). But sex nevertheless remains an "insidious presence"[151] in contemporary understandings of unfree labor, even if the explicit language of unfree sex has fallen away somewhat. Constructions of trafficking as modern slavery therefore reestablish rather than dismantle the dualism between free labor and sexual slavery that, as we have seen in earlier chapters, has shaped the politico-economic imaginary for centuries.

To be clear, twenty-first-century appeals to the imperative of free labor are the pretext for the radical curtailment of labor freedoms under the so-called hostile environment policy—which has led, for instance, to the Windrush scandal in which scores of people were wrongly deported on the spurious grounds that they had no legal right to reside in the United Kingdom. Unfree labor, it seems, does not count as such when it involves "excluding illegalized non-citizens from access to employment, housing, healthcare, a driving license, a bank account, and an education."[152] It is precisely the hostile environment that the APPG unambiguously endorses in *Behind Closed Doors*. Rather than advocating labor rights or legal protections for sex workers (such as, say, the right to asylum), the report instead proposes that "Britain must become a hostile place for sex traffickers and other third party profiteers of sexual exploitation," and recommends that the purchase of sex should be made into "a criminal offence in all locations."[153]

Furthermore, and given the longstanding connections between anti-prostitution and anti-immigration discourses in the United Kingdom, it is clear that the modern slavery agenda cannot be removed from the nationalistic and xenophobic imaginaries that are currently driving the Brexit agenda, and that have seen a marked increase in racist incidents since the referendum.[154] As Aida Hozić and Jacqui True contend, Brexit should first and foremost be conceived as a "scandal" since it has been "manufactured by elites but exploited through appeals to gendered identities and selves linked to affective economies constituted by desiring subjects of consumerism and frequently symbolized by the otherness of women's bodies."[155] It is perplexing that some of the politicians who are vocal in their opposition to Brexit—including the APPG's Gavin Shuker and Jess Philipps—are not also taking the opportunity to denounce the anti-trafficking agenda that helped to whip up the very anti-immigration sentiments that contributed to the referendum result. As Hozić and True also note, the absenting of women's work—and especially migrant women's work—is exactly how Brexit was able to materialize, for "it is only by keeping women's labor invisible—particularly in the globalized chains of care economies—that the world without immigrants might have appeared feasible to voters." Yet the reality is that the British economy relies on feminized migration to provide a great deal of its caring labor, with migrants making up two fifths of the social care workforce and four fifths of new entrants coming from the European Economic Area.[156] Indeed, the mobility of women from eastern Europe has been "instrumental"[157] in the reproduction of Britain's labor force and thus the body politic itself.

Yet moral panics over prostitution and trafficking are also a profitable business, tied as they are to processes of capitalist accumulation at both the national and local levels. For example, Phil Hubbard points to the connections between the use of criminal justice interventions to tackle prostitution, on the one hand, and the corporate-led gentrification of urban spaces, on the other.[158] The policing, surveillance, and criminalization of sex workers have facilitated the dislocation and relocation of already marginalized populations—such as poor and migrant communities—from well-to-do areas into impoverished, downtown districts.[159] While the stated intention may be to tackle the sexual exploitation of women, the effect of trafficking and prostitution policies in the twenty-first century is to propagate "geographies of exception and abandonment."[160] This has also involved the suppression of visibly queer spaces—such as the closure of gay saunas and clubs in major cities—as part of efforts to remove sex from plain sight to respond to "the increasingly aggressive demand of market capital."[161] Just as moral panics over the "witches" legitimized the economic privatization of common land in early modern England, the contemporary privatization of public/collective space has been advanced under the guise of protecting morality and decency for ordinary citizens.[162] Since 1979, the British state has been able to sell off vast swathes of publicly owned land to the private sector—about one tenth of the whole of Britain's land mass, and worth around £400 billion.[163] Couched as a moral project, the targeting of sex workers under the modern-day enclosures must therefore be understood as the latest in a centuries-old process of what David Harvey has famously termed "accumulation by dispossession."[164]

CONCLUSION

In *The Will to Knowledge*, Michel Foucault remarks that modern power has "wrapped the sexual body in its embrace,"[165] and the Marriage (Same Sex Couples) Act of 2013 suggests that there is still some truth to this in twenty-first-century Britain. Yet the rise of anti-trafficking campaigns that have served as a thin disguise for anti-immigration policies reveal that sexuality also continues to be deployed as a means to mark out populations for "neglect, disposal, and death."[166] Indeed, in the midst of reports that budget cuts to health and social services have led to at least 130,000 preventable deaths in just five years,[167] and with growing swathes of the population condemned quite deliberately to the "slow death"[168] of poverty and destitution, it is difficult not to conclude that the present moment is characterized less by the calculated management of life than by the calculated mismanagement of death. Moreover, as Silvia Federici makes plain, the modern-day expropriation of the commons that we are witnessing is deeply entwined with the sexual division of labor, for it is women as the "primary subjects of reproductive work" who are penalized the most by the privatization of the means of reproduction.[169] Anti-trafficking and "modern slavery" campaigns therefore do no more to advance the interests of poor and marginalized women than they do to exercise anti-capitalist politics,[170] for they are implicated in women's individual and collective subjugation, in the stripping back of the welfare state, and in the ever-upward hemorrhaging of wealth.

Conclusion

On Friday, March 8, 2019, sex workers in Britain went on strike to protest against the criminalization and denigration of their labor as part of the International Women's Strike that was held in over fifty countries. In the words of sex worker and activist Molly Smith:

> The women's strike builds solidarity across difference. We work to draw links between all the ways in which women's work is exploited or taken for granted; all the ways in which resources and autonomy are withheld from us. That means naming work in all its forms: our work on shopfloors, our work cleaning offices, our work in brothels, our work in marriage, our work in care homes and our work caring for and raising the next generation of workers. It means the work we must put in to access healthcare—the work of resisting attacks on our reproductive autonomy; the work of accessing trans healthcare. It means the work we must put in to attempt to avoid criminalisation. It means naming our reproductive and domestic work as work alongside our work outside the home. In naming all this as work, we struggle together to make visible "all the work we do as women" and to resist the exploitative conditions we are offered. We work to transform the conditions of our work and of the world.[1]

By situating paid sexual labor alongside unpaid labor in the home, and by locating feminized labor at the heart of struggles for economic and social justice, the sex workers' movement is radically contesting the terms of the capitalist order. For, as I have attempted to demonstrate in this book, capitalism profits greatly from the illusion that economy and sexuality are not just separate spheres but exist in opposition to each other. It is this

Capitalism's Sexual History. Nicola J. Smith, Oxford University Press (2020). © Oxford University Press.
DOI: 10.1093/oso/9780197530276.001.0001.

move, I have argued, that allows the sexual division of labor on which capitalism relies to appear as the natural, moral, and only way of organizing economic, political, and cultural life. Indeed, the criminalization of commercial sex might itself be understood as work that is done for capitalism, for the economy/sexuality dichotomy does not—and never did—rest on solid foundations. Instead, the case I have made is that this dichotomy is maintained and defended as much through state repression as it is through techniques of normalization: it takes an awful lot of work to transform sexual labor into non-labor, after all.

Yet I have also discussed how the economy/sexuality dichotomy has all too often been replicated in the bodies of scholarship dedicated to capitalism and sexuality respectively: international political economy (IPE) and queer theory. In IPE, sexuality has been treated as exogenous to the discipline from the outset, despite longstanding interventions from feminists in the field; and in queer theory, the analysis of sexuality has frequently come unshackled from the analysis of global capitalism, with the contributions of feminist political economists again neglected as a result. This lack of sustained dialogue means that both fields are missing important opportunities to deepen their analysis and understanding of contemporary power relations. A key aim of this book has therefore been to address this gap by bringing IPE into much closer conversation with queer theory than has hitherto been the case, and to do so by writing in—and not writing out—the invaluable insights of feminists political economists that make such a project possible in the first place.

Central to this agenda has been my contention that the study of capitalism and sexuality is most fruitfully approached as a historical project. More particularly, I have brought together the work of Michel Foucault and Silvia Federici to assemble a new framework for understanding the complex, contingent, and contradictory relations between capitalism and sexuality—one that is capable of attending to the frictions and bonds between the repression of sex and the production of sexuality (Chapter 1). This has enabled me to investigate how capitalism both needs and obscures its relationship with sexuality, not least by harnessing women's reproductive labor while hiding the existence of such labor. Through the suppression and stimulation of sexual deviance, the sexual division of labor has been historically constituted as the "normal" state of affairs that must be upheld and protected, including through state-led coercion and violence.

With an empirical focus on the British case, the book has interrogated how capitalism is organized around the very dualism between sex and work that sex workers are opposing, and which has been centuries in the making. Beginning in the Middle Ages (Chapter 2), I have shown that economic and sexual life were not always conceived as opposites, for they were fused together—and very explicitly—within the medieval institution of marriage. Yet capitalist development in early modern England nevertheless utilized these distinctions, which provided the basis for a new sexual division of labor to be forged through which women's unpaid work could be appropriated. Moving into the Victorian era (Chapter 3), I have traced how the budding division between sex and work became crystalized in the public/private split that constituted bourgeois sexuality as natural and privileged through reference to the abnormality of commercial sex. The public/private split was further strengthened in the twentieth century (Chapter 4) as heteronormativity and consumerism coalesced to reproduce the "healthy" nuclear family at one end of the sexual continuum and the "pathological" prostitute at the other. Finally, I have charted how the sex/work binary continues to be deployed in the twenty-first century (Chapter 5) to justify the heightening of economic and social injustice.

Overall, I have sought to historicize and thereby politicize capitalism's sexual relations, as perhaps the most puzzling question of all is why the sexual is not already assumed to be economic. Given that heteronormativity is so obviously tied to any number of lucrative industries from pregnancy products to romantic movies, and especially given that marriage is one of the most enduring and pervasive of all economic arrangements, why is sexuality not automatically understood to be a matter of political economy? The answer offered in this book is that sexuality is absent because it has been absented—and it has been absented because this makes possible one of capitalism's most profitable enterprises, the sexual division of labor, as a seemingly endless source of "free" labor power. Indeed, reproductive labor is, for the most part, done for free precisely because it is constituted as something that is—and must be—done freely (in the sense that the ideal sexual subject is depicted as a reproductive subject who embodies freedom). Thus, as the book has also sought to establish, the sexual division of labor itself hinges on the regulation of sexuality that is, in turn, constituted in and through discourses of sex work as the embodiment of all that is unfree. As Silvia Federici writes of early modern Europe, "once women's activities were defined as non-work, women's labor began to appear as a natural resource, available to all, no less than the air we breathe or the water we drink."[2] It is clear that women's labor is still regarded very much as a natural resource both within the home and outside of it, for it is women—and especially migrant women and women of color—who perform a disproportionate share of both unpaid reproductive labor and low-paid productive labor.[3] And what all of this suggests is that, when abolitionist feminists (and Hollywood stars) align themselves with governments to rally against the "unfreedom" of paid sexual labor, they are focusing on entirely the wrong target.

While this book has involved a great deal of "looking backward,"[4] a major question therefore remains: where to go from here? For sex worker activists and allies, the most pressing issue is the full decriminalization of commercial sex so as to combat "the sexist, racist and criminal laws and whore stigma that jeopardize [sex workers'] lives."[5] But, over the longer term, the sex workers' movement is also calling for access to universal health care, affordable housing, social protection, safe working conditions, decent pay, and freedom from state repression for all workers, including migrant workers.[6] This is a project that is directly compatible with the "new queer agenda"[7] that queer scholars and activists have been pursuing in recent years, which focuses on questions of material (in)justice such as welfare policies, health care, employment rights, homelessness, and incarceration.[8] While queer theory and politics have, in the main, stayed silent about the question of sex work,[9] this is beginning to change. In July 2018, for instance, Queer Strike marched alongside the English Collective of Prostitutes at Trans Pride Brighton to oppose proposals to close down online platforms that sex workers use to advertise. And in March 2019, the International Lesbian, Gay, Bisexual, Trans and Intersex Association, encompassing over 1,500 organizations from across the world, passed a resolution in support of the full decriminalization of commercial sex.[10]

If—as this book has sought to show—the removal of sexuality from economy is exactly how sexual injustice is produced, then queer studies and activism would certainly do well to reposition sex work as a central, not marginal, concern. As noted in Chapter 1, some have begun to approach sex work as a question of queer fluidity (e.g., by troubling the female worker/male client binary), but this book also elucidates the need for queer theorists to take up commercial sex as a constitutive element in the making and writing of queer histories as well as queer political economies. By the same token, if the history of sex work has been interlaced with the history of homosexuality—as this book has also tried to uncover—then it makes sense for feminist debates about commercial sex to draw and gain much more from the wealth of queer insights into sexuality than they have to date. This would enable feminist scholars to better understand how the sex/work split is entangled with heteronormative logics that, at times, feminists themselves have reproduced in controversies over the "truth" of sex and work. By bringing together the intellectual and political projects of queer, feminist, and political economy scholars, my hope with this book is not to offer any kind of last word on these fields but, on the contrary, to invite them to question, listen to, and ultimately learn from each other going forward.

This is not to underplay the clear tensions and sticking points within and between queer, feminist, and leftist agendas. One challenging question that warrants further research is how (and indeed if) the "politics of refusal" embodied by queer anti-social theory can be pursued alongside the "politics of redistribution" and the "politics of recognition."[11] As Kathi Weeks notes, feminists have often called either for greater access to paid work in the workplace or for greater recognition of their domestic and caring labor, and yet perhaps the most significant struggle to be waged is not just "for more work and better work, but also for less work."[12] In a similar vein, Heather Berg draws on queer anti-social theory to argue that— since productive and reproductive labor are the main sources of capitalism's profitability—feminists should question the "(re)productivism" of the premise that social reproduction is "self-evidently good and necessary." Indeed, one of the most insidious ways in which capitalism is able to extract value from workers is through appeals to the social necessity of their labor, with workers in a variety of contexts (e.g., teachers, nurses, office workers) placed under ever-growing pressure to adhere to the strictures of mutual responsibility in what amounts to a mode of corporate emotional extortion. Instead, Berg asks for feminists to open up more conceptual and political space for workers, both paid and unpaid, to refuse to service what she terms the "social necessity debt" that capitalism so depends on.[13] This is, moreover, a specifically gendered issue that needs to be interrogated as such. As Lisa Downing lays bare, feminist accounts often valorize altruism, caring labor, and collective forms of work and action, and yet this can reinforce rather than destabilize cultural expectations that women must prioritize care-for-others above self-care (i.e., that women must literally be self-less).[14] Given feminist contentions that one of the cornerstones of patriarchal power relations is that women belong to others, this is indeed a troubling irony that highlights the need for further reflection on the possibilities for feminist refusal (or what Jack Halberstam terms "antisocial feminism"[15]).

At the same time, there is more work to be done on the work involved in acts of refusal for, as the feminist political economy literature reminds us, no mode of human (in)action is not already beholden to others' labor.[16] Given that those at the bottom of gendered, racialized, classed, and territorialized hierarchies perform the bulk of unpaid and low-paid productive and reproductive labor,[17] and yet they are also structurally positioned as the least able to practice refusal, it is unclear how individualized acts of refusal alone can address such systemic inequalities.[18] To borrow from

Jasbir Puar, "what material conditions of possibility are necessary" to exercise refusal, and "what happens when those conditions are not available"?[19] One way forward, as Wanda Vrasti highlights, might be refusal "from below" involving collective, autonomous forms of resistance to the primacy of waged labor. Since the roots of waged labor lie in the privatization of the means of production and reproduction, then such refusal would mean regaining the commons while also opposing the division between productive and reproductive labor.[20] In this way, the politics of refusal, recognition, and redistribution might work together to reconstitute what it means to work together and, in so doing, to offer a "plurality of resistances."[21]

Above all, since capitalism is structured by sexual injustice, as this volume has shown, no leftist agenda can (continue to) marginalize sexuality if it is to genuinely challenge capitalist structures, just as no struggles for sexual justice can afford to overlook how sexuality is both a product of, and productive of, capitalist power relations. As I come to the end of writing this book, I am struck by the proliferation of discourses (largely but not only online) surrounding something called "queer theory" as the instigator of something called "identity politics" that, it is said, is fracturing something called "the left." Not only do such claims fundamentally misread the history of queer, but they perpetuate the very same logics that queer theory emerged to contest. From the outset, as Jack Halberstam writes, queer meant "a commitment to coalition, a vision of alternative worlds"[22]—and it is clear that coalitions and alternative visions are needed as much now as they ever have been. For it is only through working together that queer, feminist, antiracist, and leftist agendas can hope to combat the (seemingly inexorable) economic, political, social, and environmental destruction that is currently being wrought. Perhaps, if we can find new ways to forge solidarity across difference(s), then neoliberal capitalism—along with its systemic cruelties and gross inequities—might even become a thing of the past.

NOTES

INTRODUCTION

1. Magdy Abdel-Hamid et al., "Letter to Salil Shetty, Steven W. Hawkins and the Amnesty International Board of Directors," July 17, 2015, from http://catwinternational.org/Content/Images/Article/621/attachment.pdf.

2. Julie Bindel, "Prostitution Is Not a Job. The Inside of a Woman's Body Is Not a Workplace," *The Guardian*, April 30, 2018.

3. Cynthia Enloe, *Bananas, Beaches and Bases: Making Feminist Sense of International Politics* (Oakland: University of California Press, 1990); Jan Jindy Pettman, "Body Politics: International Sex Tourism," *Third World Quarterly* 18, no. 1 (1997): 93–108; Gillian Youngs, "Embodied Political Economy or an Escape from Disembodied Knowledge," in *Political Economy, Power and the Body*, ed. Gillian Youngs (Basingstoke, UK: Palgrave, 2000), 11–30; V. Spike Peterson, *A Critical Rewriting of Global Political Economy: Integrating Reproductive, Productive and Virtual Economies* (Abingdon, UK: Routledge, 2003); Anna Agathangelou, *The Global Political Economy of Sex: Desire, Violence, And Insecurity in Mediterranean Nation States* (Basingstoke, UK: Palgrave, 2005); Kate Bedford and Shirin Rai, "Feminists Theorize International Political Economy," *Signs: Journal of Women in Culture and Society* 36, no. 1 (2010): 1–18; J. Ann Tickner, *A Feminist Voyage Through International Relations* (New York: Oxford University Press, 2014); Jacqui True and Aida Hozić, eds., *Scandalous Economics: Gender and the Politics of Financial Crisis* (New York: Oxford University Press, 2016).

4. Nicola Smith and Donna Lee, "Corporeal Capitalism: The Body in International Political Economy," *Global Society* 29, no. 1 (2015): 64–69; see also Pettman, "Body Politics"; Youngs, "Embodied Political Economy"; Sébastien Rioux, "Embodied Contradictions: Capitalism, Social Reproduction and Body Formation," *Women's Studies International Forum* 48 (2015): 194–202; Juanita Elias and Adrienne Roberts, eds., *Feminist Global Political Economies of the Everyday* (London: Routledge, 2018).

5. Adam David Morton, "Social Forces in the Struggle over Hegemony: Neo-Gramscian Perspectives in International Political Economy," *Rethinking Marxism* 15, no. 2 (2003): 153–179; Matthew Watson, *Foundations of International Political Economy* (Basingstoke, UK: Palgrave, 2005); John M. Hobson and Leonard Seabrooke, eds., *Everyday Politics of the World Economy* (Cambridge, UK: Cambridge University Press, 2007); Adrian Budd, *Class, States and International Relations: A Critical Appraisal of Robert Cox and Neo-Gramscian Theory* (Abingdon, UK: Routledge, 2013); although see Stuart Shields, Ian Bruff,

and Huw Macartney, eds., *Critical International Political Economy: Dialogue, Debate, and Dissensus* (Basingstoke, UK: Palgrave, 2011).

6. Jill Steans and Daniela Tepe, "Gender in the Theory and Practice of International Political Economy: The Promise and Limitations of Neo-Gramscian Approaches," in *Gramsci, Political Economy, and International Relations Theory: Modern Princes and Naked Emperors*, ed. Alison J. Ayers (New York: Palgrave, 2008), 133–52; Bedford and Rai, "Feminists Theorize International Political Economy."

7. Judith Butler, "Merely Cultural," *Social Text* 15, no. 3/4 (1997): 265.

8. For an excellent critique of "dividing" practices, see Penny Griffin, "Gender, IPE and Poststructuralism: Problematizing the Material/Discursive Divide," in *Handbook on the International Political Economy of Gender*, ed. Juanita Elias and Adrienne Roberts (Cheltenham, UK: Edward Elgar, 2018), 86–101.

9. This will be discussed in detail in Chapter 1, but examples of work in this vein include Richard Cornwall, "Queer Political Economy: The Social Articulation of Desire," in *Homo Economics: Capitalism, Community, and Lesbian and Gay Life*, ed. Amy Gluckman and Betsy Reed (New York: Routledge, 1997), 89–122; Rosemary Hennessy, *Profit and Pleasure: Sexual Identities in Late Capitalism* (Abingdon, UK: Routledge, 2000); Lisa Duggan, *The Twilight of Equality? Neoliberalism, Cultural Politics, and the Attack on Democracy* (Boston: Beacon Press, 2003); Kevin Floyd, *The Reification of Desire: Toward a Queer Marxism* (Minneapolis: University of Minnesota Press, 2009); Suzanne Bergeron and Jyoti Puri, "Sexuality Between State and Class: An Introduction," *Rethinking Marxism* 24, no. 4 (2012): 491–98; Jon Binnie, *The Globalization of Sexuality* (London: Sage, 2010); Christina Crosby et al., "Queer Studies, Materialism, and Crisis: A Roundtable Discussion," *GLQ: A Journal of Lesbian and Gay Studies* 18, no. 1 (2012): 127–147; Anna Agathangelou, "Neoliberal Geopolitical Order and Value: Queerness as a Speculative Economy and Anti-Blackness as Terror," *International Feminist Journal of Politics* 15, no. 4 (2013): 453–476; V. Spike Peterson, "Family Matters: How Queering the Intimate Queers the International," *International Studies Review* 16, no. 4 (2014): 604–608; Rahul Rao, "Global Homocapitalism," *Radical Philosophy* 194 (2015): 38–49; Nikita Dhawan et al., eds., *Global Justice and Desire: Queering Economy* (Abingdon, UK: Routledge, 2015); Peter Drucker, *Warped: Gay Normality and Queer Anti-Capitalism* (Leiden: Brill, 2015).

10. Pettman, "Body Politics"; Youngs, "Embodied Political Economy"; Jill Steans, "Engaging from the Margins: Feminist Encounters with the 'Mainstream' of International Relations," *British Journal of Politics and International Relations* 5, no. 3 (2003): 428–454; Agathangelou, *The Global Political Economy of Sex*.

11. This endeavor is very much inspired by Cynthia Weber's approach to forging conversations between international relations (IR) and queer theory (including the clarifications offered on pp. 201–202). Cynthia Weber, *Queer International Relations: Sovereignty, Sexuality and the Will to Knowledge* (New York: Oxford University Press, 2016). On the need to foster dialogue between queer theory and political science, see Nicola Smith and Donna Lee, "What's Queer About Political Science?", *British Journal of Politics & International Relations* 17, no. 1 (2015): 49–63.

12. Peterson, *A Critical Rewriting of Global Political Economy*; see also Diane Elson, "Labor Markets as Gendered Institutions: Equality, Efficiency and Empowerment Issues," *World Development* 27, no. 3 (March 1999): 611–627; Meg Luxton and Kate Bezanson, *Social Reproduction: Feminist Political Economy Challenges Neo-Liberalism* (Montreal: McGill Queens University Press, 2006); Jill Steans, *Gender*

and *International Relations* (London: Polity, 2013); Tickner, *A Feminist Voyage Through International Relations*.

13. Silvia Federici, *Caliban and the Witch: Women, the Body and Primitive Accumulation* (New York: Autonomedia, 2004), 115.

14. Notable exceptions include Corina McKay, "Is Sex Work Queer?", *Social Alternatives* 18, no. 3 (1999): 48–53; Roderick A. Ferguson, *Aberrations in Black: Toward a Queer of Color Critique* (Minneapolis: University of Minnesota Press, 2004); Anna Carline, "Criminal Justice, Extreme Pornography and Prostitution: Protecting Women or Promoting Morality?", *Sexualities* 14, no. 3 (2011): 312–333; Nick Mai, "The Fractal Queerness of Non-Heteronormative Migrants Working in the UK Sex Industry," *Sexualities* 15, no. 5–6 (2012): 570–585; Noelle M. Stout, *After Love: Queer Intimacy and Erotic Economies in Post-Soviet Cuba* (Durham, NC: Duke University Press, 2014); Mary Laing, Katy Pilcher, and Nicola Smith, eds., *Queer Sex Work* (Abingdon, UK: Routledge, 2015); Brooke M. Beloso, "Queer Theory, Sex Work, and Foucault's Unreason," *Foucault Studies* 23 (2017): 141–166.

15. Kathleen Barry, *The Prostitution of Sexuality: The Global Exploitation of Women* (New York: NYU Press, 1995); Donna Dickinson, "Philosophical Assumptions and Presumptions about Trafficking for Prostitution," in *Trafficking and Women's Rights*, ed. Christien van den Anker (Basingstoke, UK: Palgrave, 2006), 43–53; Kat Banyard, *Pimp State: Sex, Money, and the Future of Equality* (London: Faber & Faber, 2016); Julie Bindel, *The Pimping of Prostitution* (London: Palgrave, 2017).

16. That is, individuals should have "equal freedom to choose how they earn their living and freedom to choose what they do with their own body." Ava Caradonna, "Sex Work Without Apology," April 13, 2008, http://libcom.org/forums/organise/sex-work-without-apology-13042008; see also Camille Paglia, *Vamps and Tramps: New Essays* (London: Penguin, 1994); Carol Queen, "Sex Radical Politics, Sex-Positive Feminist Thought, and Whore Stigma," in *Whores and Other Feminists*, ed. Jill Nagle (New York: Routledge, 1997), 125–235; Drew Campbell, "Confessions of a Fat Sex Worker," in *Whores and Other Feminists*, 189–190; Theresa Reed, "Private Acts Versus Public Art: Where Prostitution Ends and Pornography Begins," in *Prostitution and Pornography: Philosophical Debates About the Sex Industry*, ed. Jessica Spector (Stanford: Stanford University Press, 2006), 249–257.

17. For a critique of the "oppression/liberation dichotomy" in sex work research, see Nicola J. Smith, "The International Political Economy of Commercial Sex," *Review of International Political Economy* 18, no. 4 (2011): 537; see also Shannon Bell, *Reading, Writing, and Rewriting the Prostitute Body* (Bloomington: Indiana University Press, 1994); Noah D. Zatz, "Sex Work/Sex Act: Law, Labor, and Desire in Constructions of Prostitution," *Signs*, 1997, 277–308; Jane Scoular, "The 'Subject' of Prostitution," *Feminist Theory* 5, no. 3 (2004): 343–355. For a discussion of this dichotomy in feminist debates more widely, see Amelia Morris, *The Politics of Weight: Feminist Dichotomies of Power in Dieting* (Basingstoke, UK: Palgrave, 2019).

18. On which see also Zatz, "Sex Work/Sex Act'; Prabha Kotiswaran, *Dangerous Sex, Invisible Labor: Sex Work and the Law in India* (Princeton, NJ: Princeton University Press, 2011); Molly Smith and Juno Mac, *Revolting Prostitutes: The Fight for Sex Workers' Rights* (London: Verso, 2018).

19. Smith and Mac, *Revolting Prostitutes*, 3–4.

20. Michel Foucault, *The History of Sexuality: The Will to Knowledge* (translated by Robert Hurley) (New York: Pantheon, 1978), 36.

21. Michel Foucault, *The Birth of Biopolitics: Lectures at the Collège de France, 1978–1979* (translated by Graham Burchell) (Basingstoke, UK: Palgrave, 2008), 21.

22. On which see Nicola Smith, Mary Laing, and Katy Pilcher, "Being, Thinking and Doing 'Queer' in Debates About Commercial Sex," in *Queer Sex Work*, 1–9.

23. Nicola Smith, "Queer in/and Sexual Economies," in *Queer Sex Work*, 13–22.

24. On the need for queer theory and feminist political economy to align forces in and around sex work research see Smith, "Queer in/and Sexual Economies."

25. Recent exceptions include V. Spike Peterson, "Sex Matters: A Queer History of Hierarchies," *International Feminist Journal of Politics* 16, no. 3 (2014): 389–409; Alison Phipps, *The Politics of the Body: Gender in a Neoliberal and Neoconservative Age* (Hoboken, NJ: John Wiley & Sons, 2014); Jemima Repo, *The Biopolitics of Gender* (New York: Oxford University Press, 2015); Angus Cameron, Nicola Smith, and Daniela Tepe-Belfrage, "Household Wastes: Disciplining the Family in the Name of Austerity," *British Politics* 11, no. 4 (2016): 396–417; Robbie Shilliam, *Race and the Undeserving Poor: From Abolition to Brexit* (Newcastle Upon Tyne, UK: Agenda, 2018).

26. Laura Jenkins, "The Difference Genealogy Makes: Strategies for Politicisation or How to Extend Capacities for Autonomy," *Political Studies* 59, no. 1 (2011): 156–174.

27. Joanna K. Fadyl and David A. Nicholls, "Foucault, the Subject and the Research Interview: A Critique of Methods," *Nursing Inquiry* 20, no. 1 (2013): 24.

28. Michel Foucault, "Nietzsche, Genealogy, History," *Semiotexte* 3, no. 1 (1978): 76–77.

29. Michel Foucault, *Society Must Be Defended: Lectures at the Collège de France, 1975–76* (translated by David Macey) (New York: Picador, 2003), 9–10. As Foucault clarifies, this is not to reject knowledge per se nor to "demand the lyrical right to be ignorant" but rather to "fight the power-effects characteristic of any discourse that is regarded as scientific . . . What types of knowledge are you trying to disqualify when you say that you are a science? What speaking subject, what discursive subject, what subject of experience and knowledge are you trying to minorize when you begin to say: 'I speak this discourse, I am speaking a scientific discourse, and I am a scientist.'" Foucault, *Society Must Be Defended*, 9–10.

30. Michel Foucault, *Discipline and Punish* (translated by Alan Sheridan) (New York: Vintage, 1979), 31.

31. Jacinda Swanson, "Recognition and Redistribution: Rethinking Culture and the Economic," *Theory, Culture & Society* 22, no. 4 (2005): 88.

32. Mark Olssen, "Foucault and Marxism: Rewriting the Theory of Historical Materialism," *Policy Futures in Education* 2, no. 3 (2004): 454–482, 454.

33. Fadyl and Nicholls, "Foucault, the Subject and the Research Interview," 24.

34. Bergeron and Puri, "Sexuality Between State and Class," 491.

35. Repo, *The Biopolitics of Gender*, 19. To take another example, Robbie Shilliam's analysis of the relations between race and class focuses specifically on the emergence of distinctions between the "deserving" white working class and the "undeserving" racialized poor in Britain over the past two centuries. Shilliam, *Race and the Undeserving Poor*.

36. As a researcher, I am also greatly influenced and energized by Jack Halberstam's brilliant quip that his queer research forms "part of a much smaller project." Halberstam in Carolyn Dinshaw et al., "Theorizing Queer Temporalities: A Roundtable Discussion," *GLQ: A Journal of Lesbian and Gay Studies* 13, no. 2 (2007): 182.

37. J. Ann Tickner, "Gendering a Discipline: Some Feminist Methodological Contributions to International Relations," *Signs: Journal of Women in Culture and Society* 30, no. 4 (2005): 2173–2188; Mary Hawkesworth, *Feminist Inquiry: From Political Conviction to Methodological Innovation* (New Brunswick, NJ: Rutgers University Press, 2006); Celine-Marie Pascale, *Making Sense of Race, Class, and Gender: Commonsense, Power, and Privilege in the United States* (New York: Routledge, 2007); Kath Browne and Catherine J. Nash, "Queer Methods and Methodologies: An Introduction," in *Queer Methods and Methodologies: Intersecting Queer Theories and Social Science Research*, ed. Kath Browne and Catherine J. Nash (Farnham, UK: Ashgate, 2010), 1–23; Laura Sjoberg, "What's Lost in Translation? Neopositivism and Critical Research Interests," *Millennium* 43, no. 3 (2015): 1007–1010.

38. Judith Butler, "Contingent Foundations: Feminism and the Question of 'Postmodernism,'" in *Feminists Theorize the Political*, ed. Judith Butler and Joan Wallach (New York: Routledge, 1992), 6.

39. Annick Wibben, *Feminist Security Studies: A Narrative Approach* (Abingdon, UK: Routledge, 2011), 2. Western feminist theories of the state, for instance, have often taken on a "universalizing language" rather than attending to the historical specificity of particular state forms. Shirin Rai, "Women and the State in the Third World," in *Women and Politics in the Third World*, ed. Haleh Afshar (Abingdon, UK: Routledge, 1996), 26–40, 26.

40. See for instance Thanh-Dam Truong, *Sex, Money and Morality: Prostitution and Tourism in Southeast Asia* (London: Zed, 1990); Barbara Ehrenreich and Arlie Russell Hochschild, eds., *Global Woman: Nannies, Maids and Sex Workers in the New Economy* (London: Granta Books, 2002); Agathangelou, *The Global Political Economy of Sex*; Kate Hardy, "Uneven Divestment of the State: Social Reproduction and Sex Work in Neo-Developmentalist Argentina," *Globalizations*, 2016, 1–14. The term "Western" can be read as "indicative of a historically and socially contingent package of ideas and ideals rather than as a geographically specific location." Laura J. Shepherd and Laura Sjoberg, "Trans-Bodies in/of War(s): Cisprivilege and Contemporary Security Strategy," *Feminist Review* 101, no. 1 (2012): 5–23, 7.

41. Elizabeth Bernstein, *Temporarily Yours: Intimacy, Authenticity, and the Commerce of Sex* (Chicago: University of Chicago Press, 2007).

42. Jessica Jacobs, *Sex, Tourism and the Postcolonial Encounter: Landscapes of Longing in Egypt* (Farnham, UK: Ashgate, 2012).

43. To borrow here from Adrienne Roberts's argument regarding financial consumers in the Global South. Adrienne Roberts, "Gender, Financial Deepening and the Production of Embodied Finance: Towards a Critical Feminist Analysis," *Global Society* 29, no. 1 (2015): 111.

44. Charlotte Hooper, "Disembodiment, Embodiment and the Construction of Hegemonic Masculinity," in *Political Economy, Power and the Body*, 31–51, 39.

45. Luise White, *The Comforts of Home: Prostitution in Colonial Nairobi* (Chicago: University of Chicago Press, 1990); Kamala Kempadoo, *Sun, Sex, and Gold: Tourism and Sex Work in the Caribbean* (Lanham, MD: Rowman & Littlefield, 1999); Ratna Kapur, "Post-Colonial Economies of Desire: Legal Representations of the Sexual Subaltern," *Denver University Law Review* 78 (2000): 855; Laura María Agustín, *Sex at the Margins: Migration, Labour Markets and the Rescue Industry* (London: Zed, 2007); Amalia L. Cabezas, *Economies of Desire: Sex and Tourism in Cuba and the Dominican Republic* (Philadelphia: Temple University

Press, 2009); Kotiswaran, *Dangerous Sex, Invisible Labor*; Christine Chin, *Cosmopolitan Sex Workers: Women and Migration in a Global City* (Oxford: Oxford University Press, 2013); Svati Shah, *Street Corner Secrets: Sex, Work, and Migration in the City of Mumbai* (Durham, NC: Duke University Press, 2014); Megan Daigle, *From Cuba with Love: Sex and Money in the Twenty-First Century* (Oakland: University of California Press, 2015).

46. Sara Meger develops the concept of fetishization to explore how sexual violence is "decontextualized from local/global power relations" and "objectified as a 'thing' in media, advocacy, policy and scholarly discourses." Sara Meger, "The Fetishization of Sexual Violence in International Security," *International Studies Quarterly* 60, no. 1 (2016): 4. The decontextualization and objectification of sex trafficking will be explored in Chapter 5.

47. Stuart Hall, "Castaway: Stuart Hall in His Own Words," OpenDemocracy, February 20, 2014, https://www.opendemocracy.net/shinealight/stuart-hall/castaway-stuart-hall-in-his-own-words.

48. Bridget Byrne, "Crisis of Identity: Englishness, Britishness, and Whiteness," in *Empire and After: Englishness in Postcolonial Perspective* (Oxford: Berghahn, 2007), 139–158; Krishan Kumar, "Negotiating English Identity: Englishness, Britishness, and the Future of the United Kingdom," *Nations and Nationalism* 16, no. 3 (2010): 469–487; Shilliam, *Race and the Undeserving Poor*.

49. Ellen Meiksins Wood, *The Origin of Capitalism: A Longer View* (London: Verso, 2002), 142.

50. John M. Hobson, *The Eastern Origins of Western Civilisation* (Cambridge, UK: Cambridge University Press, 2004); Alexander Anievas and Kerem Nisancioglu, *How the West Came to Rule: The Geopolitical Origins of Capitalism* (London: Pluto, 2015).

51. See *inter alia* Lance E. Davis and Robert A. Huttenback, *Mammon and the Pursuit of Empire: The Political Economy of British Imperialism, 1860–1912* (Cambridge, UK: Cambridge University Press, 1986); W. D. Rubenstein, *Capitalism, Culture, and Decline in Britain, 1750–1990* (London: New York, 1993); Spencer Dimmock, *The Origin of Capitalism in England, 1400–1600* (Leiden: Brill, 2014).

52. Likewise, the study of sexuality remains marginalized in the British politics literature, as the lack of dedicated chapters in state-of-the-art textbooks reveals. Smith and Lee, "What's Queer About Political Science."

53. Foucault, *The Will to Knowledge*, 69.

54. This is in contrast to the bulk of the literature on commercial sex. Jo Doezema, *Sex Slaves and Discourse Masters: The Construction of Trafficking* (London: Zed Books, 2010).

55. Michel Foucault, *Archaeology of Knowledge* (translated by A. M. Sheridan Smith) (Abingdon, UK: Routledge, 1989), 54.

56. Jeff Hearn, "From Hegemonic Masculinity to the Hegemony of Men," *Feminist Theory* 5 (2004): 49–72; Lauren B. Wilcox, *Bodies of Violence: Theorizing Embodied Subjects in International Relations* (New York: Oxford University Press, 2015); Penny Griffin, *Popular Culture, Political Economy, and the Death of Feminism: Why Women Are in Refrigerators and Other Stories* (Abingdon, UK: Routledge, 2015).

57. Laura J. Shepherd, *Gender, UN Peacebuilding, and the Politics of Space: Locating Legitimacy* (New York: Oxford University Press, 2017), 22–23.

58. My inability to speak either Latin or Middle English means that I am especially indebted to the prior scholarship of medieval historians such as Ruth Mazo

Karras (who conducted exhaustive primary research into commercial sex in medieval England), which I draw on in Chapter 2.

59. Foucault, *Society Must Be Defended*, 10.
60. Foucault, *The Will to Knowledge*, 100.
61. Pascale, *Making Sense of Race, Class, and Gender*, 20.
62. Laura J. Shepherd, "'To Save Succeeding Generations from the Scourge of War': The US, UN and the Violence of Security," *Review of International Studies* 34, no. 2 (2008): 297.
63. With a specific focus on Volume 1, *The Will to Knowledge*.
64. The Middle Ages roughly spans a thousand years but I begin my analysis in late medieval times (a period that lasted from the thirteenth century to the fifteenth century).
65. Hennessy, *Profit and Pleasure*, 97.
66. Jasbir Puar, *Terrorist Assemblages: Homonationalism in Queer Times* (Durham, NC: Duke University Press, 2008), xv.
67. Weber, *Queer International Relations*, 38.
68. Lisa Downing, "Perversion and the Problem of Fluidity and Identity," in *Clinical Encounters in Sexuality: Psychoanalytic Practice and Queer Theory*, ed. Noreen Giffney and Eve Watson (Goleta, CA: punctum books, 2017), 139.
69. Lisa Downing and Robert Gillett, "For an Anti-Post-Queer Agenda" (Critical Sexology Seminar in Birmingham, University of Birmingham, 2016); see also Downing, "Perversion and the Problem of Fluidity and Identity"; Robert Gillett, "Foucault's Genealogy," in *After Foucault: Culture, Theory, and Criticism in the Twenty-First Century*, ed. Lisa Downing (Cambridge, UK: Cambridge University Press, 2018), 17–30.
70. Readers may also notice that I use the term "queer political economy" rather than "queer international political economy" or "queer IPE." I do so deliberately because, although this book seeks to encourage closer engagement between IPE and queer theory, my aim is not to (re)position queer work on capitalism as a distinct subdiscipline of IPE. This is not only because queer theory is a huge field that spans a large number of disciplines while actively resisting "disciplining" (i.e., it is both interdisciplinary and anti-disciplinary). It is also because, while the book certainly hopes to contribute to scholarship in IPE, it draws on and speaks to scholars who are not located in, and do not identify as, "IPE." Since those scholars tend to refer instead to the study of "global capitalism" and/ or "political economy," I use the term "queer political economy" in this loose, interdisciplinary sense rather than to denote a subsection of IPE specifically. Similarly, I refer to "feminist political economy" in recognition of the fact that some of the feminist scholars cited—such as Silva Federici—are not, strictly speaking, "IPE" scholars (even if their work has been profoundly influential in IPE). Queer and feminist political economy are considered in greater depth in Chapter 1.
71. A wonderfully expansive volume to address this lacuna is Drucker, *Warped*.
72. Cathy J. Cohen, "Punks, Bulldaggers, and Welfare Queens: The Radical Potential of Queer Politics?", *GLQ: A Journal of Lesbian and Gay Studies* 3, no. 4 (1997): 439.
73. Weber, *Queer International Relations*.
74. What Diane Richardson calls "deviant heterosexuality." Diane Richardson, *Rethinking Sexuality* (Thousand Oaks, CA: Sage, 2000), 136.

75. Barbara Creed, *The Monstrous-Feminine: Film, Feminism, Psychoanalysis* (Abingdon, UK: Routledge, 2012). On historical and contemporary representations of women as "mothers, monsters, and whores," see Laura Sjoberg and Caron E. Gentry, *Mothers, Monsters, Whores: Women's Violence in Global Politics* (London: Zed, 2007); Caron E. Gentry and Laura Sjoberg, *Beyond Mothers, Monsters, Whores: Thinking About Women's Violence in Global Politics* (London: Zed, 2015).

76. Beloso, "Queer Theory, Sex Work, and Foucault's Unreason."

77. By now it should be clear that my aim is not to identify the ontology of sex or to locate this on the inside of women's bodies but, quite the opposite, to critique the *discourses* that seek to do so, together with their material effects.

78. To borrow from Judith Butler's framing of normative sexuality in Butler, "Merely Cultural," 274.

79. Jill McCracken, *Street Sex Workers' Discourse: Realizing Material Change Through Agential Choice* (New York: Routledge, 2013); Melinda Chateauvert, *Sex Workers Unite: A History of the Movement from Stonewall to SlutWalk* (Boston: Beacon Press, 2014).

80. On which see Sjoberg and Gentry, *Mothers, Monsters, Whores*; Gentry and Sjoberg, *Beyond Mothers, Monsters, Whores*.

81. See Chapter 2.

82. Hence her quip that her book is "written neither in Latin nor in Middle English." Ruth Mazo Karras, *Common Women: Prostitution and Sexuality in Medieval England* (Oxford: Oxford University Press, 1996), 11.

83. Repo, *The Biopolitics of Gender*, 1, 180. Following Susan Stryker, I understand gender not as alignment with a "signifying sex" or "psychical disposition" but rather as "an apparatus within which all bodies are taken up." Susan Stryker, "Biopolitics," *TSQ: Transgender Studies Quarterly* 1, no. 1–2 (2014): 39. For example, historical deployments of gender have included spiritual (Chapter 2), biological (Chapter 3), and psychological (Chapter 4) elements, albeit in overlapping, contested, and contingent ways (i.e., there has been no straightforward shift from the soul to the body to the mind). While Repo similarly defines gender as an apparatus, she restricts this to "an apparatus of biopower that emerged sixty years ago in the clinic." Repo, *The Biopolitics of Gender*, 2.

84. In the Middle Ages, for instance, men and women were often conceived in terms of a one-sex model in which they were simply different variants of the same sex (see Chapter 2).

85. David Garland, "What Is a 'History of the Present'? On Foucault's Genealogies and Their Critical Preconditions," *Punishment & Society* 16, no. 4 (2014): 372.

CHAPTER 1

1. James Penney, *After Queer Theory: The Limits of Sexual Politics* (London: Pluto Press, 2014), 1, 3.

2. David V. Ruffolo, *Post-Queer Politics* (New York: Routledge, 2016), 1.

3. Michael O'Rourke, "The Afterlives of Queer Theory," *Continent* 1, no. 2 (2011): 103–104.

4. Sara Ahmed, *On Being Included: Racism and Diversity in Institutional Life* (Durham, NC: Duke University Press, 2012), 179.

5. To take just one example, a Google search for the term "queer international political economy" on March 17, 2019, brought up zero results. (I mention this

to illustrate the lack of formal dialogue between IPE and queer theory but, as noted in the Introduction, I prefer the term "queer political economy" to "queer international political economy" for the purposes of this book.)

6. Anna Agathangelou, *The Global Political Economy of Sex: Desire, Violence, and Insecurity in Mediterranean Nation States* (Basingstoke, UK: Palgrave, 2005), 7.

7. Judith Butler, "Merely Cultural," *Social Text* 15, no. 3/4 (1997): 274.

8. What is especially odd is that, elsewhere in the social sciences and humanities, queer scholarship is particularly highly cited. Nicola Smith and Donna Lee, "What's Queer About Political Science?", *British Journal of Politics & International Relations* 17, no. 1 (2015): 49–63.

9. Noreen Giffney, "Denormatizing Queer Theory: More Than (Simply) Lesbian and Gay Studies," *Feminist Theory* 5, no. 1 (2004): 73–78.

10. Michel Foucault, *The History of Sexuality: The Will to Knowledge* (translated by Robert Hurley) (New York: Pantheon, 1978).

11. Penney, *After Queer Theory*, 3, 73.

12. Ruffolo, *Post-Queer Politics*, 4.

13. Noreen Giffney, "Introduction: The 'q' Word," in *The Ashgate Research Companion to Queer Theory*, ed. Noreen Giffney and Michael O'Rourke (Abingdon, UK: Routledge, 2016), 2; see also Colin Danby, "Political Economy and the Closet: Heteronormativity in Feminist Economics," *Feminist Economics* 13, no. 2 (2007): 29–53; Kath Browne and Catherine J. Nash, "Queer Methods and Methodologies: An Introduction," in *Queer Methods and Methodologies: Intersecting Queer Theories and Social Science Research*, ed. Kath Browne and Catherine J. Nash (Farnham, UK: Ashgate, 2010), 1–23; Lauren Wilcox, "Queer Theory and the 'Proper Objects' of International Relations," *International Studies Review* 16, no. 4 (2014): 612–615.

14. Cynthia Weber, *Queer International Relations: Sovereignty, Sexuality and the Will to Knowledge* (New York: Oxford University Press, 2016), 16.

15. Browne and Nash, "Queer Methods and Methodologies."

16. As Lisa Downing writes, queer scholars would do well to rethink "the construction, and reification through the repetition of discourse, of an unhelpful binary, which risks appearing as an archaic and originary truth: fixity is always a problem; fluidity is its 'cure' (whether the antidote is political or clinical)." Lisa Downing, "Perversion and the Problem of Fluidity and Identity," in *Clinical Encounters in Sexuality: Psychoanalytic Practice and Queer Theory*, ed. Noreen Giffney and Eve Watson (Goleta, CA: punctum books, 2017), 139. See also Cathy J. Cohen, "Punks, Bulldaggers, and Welfare Queens: The Radical Potential of Queer Politics?", *GLQ: A Journal of Lesbian and Gay Studies* 3, no. 4 (1997): 437–465; Jack Halberstam, "The Anti-Social Turn in Queer Studies," *Graduate Journal of Social Science* 5, no. 2 (2008): 140–156; Ruffolo, *Post-Queer Politics*.

17. Lisa Downing and Robert Gillett, "For an Anti-Post-Queer Agenda" (Critical Sexology Seminar in Birmingham, University of Birmingham, 2016).

18. Eve Kosofsky Sedgwick, *Tendencies* (Durham, NC: Duke University Press, 1993), 8. For an alternative reading, see Weber, *Queer International Relations*.

19. On these respective themes, see for instance Judith Butler, "Critically Queer," *GLQ: A Journal of Lesbian and Gay Studies* 1 (1993): 17–32; Louisa Allen, "Queer(y)Ing the Straight Researcher: The Relationship(?) Between Researcher Identity and Anti-Normative Knowledge," *Feminism & Psychology* 20, no. 2 (2010): 147–165; Jason Ritchie, "Pinkwashing, Homonationalism, and Israel–Palestine: The Conceits of Queer Theory and the Politics of the

Ordinary," *Antipode* 47, no. 3 (2015): 616–634; Alison Kafer, *Feminist, Queer, Crip* (Bloomington: Indiana University Press, 2013); Lee Edelman, *No Future: Queer Theory and the Death Drive* (Durham, NC: Duke University Press, 2004); Brooke M. Beloso, "Queer Theory, Sex Work, and Foucault's Unreason," *Foucault Studies* 23 (2017): 141–166; Jack Halberstam, *The Queer Art of Failure* (Durham, NC: Duke University Press, 2011); David Eng, *The Feeling of Kinship: Queer Liberalism and the Racialization of Intimacy* (Durham, NC: Duke University Press, 2010); José Esteban Muñoz, *Cruising Utopia: The Then and There of Queer Futurity* (New York: NYU Press, 2009).

20. David Eng, Jack Halberstam, and José Esteban Muñoz, "Introduction: What's Queer About Queer Studies Now?", *Social Text* 23, no. 3–4 (2005): 1. Similarly, Judith Butler writes that queer is "never fully owned, but always and only redeployed, twisted." Butler, "Critically Queer," 19.

21. Browne and Nash, "Queer Methods and Methodologies."

22. Janet R. Jakobsen, "Queer Is? Queer Does? Normativity and the Problem of Resistance," *GLQ: A Journal of Lesbian and Gay Studies* 4, no. 4 (1998): 511–536; Nikki Sullivan, *A Critical Introduction to Queer Theory* (New York: NYU Press, 2003). On theory-as-verb, see Marysia Zalewski, "'All These Theories Yet the Bodies Keep Piling Up': Theory, Theorists, Theorising," in *International Theory: Positivism and Beyond*, ed. Ken Booth, Steve Smith, and Marysia Zalewski (Cambridge, UK: Cambridge University Press, 1996), 340–353.

23. Browne and Nash, "Queer Methods and Methodologies," 4; see also Laura Sjoberg, "Queering the 'Territorial Peace'? Queer Theory Conversing With Mainstream International Relations," *International Studies Review* 16, no. 4 (2014): 608–12.

24. Lisa Duggan and Richard Kim, "Preface: A New Queer Agenda," *S&F Online* 10, no. 1–2 (2012): 1, http://sfonline.barnard.edu/a-new-queer-agenda/preface/ ; see also Christina Crosby et al., "Queer Studies, Materialism, and Crisis: A Roundtable Discussion," *GLQ: A Journal of Lesbian and Gay Studies* 18, no. 1 (2012): 127–147; John Elia and Gust Yep, "Sexualities and Genders in an Age of Neoterrorism," *Journal of Homosexuality* 59, no. 7 (2012): 879–889; Grace Kyungwon Hong, "Existentially Surplus: Women of Color Feminism and the New Crises of Capitalism," *GLQ: A Journal of Lesbian and Gay Studies* 18, no. 1 (2012): 87–106; Jordana Rosenberg and Amy Villarejo, "Queerness, Norms, Utopia," *GLQ: A Journal of Lesbian and Gay Studies* 18, no. 1 (2012): 1–18; Morgan Bassichis, Alexander Lee, and Dean Spade, "Building an Abolitionist, Trans and Queer Movement with Everyone We've Got," in *The Transgender Studies Reader* 2, ed. Susan Stryker and Aren Z. Aizura (Abingdon, UK: Routledge, 2013), 653–667; Nikita Dhawan et al., eds., *Global Justice and Desire: Queering Economy* (Abingdon, UK: Routledge, 2015).

25. Joseph DeFilippis, "Common Ground: The Queerness of Welfare Policy," *S&F Online* 10, no. 1–2 (2012), http://sfonline.barnard.edu/a-new-queer-agenda/common-ground-the-queerness-of-welfare-policy/.

26. Lisa Duggan, "After Neoliberalism? From Crisis to Organizing for Queer Economic Justice," *S&F Online* 10, no. 1–2 (2012), http://sfonline.barnard.edu/a-new-queer-agenda/after-neoliberalism-from-crisis-to-organizing-for-queer-economic-justice/.

27. Kevin Floyd, *The Reification of Desire: Toward a Queer Marxism* (Minneapolis: University of Minnesota Press, 2009); Petrus Liu, *Queer Marxism in Two Chinas* (Durham, NC: Duke University Press, 2015).

28. J. K. Gibson-Graham, *The End of Capitalism (As We Knew It): A Feminist Critique of Political Economy* (Minneapolis: University of Minnesota Press, 1996); V. Spike Peterson, "Political Identities/Nationalism as Heterosexism," *International Feminist Journal of Politics* 1, no. 1 (1999): 34–65; Rosemary Hennessy, *Profit and Pleasure: Sexual Identities in Late Capitalism* (Abingdon, UK: Routledge, 2000); see also Anna Agathangelou, Daniel Bassichis, and Tamara L. Spira, "Intimate Investments: Homonormativity, Global Lockdown, and Seductions of Empire," *Radical History Review* 100 (2008): 120; Kate Bedford, *Developing Partnerships: Gender, Sexuality, and the Reformed World Bank* (Minneapolis: University of Minnesota Press, 2009); Penny Griffin, *Gendering the World Bank: Neoliberalism and the Gendered Foundations of Global Governance* (Basingstoke, UK: Palgrave, 2009); Amy Lind, ed., *Development, Sexual Rights and Global Governance* (London: Routledge, 2010); Susie Jacobs and Christian Klesse, "Gender, Sexuality and Political Economy," *International Journal of Politics, Culture and Society* 27 (2013): 129–152; Nicola Smith, "Queer in/and Sexual Economies," in *Queer Sex Work*, ed. Mary Laing, Katy Pilcher, and Nicola Smith (Abingdon, UK: Routledge, 2015), 13–22.

29. Michael Warner, "Introduction," in *Fear of a Queer Planet: Queer Politics and Social Theory*, ed. Michael Warner (Minneapolis: University of Minnesota Press, 1993), vii.

30. Butler "Merely Cultural," 217.

31. V. Spike Peterson, *A Critical Rewriting of Global Political Economy: Integrating Reproductive, Productive and Virtual Economies* (Abingdon, UK: Routledge, 2003); Georgina Waylen, "You Still Don't Understand: Why Troubled Engagements Continue Between Feminists and (Critical) IPE," *Review of International Studies* 32, no. 1 (2006): 145–164; Griffin, *Gendering the World Bank*; Juanita Elias, "Critical Feminist Scholarship and IPE," in *Critical International Political Economy: Dialogue, Debate and Dissensus*, ed. Stuart Shields, Ian Bruff, and Huw Macartney (Basingstoke, UK: Palgrave, 2011), 99–113.

32. Meg Luxton and Kate Bezanson, *Social Reproduction: Feminist Political Economy Challenges Neo-Liberalism* (Montreal: McGill Queens University Press, 2006); Lourdes Beneria, "Neoliberalism and the Global Economic Crisis: A View from Feminist Economics," in *Under Development: Gender*, ed. Christine Verschuur, Isabelle Guerin, and Helene Guetat-Bernard (New York: Palgrave, 2014), 257–285; Ruth Pearson, "Gender, Globalization and the Reproduction of Labor: Bringing the State Back In," in *New Frontiers in Feminist Political Economy*, ed. Shirin Rai and Georgina Waylen (New York: Routledge, 2014), 19–42.

33. Diane Elson, *Male Bias in the Development Process* (Manchester: Manchester University Press, 1995), 276; see also Georgina Waylen, "Gender, Feminism and Political Economy," *New Political Economy* 2, no. 2 (1997): 205–220; Peterson, *A Critical Rewriting of Global Political Economy*; Agathangelou, *The Global Political Economy of Sex*; J. Ann Tickner, *A Feminist Voyage Through International Relations* (New York: Oxford University Press, 2014); Gülay Çağlar, "Constructivist Thought in Feminist IPE: Tracking Gender Norms," in *Handbook on the International Political Economy of Gender*, ed. Juanita Elias and Adrienne Roberts (Cheltenham, UK: Edward Elgar, 2018), 73–85.

34. Kate Bezanson, *Gender, the State, and Social Reproduction: Household Insecurity in Neo-Liberal Times* (Toronto: University of Toronto Press, 2006); Elias, "Critical Feminist Scholarship and IPE"; Meg Luxton, "The Production of Life Itself: Gender, Social Reproduction and IPE," in *Handbook on the International*

Political Economy of Gender, 37–49; Nancy Fraser, Tithi Bhattacharya, and Cinzia Arruzza, "Notes for a Feminist Manifesto," *New Left Review* 114 (2018): 113–134.

35. Isabella Bakker and Rachel Silvey, *Beyond States and Markets: The Challenges of Social Reproduction* (Abingdon, UK: Routledge, 2012), 2–3.

36. Nancy Fraser, "A Feminism Where 'Lean In' Means Leaning On Others," *Opinionator*, October 15, 2015, http://opinionator.blogs.nytimes.com/2015/10/15/a-feminism-where-leaning-in-means-leaning-on-others/.

37. Silvia Federici, *Wages Against Housework* (London: Power of Women Collective, 1975), 3, 7.

38. In V. Spike Peterson's words, women's work is "variously unpaid, underpaid, trivialized, denigrated, obscured and uncounted." V. Spike Peterson, "How (the Meaning of) Gender Matters in Political Economy," *New Political Economy* 10, no. 4 (2005): 507.

39. Peterson, *A Critical Rewriting of Global Political Economy*.

40. Shirin M. Rai, Catherine Hoskyns, and Dania Thomas, "Depletion: The Cost of Social Reproduction," *International Feminist Journal of Politics* 16, no. 1 (2014): 86.

41. Federici, *Wages Against Housework*, 3.

42. Indeed, this absenting of feminist political economy is so prevalent that even post-queer accounts fail to spot it. For example, Penney argues that "[a]ll the valuable points queer theory has made about human sexuality were previously made by Freud" (rather than by feminists) and, despite claiming that sexual politics must interrogate the "organization of production," he offers no discussion of how such an agenda is already central to feminist theories of productive and reproductive labor. Penney, *After Queer Theory*, 5, 67.

43. Halberstam, "The Anti-Social Turn in Queer Studies," 140.

44. Lisa Downing, *The Subject of Murder: Gender, Exceptionality, and the Modern Killer* (Chicago: University of Chicago Press, 2013).

45. Leo Bersani, "Is the Rectum a Grave?," *October* 43 (1987): 197.

46. Edelman, *No Future*, 2, 31.

47. Edelman, *No Future*, 29.

48. Noreen Giffney, "Queer Apocal(o)ptic/ism: The Death Drive and the Human," in *Queering the Non/Human: Queer Interventions*, ed. Myra J. Hird (Farnham, UK: Ashgate, 2008), 60.

49. Anca Parvulescu, *Traffic in Women's Work: East European Migration and the Making of Europe* (Chicago: University of Chicago Press, 2014), 11.

50. James Bliss, "Hope Against Hope: Queer Negativity, Black Feminist Theorizing, and Reproduction without Futurity," *Mosaic: A Journal for the Interdisciplinary Study of Literature* 48, no. 1 (2015): 85.

51. Elahe Haschemi Yekani, Elaine Kilian, and Beatrice Michaelis, "Introducing Queer Futures," in *Queer Futures: Reconsidering Ethics, Activism and the Political*, ed. Elahe Haschemi Yekani, Elaine Kilian, and Beatrice Michaelis (Farnham, UK: Ashgate, 2013), 1–15.

52. Halberstam, "The Anti-Social Turn in Queer Studies," 154.

53. Alan Sears, "Situating Sexuality in Social Reproduction," *Historical Materialism* 24, no. 2 (2016): 139.

54. On "queer feminist criticism" as the "forging [of] projects from within a set of shared political and theoretical genealogies," see Robyn Wiegman, "The Times We're in: Queer Feminist Criticism and the Reparative 'Turn,'" *Feminist Theory* 5, no. 1 (2014): 19–20.

55. Samuel A. Chambers and Terrell Carver, *Judith Butler and Political Theory: Troubling Politics* (Abingdon, UK: Routledge, 2008), 155.

56. Danby, "Political Economy and the Closet"; Suzanne Bergeron, "Querying Economics' Straight Path to Development: Household Models Reconsidered," in *Development, Sexual Rights and Global Governance*, ed. Amy Lind (London: Routledge, 2010), 54–64; Amy Lind, "Introduction: Development, Global Governance and Sexual Subjectivities," in *Development, Sexual Rights and Global Governance*, 1–20.

57. Danby, "Political Economy and the Closet."

58. Danby, "Political Economy and the Closet"; Chambers and Carver, *Judith Butler and Political Theory*; Griffin, *Gendering the World Bank*; Browne and Nash, "Queer Methods and Methodologies."

59. Penny Griffin, "Sexuality, Power and Global Social Justice," in *Global Social Justice*, ed. Heather Widdows and Nicola Smith (Abingdon, UK: Routledge, 2011), 138–150.

60. Shannon Winnubst, "The Queer Thing About Neoliberal Pleasure: A Foucauldian Warning," *Foucault Studies*, no. 14 (2012): 80.

61. Nicola Smith, "Toward a Queer Political Economy of Crisis," in *Scandalous Economics: Gender and the Politics of Financial Crisis*, ed. Jacqui True and Aida Hozić (New York: Oxford University Press, 2016), 231–247. On queer theory and the unproductive and/or unreproductive, see for instance Joseba Gabilondo, "Like Blood for Chocolate, Like Queers for Vampires: Border and Global Consumption in Rodríguez, Tarantino, Arau, Esquivel, and Troyano (Notes on Baroque, Camp, Kitsch, and Hybridization)," in *Queer Globalizations: Citizenship and the Afterlife of Colonialism*, ed. Arnaldo Cruz-Malavé and F. Manalansan IV (New York: New York University Press, 2002), 236–264; Roderick A. Ferguson, *Aberrations in Black: Toward a Queer of Color Critique* (Minneapolis: University of Minnesota Press, 2004); Lisa Downing, "Heteronormativity and Repronormativity in Sexological 'Perversion Theory' and the DSM-5's 'Paraphilic Disorder' Diagnoses," *Archives of Sexual Behavior* 44, no. 5 (2015): 1139–1145; Grace Kyungwon Hong, *Death Beyond Disavowal: The Impossible Politics of Difference* (Minneapolis: University of Minnesota Press, 2015); Ilan Kapoor, "The Queer Third World," *Third World Quarterly* 36, no. 9 (2015): 1611–1628; Rahul Rao, "Global Homocapitalism," *Radical Philosophy* 194 (2015): 38–49; Weber, *Queer International Relations*; Jasbir Puar, *The Right to Maim: Debility, Capacity, Disability* (Durham, NC: Duke University Press, 2017).

62. On queer theory and value, see Meg Wesling, "Queer Value," *GLQ: A Journal of Lesbian and Gay Studies* 18, no. 1 (2012): 107–125.

63. Ferguson, *Aberrations in Black*, 87.

64. Bliss, "Hope Against Hope," 86.

65. Kafer, *Feminist, Queer, Crip*, 28, 34.

66. Hong, "Existentially Surplus," 91.

67. See for instance Jemima Repo's perceptive critique of Judith Butler's "genealogy of gender ontology" in Repo, *The Biopolitics of Gender* (New York: Oxford University Press, 2015), 7.

68. Ida Danewid, "White Innocence in the Black Mediterranean: Hospitality and the Erasure of History," *Third World Quarterly* 38, no. 7 (2017): 1674–1689.

69. Danewid, "White Innocence in the Black Mediterranean," 3, 10.

70. Halberstam, "The Anti-Social Turn in Queer Studies," 143.

71. I am indebted to Downing and Gillett for their mind-expanding discussion of the need to reclaim queer's oft-forgotten legacies by utilizing "queer" as a mode of historical critique rather than as the study of fluidity. Downing and Gillett, "For an Anti-Post-Queer Agenda." On history in/and queer theory, see for instance Heather Love, *Feeling Backward: Loss and the Politics of Queer History* (Cambridge, MA: Harvard University Press, 2009); Lynne Huffer, *Mad for Foucault: Rethinking the Foundations of Queer Theory* (New York: Columbia University Press, 2010); V. Spike Peterson, "Sex Matters: A Queer History of Hierarchies," *International Feminist Journal of Politics* 16, no. 3 (2014): 389–409; Robert Gillett, "Foucault's Genealogy," in *After Foucault: Culture, Theory, and Criticism in the Twenty-First Century*, ed. Lisa Downing (Cambridge, UK: Cambridge University Press, 2018), 17–30.

72. Love, *Feeling Backward*, 10, 28.

73. Adrienne Roberts, *Gendered States of Punishment and Welfare: Feminist Political Economy, Primitive Accumulation and the Law* (Abingdon, UK: Routledge, 2016), 13.

74. Gillian Youngs, "Embodied Political Economy or an Escape from Disembodied Knowledge," in *Political Economy, Power and the Body*, ed. Gillian Youngs (Basingstoke, UK: Palgrave, 2000), 19.

75. Downing and Gillett, "For an Anti-Post-Queer Agenda."

76. Foucault, *The Will to Knowledge*; Michel Foucault, *The History of Sexuality: The Use of Pleasure* (translated by Robert Hurley) (New York: Vintage, 1985); Michel Foucault, *The History of Sexuality: The Care of the Self* (translated by Robert Hurley) (New York: Pantheon, 1986). For an overview of Foucault's corpus of work, see Lisa Downing, *The Cambridge Introduction to Michel Foucault* (Cambridge, UK: Cambridge University Press, 2008).

77. For example, Jeffrey Weeks notes that Mary McIntosh had already investigated the historical contingency of sexuality in "The Homosexual Role," which was published nearly a decade before *The Will to Knowledge*. Jeffrey Weeks, "The 'Homosexual Role' After 30 Years: An Appreciation of the Work of Mary McIntosh," *Foucault* 1, no. 2 (1998): 131–152.

78. Foucault, *The Will to Knowledge*, 35.

79. Foucault, *The Will to Knowledge*, 33.

80. Foucault, *The Will to Knowledge*, 26.

81. Foucault, *The Will to Knowledge*, 35.

82. Gargi Bhattacharyya, *Sexuality and Society: An Introduction* (Abingdon, UK: Routledge, 2005), 7.

83. Foucault, *The Will to Knowledge*, 61.

84. Foucault, *The Will to Knowledge*, 34.

85. Foucault, *The Will to Knowledge*, 25.

86. Foucault, *The Will to Knowledge*, 25.

87. Downing, *The Cambridge Introduction to Michel Foucault*, 89.

88. Foucault, *The Will to Knowledge*, 36–38.

89. Foucault, *The Will to Knowledge*, 38–40.

90. Foucault, *The Will to Knowledge*, 40, 44.

91. Foucault, *The Will to Knowledge*, 140. That said, the term "capitalism" appears just five times in *The Will to Knowledge*.

92. Foucault, *The Will to Knowledge*, 140–141.

93. Foucault, *The Will to Knowledge*, 145–146.

94. Foucault, *The Will to Knowledge*, 125. On Foucauldian biopolitics, see also Downing, *The Cambridge Introduction to Michel Foucault*; Huffer, *Mad for Foucault*;

Repo, *The Biopolitics of Gender*; Hannah Richter, ed., *Biopolitical Governance: Race, Gender, and Economy* (London: Rowman & Littlefield International, 2018).

95. Silvia Federici, *Caliban and the Witch: Women, the Body and Primitive Accumulation* (New York: Autonomedia, 2004).

96. The Wages for Housework campaign, for example, had challenged how housework is "transformed into a natural attribute of our female physique and personality, an internal need, an aspiration, supposedly coming from the depth of our female character." Federici, *Wages Against Housework*, 77.

97. Repo, *The Biopolitics of Gender*, 10.

98. Federici, *Caliban and the Witch*, 15.

99. On Foucault in/and feminism, see for instance Lee Quinby and Irene Diamond, *Feminism and Foucault: Reflection on Resistance* (Boston: Northeastern University Press, 1988); Caroline Ramazanoglu, ed., *Up Against Foucault: Explorations of Some Tensions Between Foucault and Feminism* (New York: Routledge, 2002); Dianna Taylor and Karen Vintges, *Feminism and the Final Foucault* (Champaign: University of Illinois Press, 2004); Margaret A. McLaren, *Feminism, Foucault, and Embodied Subjectivity* (Albany: SUNY Press, 2012); Amelia Morris, *The Politics of Weight: Feminist Dichotomies of Power in Dieting* (Basingstoke, UK: Palgrave, 2019).

100. Susan Stryker, "Biopolitics," *TSQ: Transgender Studies Quarterly* 1, no. 1–2 (2014): 39.

101. Huffer, *Mad for Foucault*, 7.

102. Repo, *The Biopolitics of Gender*, 9.

103. Megan Mackenzie, "I Broke Up with Michel Foucault," Duck of Minerva, September 6, 2016, http://duckofminerva.com/2016/09/i-broke-up-with-michel-foucault.html.

104. Downing, *The Cambridge Introduction to Michel Foucault*.

105. Imogen Tyler, *Revolting Subjects: Social Abjection and Resistance in Neoliberal Britain* (London: Zed, 2013); see also Federici, *Caliban and the Witch*.

106. Huffer, *Mad for Foucault*.

107. Federici, *Caliban and the Witch*, 13, 15.

108. Federici, *Caliban and the Witch*, 21–22.

109. Federici, *Caliban and the Witch*, 15–16.

110. Federici, *Caliban and the Witch*, 8.

111. Despite early claims that millions of people were killed as witches in Europe and colonial America, this is "without any basis in fact." Steven T. Katz, *Historicism, the Holocaust, and Zionism: Critical Studies in Modern Jewish Thought and History* (New York: NYU Press, 1993), 113. Research based on archival evidence of the trials suggests that up to sixty thousand people were put to death for witchcraft in Europe—a figure that, there can be no doubt, "remains large enough to instill a sense of horror in its own right." Robert Poole, *The Lancashire Witches: Histories and Stories* (Manchester: Manchester University Press, 2002), 192. Around half of these European executions occurred within the borders of the Holy Roman Empire. In some areas, around three quarters were not executed but were banished, imprisoned, or otherwise severely punished; and others were accused but not prosecuted. Brian P. Levack, "Introduction," in *The Oxford Handbook of Witchcraft in Early Modern Europe and Colonial America*, ed. Brian P. Levack (Oxford: Oxford University Press, 2013), 1–10.

112. Federici, *Caliban and the Witch*, 11, 22.

113. Ann Laura Stoler, *Race and the Education of Desire: Foucault's History of Sexuality and the Colonial Order of Things* (Durham, NC: Duke University Press, 1995); Achille Mbembe, "Necropolitics," *Public Culture* 15 (2003): 11–40; Couze Venn, "Neoliberal Political Economy, Biopolitics and Colonialism: A Transcolonial Genealogy of Inequality," *Theory, Culture & Society* 26, no. 6 (2009): 206–233; Alison Howell and Melanie Richter-Montpetit, "Racism in Foucauldian Security Studies: Biopolitics, Liberal War, and the Whitewashing of Colonial and Racial Violence," *International Political Sociology* 13, no. 1 (2018): 2–19.

114. Federici, *Caliban and the Witch*, 17; see also Luise White, *The Comforts of Home: Prostitution in Colonial Nairobi* (Chicago: University of Chicago Press, 1990); Ann Laura Stoler, *Carnal Knowledge and Imperial Power: Race and the Intimate in Colonial Rule* (Oakland: University of California Press, 2002); bell hooks, *Ain't I a Woman: Black Women and Feminism* (New York: Routledge, 2015); Gargi Bhattacharyya, *Rethinking Racial Capitalism: Questions of Reproduction and Survival* (London: Rowman & Littlefield International, 2018); Alys Eve Weinbaum, *The Afterlife of Reproductive Slavery: Biocapitalism and Black Feminism's Philosophy of History* (Durham, NC: Duke University Press, 2019).

115. Stryker, "Biopolitics," 39.

116. Foucault, *The Will to Knowledge*, 140.

117. Laura J. Shepherd, *Gender, Violence and Security: Discourse as Practice* (London: Zed, 2008), 49.

118. Federici, *Caliban and the Witch*, 16.

119. Federici, *Caliban and the Witch*, 88. Alison Rowlands, for instance, rejects such claims as "polemical and historically inaccurate." Alison Rowlands, "Witchcraft and Gender in Early Modern Europe," in *The Oxford Handbook of Witchcraft in Early Modern Europe and Colonial America*, 450. See also Lara Apps and Andrew Gow, *Male Witches in Early Modern Europe* (Manchester: Manchester University Press, 2003); Malcolm Gaskill, "Witchcraft Trials in England," in *The Oxford Handbook of Witchcraft in Early Modern Europe and Colonial America*, 283–299.

120. Apps and Gow, *Male Witches in Early Modern Europe*; Rowlands, "Witchcraft and Gender in Early Modern Europe"; Angus Cameron, "The Fool and the Witch," in *Sorcières: Pourchassés, Assumées, Puissantes, Queer*, ed. Anna Colin (Montreuil: Paris and La Maison Populaire, 2013), 6–113.

121. Gaskill, "Witchcraft Trials in England"; Levack, "Introduction."

122. Louise Jackson, "Witches, Wives and Mothers: Witchcraft Persecution and Women's Confessions in Seventeenth-Century England," *Women's History Review* 4, no. 1 (1995): 63–84; Willem De Blécourt, "The Making of the Female Witch: Reflections on Witchcraft and Gender in the Early Modern Period," *Gender & History* 12, no. 2 (2000): 287–309.

123. Foucault, *The Will to Knowledge*, 10.

124. Foucault, *The Will to Knowledge*, 114.

125. Foucault, *The Will to Knowledge*, 11–12.

126. Federici, *Caliban and the Witch*, 139, 149.

127. Foucault, *The Will to Knowledge*, 138, 142–143. Indeed, sex is "imbued with the death instinct" in that life itself can be extinguished for the "truth and sovereignty of sex." Foucault, 156. On the relationship between life, death, and sexuality in Foucault's work, see also Jemima Repo, "The Life Function: The Biopolitics of Sexuality and Race Revisited," in *Biopolitical Governance: Race, Gender and Economy*, ed. Hannah Richter (London: Rowman & Littlefield International, 2018), 41–57.

128. Federici, *Caliban and the Witch*, 16.
129. Lauren Berlant, "Slow Death (Sovereignty, Obesity, Lateral Agency)," *Critical Inquiry* 33, no. 4 (2007): 154; see also Puar, *The Right to Maim*.
130. Repo, "The Life Function," 41.
131. Although both volumes do touch on it in places—see for example Foucault, *The Will to Knowledge*, 4, 27; Federici, *Caliban and the Witch*, 93–95.
132. Beloso, "Queer Theory, Sex Work, and Foucault's Unreason."
133. See for instance the various contributions in Nicola Smith and Mary Laing, eds., "Special Issue: Working Outside the (Hetero) Norm? Lesbian, Gay, Bisexual, Transgender and Queer (LGBTQ) Sex Work," *Sexualities* 15, no. 5–6 (2012); and *Queer Sex Work*.
134. For example, heterosexuality has often been treated as "that which explains" rather than "that which is to be explained" in the feminist political economy literature on commercial sex. Smith, "Queer in/and Sexual Economies," 17.
135. Coalition Against Trafficking in Women, "Prostitution Is Not 'Sex Work,'" February 21, 2011, http://www.catwinternational.org/Content/Images/Article/254/attachment.pdf; see also Sheila Jeffreys, *The Industrial Vagina: The Political Economy of the Global Sex Trade* (Abingdon, UK: Routledge, 2008); Janice G. Raymond, *Not a Choice, Not a Job: Exposing the Myths about Prostitution and the Global Sex Trade* (Lincoln, NE: Potomac Books, 2013); Julie Bindel, *The Pimping of Prostitution* (London: Palgrave, 2017); Amarjeet Kaur, "Prostitution Is Not Work: A Trade Unionist's Perspective," *ANTYAJAA: Indian Journal of Women and Social Change* 2, no. 2 (2018): 160–165.
136. Global Network of Sex Work Projects, "Policy Brief: Sex Work as Work," 2017, http://www.nswp.org/sites/nswp.org/files/policy_brief_sex_work_as_work_nswp_-_2017.pdf.
137. Wendy Chapkis, *Live Sex Acts: Women Performing Erotic Labor* (London: Routledge, 1997); see also Heather Berg, "An Honest Day's Wage for a Dishonest Day's Work: (Re)Productivism and Refusal," *WSQ: Women's Studies Quarterly* 42, no. 1 (2014): 161–177 for a brilliant critique of "(re)productivism" in sex work debates.
138. On sex work as work, see for instance Laura María Agustín, *Sex at the Margins: Migration, Labour Markets and the Rescue Industry* (London: Zed, 2007); Melissa Gira Grant, *Playing the Whore: The Work of Sex Work* (London: Verso, 2014); Prabha Kotiswaran, *Dangerous Sex, Invisible Labor: Sex Work and the Law in India* (Princeton, NJ: Princeton University Press, 2011); Svati Shah, *Street Corner Secrets: Sex, Work, and Migration in the City of Mumbai* (Durham, NC: Duke University Press, 2014); Molly Smith and Juno Mac, *Revolting Prostitutes: The Fight for Sex Workers' Rights* (London: Verso, 2018); Sharron A. FitzGerald and Kathryn McGarry, eds., *Realizing Justice for Sex Workers: An Agenda for Change* (London: Rowman & Littlefield International, 2018); Sara Kallock, *Livable Intersections: Re/Framing Sex Work at the Frontline* (London: Rowman & Littlefield International, 2019).
139. Heather Berg, "Working for Love, Loving for Work: Discourses of Labor in Feminist Sex-Work Activism," *Feminist Studies* 40, no. 3 (2014): 701.
140. Johanna Oksala, "Affective Labor and Feminist Politics," *Signs* 41, no. 2 (2016): 281–303.
141. Guillermina Altomonte, "Affective Labor in the Post-Fordist Transformation," *Public Seminar*, May 8, 2015, http://www.publicseminar.org/2015/05/affective-labor-in-the-post-fordist-transformation/.

142. Jeffreys, *The Industrial Vagina*, 3, 7.
143. Jeffreys, *The Industrial Vagina*, 199.
144. Alison Phipps, *The Politics of the Body: Gender in a Neoliberal and Neoconservative Age* (Hoboken, NJ: John Wiley & Sons, 2014), 77.
145. Noah D. Zatz, "Sex Work/Sex Act: Law, Labor, and Desire in Constructions of Prostitution," *Signs* 22, no. 2 (1997), 290.
146. Foucault, *The Will to Knowledge*, 4.
147. Foucault, *The Will to Knowledge*, 12.
148. Foucault, *The Will to Knowledge*, 40. On the discursive production of sex work, see also Shannon Bell, *Reading, Writing, and Rewriting the Prostitute Body* (Bloomington: Indiana University Press, 1994); Zatz, "Sex Work/Sex Act"; Jane Scoular, *The Subject of Prostitution: Sex Work, Law and Social Theory* (Abingdon, UK: Routledge, 2015).
149. Jin-kyung Lee, for instance, describes commercial sex as a form of necropolitical labor on the grounds that it entails the "figurative erasure or symbolic murder" of human subjectivity. Jin-kyung Lee, *Service Economies: Militarism, Sex Work, and Migrant Labor in South Korea* (Minneapolis: University of Minnesota Press, 2010), 7; see also Julia O'Connell Davidson, *Prostitution, Power and Freedom* (Minneapolis: University of Michigan Press, 1998); Elina Penttinen, *Globalization, Prostitution and Sex-Trafficking: Corporeal Politics* (Abingdon, UK: Routledge, 2008). In a rather different vein, Sara Kallock situates sex work within a "politics of livability . . . geared toward openness, fluidity, temporality, and vulnerability." Kallock, *Livable Intersections*, 26; see also Sara Kallock, "Livability: A Politics for Abnormative Lives," *Sexualities* 21, no. 7 (2018): 1170–1193.
150. Smith and Mac, *Revolting Prostitutes*, 49.
151. Maggie O'Neill et al., "Living with the Other: Street Sex Work, Contingent Communities, and Degrees of Tolerance," *Crime, Media, Culture* 4, no. 1 (2008): 75.
152. Jasbir Puar, *Terrorist Assemblages: Homonationalism in Queer Times* (Durham, NC: Duke University Press, 2008), 36; also cited in Weber, *Queer International Relations*, 135. On sex work and biopolitics, see also Sharron A. Fitzgerald, "Biopolitics and the Regulation of Vulnerability: The Case of the Female Trafficked Migrant," *International Journal of Law in Context* 6, no. 3 (2010): 277–294; John Scott, "Governing Prostitution: Differentiating the Bad from the Bad," *Current Issues in Criminal Justice* 23, no. 1 (2011); Jane Scoular, *The Subject of Prostitution: Sex Work, Law and Social Theory* (Abingdon, UK: Routledge, 2015).

CHAPTER 2
1. John Carpenter, *Liber Albus: The White Book of the City of London (Compiled AD 1419)* (translated by Thomas Riley) (London: Griffin, 1861), 394–395.
2. Ruth Mazo Karras, *Common Women: Prostitution and Sexuality in Medieval England* (Oxford: Oxford University Press, 1996); John Scott, "Governing Prostitution: Differentiating the Bad from the Bad," *Current Issues in Criminal Justice* 23, no. 1 (2011): 53–72.
3. Karras, *Common Women*; Scott, "Governing Prostitution"; Michelle M. Sauer, *Gender in Medieval Culture* (London: Bloomsbury, 2015).
4. Karras, *Common Women*; Gary F. Jensen, *The Path of the Devil: Early Modern Witch Hunts* (Lanham: Rowman & Littlefield, 2007); Scott, "Governing Prostitution."

5. Lotte Van de Pol, *The Burgher and the Whore: Prostitution in Early Modern Amsterdam* (New York: Oxford University Press, 2011).

6. Carpenter, *Liber Albus*, 394.

7. Karras, *Common Women*, 132.

8. Silvia Federici, *Caliban and the Witch: Women, the Body and Primitive Accumulation* (New York: Autonomedia, 2004); Peter Drucker, *Warped: Gay Normality and Queer Anti-Capitalism* (Leiden: Brill, 2015).

9. R. H. Hilton, *The Decline of Serfdom in Medieval England* (London: Macmillan, 1969), 10.

10. Federici, *Caliban and the Witch*.

11. Christopher Middleton, "The Sexual Division of Labor in Feudal England," *New Left Review*, 113–114 (1979): 153.

12. Martha C. Howell, "Gender in the Transition to Merchant Capitalism," in *The Oxford Handbook of Women and Gender in Medieval Europe*, ed. Judith M. Bennett and Ruth Mazo Karras (Oxford: Oxford University Press, 2013), 561.

13. Theo Van der Meer, "Medieval Prostitution and the Case of a (Mistaken?) Sexual Identity," *Journal of Women's History* 11, no. 2 (1999): 180.

14. Viviana A. Zelizer, *The Purchase of Intimacy* (Princeton, NJ: Princeton University Press, 2005), 22.

15. Karras, *Common Women*.

16. Howell, "Gender in the Transition to Merchant Capitalism."

17. For a detailed analysis of how and why it is meaningful to refer to "race" in the Middle Ages, see Geraldine Heng, *The Invention of Race in the European Middle Ages* (Cambridge, UK: Cambridge University Press, 2018).

18. Alfred Thomas, "Reading the Other: Teaching Chaucer's The Prioress's Tale in Its Late Medieval Context," in *Jews in Medieval England: Teaching Representations of the Other*, ed. Miriamne Ara Krummel and Tison Pugh (Basingstoke, UK: Palgrave, 2017), 134.

19. Van der Meer, "Medieval Prostitution," 183.

20. Drucker, *Warped*, 73.

21. Michel Foucault, *The History of Sexuality: The Will to Knowledge* (translated by Robert Hurley) (New York: Pantheon, 1978), 38.

22. Karras, *Common Women*, 86. On medieval marriage in England, see also Frederik Pedersen, *Marriage Disputes in Medieval England* (London: Hambledon Press, 2000); Conor McCarthy, *Marriage in Medieval England: Law, Literature, and Practice* (Woodbridge, UK: Boydell Press, 2004); R. H. Helmholz, *Marriage Litigation in Medieval England* (Cambridge, UK: Cambridge University Press, 2007).

23. Nancy Folbre, *Greed, Lust and Gender: A History of Economic Ideas* (Oxford: Oxford University Press, 2009), 6.

24. Karras, *Common Women*.

25. Foucault, *The Will to Knowledge*, 37. This was explicitly gendered since "priests were cautioned against the dangers of hearing women's confessions, and they were often suspected of breaching their oaths of celibacy as a result of this special access." Sarah Rees Jones, "Public and Private Space and Gender in Medieval Europe," in *The Oxford Handbook of Women and Gender in Medieval Europe*, 246–261, 253.

26. Folbre, *Greed, Lust and Gender*.

27. Sauer, *Gender in Medieval Culture*.

28. Marianna Muravyeva and Raisa Maria Toivo, "Introduction: Why and How Gender Matters?", in *Gender in Late Medieval and Early Modern Europe*, ed. Marianna Muravyeva and Raisa Maria Toivo (Abingdon, UK: Routledge, 2013), 1–18.

29. Sauer, *Gender in Medieval Culture*, 3–4; see also Dyan Elliott, "Gender and the Christian Traditions," in *The Oxford Handbook of Women and Gender in Medieval Europe*, 21–35; Muravyeva and Toivo, "Introduction."

30. Charlotte Rose Millar, "Witchcraft and Deviant Sexuality: A Case Study of Dr Lambe," in *The British World: Religion, Memory, Society, Culture*, ed. Marcus Harmes et al. (Toowoomba: University of Southern Queensland, 2012), 51–62.

31. Barbara Hanawalt, *Of Good and Ill Repute: Gender and Social Control in Medieval England* (New York: Oxford University Press, 1998); Van der Meer, "Medieval Prostitution"; David Gary Shaw, *Necessary Conjunctions: The Social Self in Medieval England* (Basingstoke, UK: Palgrave, 2005).

32. Sauer, *Gender in Medieval Culture*, 8.

33. Janet L. Nelson and Alice Rio, "Women and Laws in Early Medieval Europe," in *The Oxford Handbook of Women and Gender in Medieval Europe*, 109.

34. Karras, *Common Women*; Jones, "Public and Private Space and Gender in Medieval Europe."

35. Van der Meer, "Medieval Prostitution," 183.

36. In the words of the English theologian, Thomas of Chobham. Cited in Karras, *Common Women*, 27.

37. Henry Ansgar Kelly, "Bishop, Prioress, and Bawd in the Stews of Southwark," *Speculum* 75, no. 2 (2000): 342–388.

38. Karras, *Common Women*; Belinda Brooks-Gordon, *The Price of Sex: Prostitution, Policy, and Society* (London: Routledge, 2013).

39. Karras, *Common Women*; Ruth Mazo Karras, *Sexuality in Medieval Europe: Doing Unto Others* (New York: Routledge, 2017); Mara Amster, "Introductory Note," in *The Early Modern Englishwoman: A Facsimile Library of Essential Works: Volume 5: Texts on Prostitution, 1592–1633* (Aldershot, UK: Ashgate, 2007), ix–xxxii.

40. Karras, *Common Women*.

41. Ruth Mazo Karras, "The Regulation of Brothels in Later Medieval England," *Signs* 14, no. 2 (1989): 399–433; Karras, *Common Women*.

42. Karras, *Common Women*.

43. Karras, *Common Women*.

44. Karras, *Sexuality in Medieval Europe*, 8. On medieval trans histories, see for instance Karl Whittington, "Medieval," *TSQ: Transgender Studies Quarterly* 1, no. 1–2 (2014): 125–129; Robert Mills, *Seeing Sodomy in the Middle Ages* (Chicago: University of Chicago Press, 2015); Robert Mills, "Visibly Trans? Picturing Saint Eugenia in Medieval Art," *TSQ: Transgender Studies Quarterly* 5, no. 4 (2018): 540–564; Blake Gutt, "Transgender Genealogy in Tristan de Nanteuil," *Exemplaria: Medieval, Early Modern, Theory* 30, no. 2 (2018): 129–146; Anna Kłosowska, "Premodern Trans and Queer in French Manuscripts and Early Printed Texts," *Postmedieval* 9, no. 3 (2018): 349–366. On the study of trans history, see Susan Stryker, *Transgender History* (Berkeley: Seal Press, 2008).

45. Translated in David Lorenzo Boyd and Ruth Mazo Karras, "The Interrogation of a Male Transvestite Prostitute in Fourteenth-Century London," *GLQ: A Journal of Lesbian and Gay Studies* 1, no. 4 (1995): 459–465, 482–483.

46. Ruth Mazo Karras, "Prostitution and the Question of Sexual Identity in Medieval Europe," *Journal of Women's History* 11, no. 2 (1999): 159–198; Katherine L. French, "Genders and Material Culture," in *The Oxford Handbook of Women and Gender in Medieval Europe*, 197–212; Isaac Bershady, "Sexual Deviancy and Deviant Sexuality in Medieval England," *Primary Source* 5, no. 1 (2014): 12. While the authorities at the time identified Eleanor by another name (and many contemporary accounts either use that name or speculate as to her "real" name), the legal records clearly indicate that Eleanor called herself "Eleanor" and so her true name is already known to us. Kadin Henningsen, "'Calling [Herself] Eleanor': Gender Labor and Becoming a Woman in the Rykener Case," *Medieval Feminist Forum* 55, no. 1 (2019): 249–266. For the original and translated versions of the legal records, see Boyd and Karras, "The Interrogation of a Male Transvestite Prostitute."

47. Karras, "Prostitution and the Question of Sexual Identity"; see also Shannon Bell, *Reading, Writing, and Rewriting the Prostitute Body* (Bloomington: Indiana University Press, 1994).

48. Karras, *Common Women*, 18, 135.

49. Karras, "Prostitution and the Question of Sexual Identity," 164.

50. Karras, *Common Women*; Sauer, *Gender in Medieval Culture*.

51. Carpenter, *Liber Albus*, 395.

52. Reproduced in Paul Hair, *Before the Bawdy Court: Selections from Church Court and Other Records Relating to the Correction of Moral Offences in England, Scotland and New England, 1300–1800* (London: Elek, 1972), 205.

53. Karras, *Common Women*; Hanawalt, *Of Good and Ill Repute*.

54. Carpenter, *Liber Albus*; see also Bershady, "Sexual Deviancy and Deviant Sexuality in Medieval England."

55. Louis Crompton, *Homosexuality and Civilization* (Cambridge, MA: Harvard University Press, 2003), 361.

56. Jensen, *The Path of the Devil*; Drucker, *Warped*.

57. Crompton, *Homosexuality and Civilization*; Martin Ingram, *Carnal Knowledge: Regulating Sex in England, 1470–1600* (Cambridge, UK: Cambridge University Press, 2017).

58. Drucker, *Warped*.

59. In England, syphilis was blamed initially on lepers but, by 1502, medical doctors were starting to associate syphilis with lechery, and leprosy itself began to be constructed as a carnal (as opposed to a spiritual) sin. Bryon Lee Grigsby, *Pestilence in Medieval and Early Modern English Literature* (Abingdon, UK: Routledge, 2004).

60. Stanley D. Nash, *Prostitution in Great Britain 1945–1901* (London: The Scarecrow Press Inc., 1994).

61. Thomas Becon, *The Catechism of Thomas Becon: With Other Pieces Written by Him in the Reign of King Edward the Sixth* (Cambridge, UK: Printed at the University Press, 1844), 342–343.

62. Nash, *Prostitution in Great Britain*.

63. Philip Stubbes, *The Anatomy of Abuses* (London: W. Pickering, 1836), 103.

64. Karras, "The Regulation of Brothels in Later Medieval England."

65. Henry VIII, "Ordering London Brothels Closed [Westminster, April 13, 1546, 37]," in *Tudor Royal Proclamations: Volume 1: The Early Tudors (1485–1553)*, ed. Paul L. Hughes and James F. Larkin (New York: Yale University Press, 1964), 365–366, 365.

66. Ingram, *Carnal Knowledge*, 292.
67. Marjorie Keniston McIntosh, *Working Women in English Society, 1300–1620* (Cambridge, UK: Cambridge University Press, 2005).
68. Peter Marshall, *The Reformation: A Very Short Introduction* (Oxford: Oxford University Press, 2009).
69. Federici, *Caliban and the Witch*, 44.
70. Federici, *Caliban and the Witch*.
71. Spencer Dimmock, *The Origin of Capitalism in England, 1400–1600* (Leiden: Brill, 2014); John Wittich, *Catholic London* (Tenbury Wells, UK: Fowler Wright Books, 1988).
72. Federici, *Caliban and the Witch*, 47.
73. Adrienne Roberts, *Gendered States of Punishment and Welfare: Feminist Political Economy, Primitive Accumulation and the Law* (Abingdon, UK: Routledge, 2016).
74. Roberts, *Gendered States of Punishment and Welfare*.
75. Drucker, *Warped*; Roberts, *Gendered States of Punishment and Welfare*.
76. Roberts, *Gendered States of Punishment and Welfare*, 47.
77. Federici, *Caliban and the Witch*; Roberts, *Gendered States of Punishment and Welfare*.
78. Federici, *Caliban and the Witch*; Michael Welch, *Corrections: A Critical Approach* (Abingdon, UK: Routledge, 2013).
79. Welch, *Corrections*; Jessica Steinberg, "For Lust or Gain: Perceptions of Prostitutes in Eighteenth-Century London," *Journal of Gender Studies* 26, no. 6 (2017): 702–713.
80. Welch, *Corrections*; Roberts, *Gendered States of Punishment and Welfare*.
81. Roberts, *Gendered States of Punishment and Welfare*; see also Welch, *Corrections*.
82. Roberts, *Gendered States of Punishment and Welfare*. The distinction between the able and idle poor could be seen, for instance, in *The Anatomy of Abuses*, in which Stubbes wrote:

> The former sort of sturdy valiant beggars, which are able to work and will not, I would wish them to be compelled to work, or else not to have any relief given them. And if they would not work, to punish them; if that will not serve, to hang them up . . . For want of which godly order and constitution, there are infinite of the foresaid persons that die, some in ditches, some in holes, some in caves and dens, some in fields, some in one place, some in another, rather like dogs than Christian people. For not withstanding that they be never so impotent, blind, lame, sick, old, or aged, yet are they forced to walk the countries from place to place to seek their relief at every man's door. Stubbes, *The Anatomy of Abuses*, 42–43.

83. Roberts, *Gendered States of Punishment and Welfare*.
84. McIntosh, *Working Women in English Society*, 77.
85. Federici, *Caliban and the Witch*, 94.
86. Henry VIII, "Ordering London Brothels Closed," 365.
87. Federici, *Caliban and the Witch*, 95.
88. Deborah Willis, *Malevolent Nurture: Witch-Hunting and Maternal Power in Early Modern England* (Ithaca, NY: Cornell University Press, 1995); Charlotte Rose Millar, *Witchcraft, the Devil, and Emotions in Early Modern England* (Abingdon, UK: Routledge, 2017).
89. Jensen, *The Path of the Devil*.

90. Charlotte Rose Millar, "Sleeping with Devils: The Sexual Witch in Seventeenth-Century England," in *Supernatural and Secular Power in Early Modern England*, ed. Marcus Harmes and Victoria Bladen (Farnham, UK: Ashgate, 2015), 207–232, 215.

91. Millar, "Sleeping with Devils"; see also Julia M. Garrett, "Witchcraft and Sexual Knowledge in Early Modern England," *Journal for Early Modern Cultural Studies* 13, no. 1 (2012): 32–72; Malcolm Gaskill, "Witchcraft Trials in England," in *The Oxford Handbook of Witchcraft in Early Modern Europe and Colonial America*, ed. Brian P. Levack (Oxford: Oxford University Press, 2013), 283–299.

92. Louise Jackson, "Witches, Wives and Mothers: Witchcraft Persecution and Women's Confessions in Seventeenth-Century England," *Women's History Review* 4, no. 1 (1995): 63–84, 72.

93. Juliet Barker, *1381: The Year of the Peasants' Revolt* (Cambridge, MA: Harvard University Press, 2014).

94. Some sex workers and procurers were indeed from abroad (especially in the capital), and a number of brothels were Flemish- or Dutch-owned. Most were, however, English. Frederique Fouassier-Tate, "Fact Versus Fiction: The Construction of the Figure of the Prostitute in Early Modern England, Official and Popular Discourses," in *Female Transgressions in Early Modern Britain: Literary and Historical Explanations*, ed. Richard Hillman and Pauline Ruberry-Blanc (Abingdon, UK: Routledge, 2014), 71–90, 77.

95. Fouassier-Tate, "Fact Versus Fiction." The enduring practice of banishment could be seen in Henry VIII's proclamation that "all such persons as have accustomed most abominably to abuse their bodies contrary to God's law and honesty . . . [do] resort incontinently to their natural countries with their bags and baggage, upon pain of imprisonment." Henry VIII, "Ordering London Brothels Closed," 365.

96. Patricia Crawford, *Women and Religion in England: 1500–1720* (Abingdon, UK: Routledge, 1993).

97. Crawford, *Women and Religion*, 15–16.

98. Heinrich Kramer and James Sprenger, *Malleus Maleficarum* (translated by Montague Summers) (London: Arrow Books, 1971), 81, 88; see also Jensen, *The Path of the Devil*.

99. Crompton, *Homosexuality and Civilization*.

100. "An Act for the Punishment of the Vice of Buggery" (1533), https://www.bl.uk/collection-items/the-buggery-act-1533.

101. David F. Greenberg and Marcia H. Bystryn, "Capitalism, Bureaucracy and Male Homosexuality," *Contemporary Crises* 8, no. 1 (1984): 33–56.

102. An Act for the Punishment of the Vice of Buggery.

103. Crompton, *Homosexuality and Civilization*.

104. Sauer, *Gender in Medieval Culture*.

105. Crawford, *Women and Religion in England*, 7.

106. Crawford, *Women and Religion in England*, 39.

107. Crawford, *Women and Religion in England*, 8.

108. Crawford, *Women and Religion in England*.

109. Crawford, *Women and Religion in England*.

110. Becon, *The Catechism of Thomas Becon*, 342.

111. Drucker, *Warped*.

112. Greenberg and Bystryn, "Capitalism, Bureaucracy and Male Homosexuality," 37.

113. Greenberg and Bystryn, "Capitalism, Bureaucracy and Male Homosexuality"; Drucker, *Warped*.
114. Drucker, *Warped*; Roberts, *Gendered States of Punishment and Welfare*.
115. Crawford, *Women and Religion in England*, 9.
116. Becon, *The Catechism of Thomas Becon*, 343.
117. Crawford, *Women and Religion in England*.
118. Steinberg, "For Lust or Gain'.
119. Laura J. Rosenthal, *Infamous: Prostitution in Eighteenth-Century British Literature and Culture* (Ithaca, NY: Cornell University Press, 2006).
120. Rosenthal, *Infamous*, 2.
121. Jeffrey Weeks, *Sex, Politics and Society: The Regulations of Sexuality Since 1800* (Abingdon, UK: Routledge, 2014).
122. Weeks, *Sex, Politics and Society*.
123. Imogen Tyler, *Revolting Subjects: Social Abjection and Resistance in Neoliberal Britain* (London: Zed, 2013), 113–114; see also Federici, *Caliban and the Witch*.
124. Millar, *Witchcraft, the Devil, and Emotions*.
125. Crawford, *Women and Religion in England*, 6.
126. Millar, "Sleeping with Devils."
127. "An Act for Suppressing the Detestable Sins of Incest, Adultery and Fornication" (1650), https://www.british-history.ac.uk/no-series/acts-ordinances-interregnum/, pp. 387–389, 387. The legislation enacted the sexual double standard since married men could receive three months' imprisonment for fornication but, for married women, the punishment was death since this was defined as adultery rather than merely fornication. Millar, "Sleeping with Devils."
128. Nash, *Prostitution in Great Britain*.
129. Charles Horne, *Serious Thoughts on the Miseries of Seduction and Prostitution, With a Full Account of the Evils That Produce Them* (London: Swift and Son, 1783), 19, 35; see also Rosenthal, *Infamous*.
130. Jonas Hanway, *Thoughts on the Plan for a Magdalen-House for Repentant Prostitutes* (London: J. and R. Dodsley, 1759), 51.
131. Richard Champion, *Comparative Reflections on the Past and Present Political, Commercial, and Civil State of Great Britain With Some Thoughts Concerning Emigration* (London: Printed for J. Debrett, 1787), 220.
132. Steinberg, "For Lust or Gain."
133. Weeks, *Sex, Politics and Society*.
134. "Disorderly Houses Act" (1751), http://www.irishstatutebook.ie/eli/1751/act/36/section/2/enacted/en/html.
135. Roberts, *Gendered States of Punishment and Welfare*.
136. Samuel Johnson's *A Dictionary of the English Language*, for instance, defined *prostitute* as "to sell to wickedness; to expose to crimes for a reward; to expose upon vile terms." Samuel Johnson, *A Dictionary of the English Language* (Dublin: W.G. Jones, 1768). That said, Johnson did express some sympathy for sex workers on other occasions, writing that "It cannot be doubted, but that numbers follow this dreadful course of life, with shame, horror, and regret; but where can they hope for refuge?" Samuel Johnson, *The Works of Samuel Johnson, Volume 5* (London: Baynes, 1824), 231.
137. Roberts, *Gendered States of Punishment and Welfare*.
138. Roberts, *Gendered States of Punishment and Welfare*.
139. Markman Ellis and Ann Lewis, "Introduction: Venal Bodies: Prostitutes and Eighteenth-Century Culture," in *Prostitution and Eighteenth-Century Culture: Sex,*

Commerce and Morality, ed. Ann Lewis and Markman Ellis (Abingdon, UK: Routledge, 2012), 1–16, 16.

140. Steinberg, "For Lust or Gain."

141. Nash, *Prostitution in Great Britain*; Ellis and Lewis, "Introduction."

142. Robert Dingley, *Proposals for Establishing a Public Place of Reception for Penitent Prostitutes* (London: Printed by W. Faden, 1758), 6.

143. Thomas Lister, "The Prostitute," *Bath Chronicle & Weekly Gazette*, August 30, 1798.

144. Reverend Martin Madan, *An Account of the Triumphant Death of F.S. A Converted Prostitute, Who Died April 1763, Aged Twenty-Six Years* (London: Z. Fowle, 1764).

145. Reverend William Dodd, *The Magdalen, or, History of the First Penitent Prostitute Received into That Charitable Asylum* (London: Printed for Ann Lemoine, 1799), xiii.

146. Nash, *Prostitution in Great Britain*.

147. Van der Meer, "Medieval Prostitution," 182–183.

148. Foucault, *The Will to Knowledge*, 17.

149. Foucault, *The Will to Knowledge*, 19–21.

150. Van der Meer, "Medieval Prostitution," 183.

151. Steinberg, "For Lust or Gain."

152. Robbie Shilliam, *Race and the Undeserving Poor: From Abolition to Brexit* (Newcastle Upon Tyne, UK: Agenda, 2018).

153. "Act in Restraint of Appeals," c.12 § (1533).

154. Federici, *Caliban and the Witch*, 103.

155. Shilliam, *Race and the Undeserving Poor*, 7.

156. Cited in Shilliam, *Race and the Undeserving Poor*, 13.

157. Shilliam *Race and the Undeserving Poor*; see also Roberts, *Gendered States of Punishment and Welfare*; Brenna Bhandar, *Colonial Lives of Property: Law, Land, and Racial Regimes of Ownership* (Durham, NC: Duke University Press, 2018).

158. Shilliam, *Race and the Undeserving Poor*.

159. Rosenthal, *Infamous*.

160. Anon., *Thoughts on Means of Alleviating the Miseries Attendant Upon Common Prostitution* (London: Printed for T. Cadell Jun. and W. Davies, 1799), 31–32.

161. For a discussion of colonialism and sexual violence, see Sharon Block, *Rape and Sexual Power in Early America* (Chapel Hill: University of North Carolina Press, 2006).

162. Roberts, *Gendered States of Punishment and Welfare*; Tina Fernandes Botts, "Multiracial Americans and Racial Discrimination," in *Race Policy and Multiracial Americans*, ed. Kathleen Odell Korgen (Bristol, UK: Policy Press, 2016), 81–100.

163. Federici, *Caliban and the Witch*, 103.

164. Original Authors, *The Modern Part of an Universal History, from the Earliest Accounts to the Present Time, Volume 13* (London: Printed for C. Bathurst et al., 1781), 466, 472.

165. Rachel Feinstein, *When Rape Was Legal: The Untold History of Sexual Violence During Slavery* (Abingdon, UK: Routledge, 2018); see also Ann Laura Stoler, *Carnal Knowledge and Imperial Power: Race and the Intimate in Colonial Rule* (Oakland: University of California Press, 2002).

166. Christopher Tomlins, *Freedom Bound: Law, Labor, and Civic Identity in Colonizing English America, 1580–1865* (Cambridge, UK: Cambridge University Press, 2010); Botts, "Multiracial Americans and Racial Discrimination."

167. Kim F. Hall, *Things of Darkness: Economies of Race and Gender in Early Modern England* (Ithaca, NY: Cornell University Press, 1995), 240; see also bell hooks, *Ain't I a Woman: Black Women and Feminism* (New York: Routledge, 2015).

168. Mr. Holcroft, "The Dying Prostitute: An Elegy," *Hereford Journal*, April 21, 1785.

169. Federici, *Caliban and the Witch*, 103.

170. Karras, *Sexuality in Medieval Europe*.

171. Crawford, *Women and Religion in England*, 7.

172. Steinberg, "For Lust or Gain."

173. Steinberg, "For Lust or Gain."

174. Alan Bray, *Homosexuality in Renaissance England* (New York: Columbia University Press, 1995).

175. Crompton, *Homosexuality and Civilization*; Drucker, *Warped*.

176. Bray, *Homosexuality in Renaissance England*, 85; see also Crompton, *Homosexuality and Civilization*.

177. Crompton, *Homosexuality and Civilization*, 452.

178. Societies for the Reformation of Manners, *A Representation of the State of the Societies For Reformation of Manners* (London, 1715), 10–11.

179. Crompton, *Homosexuality and Civilization*.

180. L. Gilliver and J. Huggonson, *Select Trials, for Murders, Robberies, Rapes, Sodomy, Coining, Frauds, and Other Offences* (London: Printed for L. Gilliver and J. Huggonson, 1742), 362.

181. Anon., *The Trial of Charles Bradbury, for the Detestable Crime of Sodomy Said to Be Committed on the Body of James Hearne, at Justice-Hall in the Old Bailey, on Thursday the 11th of September, 1755* (London: Printed and sold by M. Cooper at the Globe, 1755), 2.

182. Crompton, *Homosexuality and Civilization*.

183. The Author of the London Spy, *The Second Part of the London Clubs; Containing the No-Nose Club, the Beaus Club, the Farting Club, the Sodomites, or Mollies Club, the Quacks Club* (London: Printed by J. Dutton, 1709), 5; see also Crompton, *Homosexuality and Civilization*.

184. Bray, *Homosexuality in Renaissance England*; Crompton, *Homosexuality and Civilization*.

185. Drucker, *Warped*; Gill Rossini, *Same Sex Love 1700–1957: A History and Research Guide* (Barnsley, UK: Pen & Sword History, 2017).

186. Anon., *Plain Reasons for the Growth of Sodomy in England* (London: Printed for A. Dodd, 1728), 9. Indeed, to be "Unmanned" was defined as "Deprived of the essential qualities of the human nature; emasculated; rendered effeminate." John Ash, *The New and Complete Dictionary of the English Language* (London: Printed for Vernor and Hood, 1795).

187. On which see Christopher A. Faraone and Laura K. McClure, eds., *Prostitutes and Courtesans in the Ancient World* (Madison: University of Wisconsin Press, 2006).

188. Federici, *Caliban and the Witch*, 97.

189. Federici, *Caliban and the Witch*.

CHAPTER 3

1. Henry Judge, *Our Fallen Sisters: The Great Social Evil: Prostitution: Its Cause, Effect, So Called Use, Decided Abuse and Only Cure or Remedy* (London: E. Marshall, 1874), 8.

2. Michel Foucault, *The History of Sexuality: The Will to Knowledge* (translated by Robert Hurley; New York: Pantheon, 1978), 147.

3. John Scott, "Governing Prostitution: Differentiating the Bad from the Bad," *Current Issues in Criminal Justice* 23, no. 1 (2011): 53–72; Jane Scoular, *The Subject of Prostitution: Sex Work, Law and Social Theory* (Abingdon, UK: Routledge, 2015).

4. Foucault, *The Will to Knowledge*, 140.

5. Scott, "Governing Prostitution"; Scoular, *The Subject of Prostitution*.

6. Norah Carlin, "The Roots of Gay Oppression," *International Socialism* 42 (1989), http://isj.org.uk/the-roots-of-gay-oppression/; Stanley D. Nash, *Prostitution in Great Britain 1945–1901* (London: The Scarecrow Press Inc., 1994).

7. Society for the Suppression of Vice, *No. III* (London: S. Gosness, Printer to the Society, 1825), 3.

8. Guardian Society for the Preservation of Public Morals, "Report of the Committee of the Guardian Society" (Mansion House, London, October 30, 1817), 35.

9. "Vagrancy Act" (1824), http://www.legislation.gov.uk/ukpga/Geo4/5/83/contents; see also Scoular, *The Subject of Prostitution*.

10. Scoular, *The Subject of Prostitution*, 27.

11. Scott, "Governing Prostitution"; Scoular, *The Subject of Prostitution*. As one commentator wrote in 1811, "I know of no crime that exceeds prostitution in its moral turpitude, nor so dreadful in its consequences as an offence against society . . . [O]ne prostitute may injure the health of others, and send to an untimely grave many promising youths. She willfully gives a mortal disease to hundreds, which may lay waste the peace of families, and ruin the health of posterity for ages yet unborn!" E. Wilson, *Hints to the Public Legislature, On the Prevalence of Vice, and on the Dangerous Effects of Seduction* (London: Published by E. Wilson, 1811), 88–89.

12. William Acton, *Prostitution Considered in Its Moral, Social, and Sanitary Aspects, in London and Other Large Cities and Garrison Towns: With Proposals for the Control and Prevention of Its Attendant Evils* (London: J. Churchill and Sons, 1870), 2–3, 50.

13. Jo Doezema, *Sex Slaves and Discourse Masters: The Construction of Trafficking* (London: Zed Books, 2010); see also Judith R. Walkowitz, *Prostitution and Victorian Society: Women, Class, and the State* (Cambridge, UK: Cambridge University Press, 1982).

14. "Act for the Prevention of Contagious Diseases" (1868), http://ozcase.library.qut.edu.au/qhlc/documents/qr_heal_act_1868_31_Vic_No40.pdf.

15. Scoular, *The Subject of Prostitution*, 45.

16. Foucault, *The Will to Knowledge*, 43.

17. Shannon Bell, *Reading, Writing, and Rewriting the Prostitute Body* (Bloomington: Indiana University Press, 1994); Silvia Federici, *Caliban and the Witch: Women, the Body and Primitive Accumulation* (New York: Autonomedia, 2004).

18. Elisabeth Bronfen, *Over Her Dead Body: Death, Femininity and the Aesthetic* (Manchester: Manchester University Press, 1992).

19. Jeffrey Weeks, *Sex, Politics and Society: The Regulations of Sexuality Since 1800* (Abingdon, UK: Routledge, 2014), 52.

20. Bell, *Reading, Writing, and Rewriting the Prostitute Body*.

21. Scoular, *The Subject of Prostitution*.

22. Stephen Parker, *Informal Marriage, Cohabitation and the Law 1750–1989* (New York: Springer, 1990).

23. Anne O'Connell and O. N. Toronto, "A Genealogy of Poverty: Race and the Technology of Population," *Critical Social Work* 11, no. 2 (2010): 29–44; Adrienne

Roberts, *Gendered States of Punishment and Welfare: Feminist Political Economy, Primitive Accumulation and the Law* (Abingdon, UK: Routledge, 2016).

24. Weeks, *Sex, Politics and Society*; Peter Drucker, *Warped: Gay Normality and Queer Anti-Capitalism* (Leiden: Brill, 2015).

25. Parker, *Informal Marriage, Cohabitation and the Law 1750–1989*; Weeks, *Sex, Politics and Society*.

26. Foucault, *The Will to Knowledge*, 122.

27. Weeks, *Sex, Politics and Society*.

28. Federici, *Caliban and the Witch*; Roberts, *Gendered States of Punishment and Welfare*.

29. Scott, "Governing Prostitution."

30. Magdalen Hospital, *A Short Account of the Magdalen Hospital* (London: Printed by W. Tew, 1823), 3–4.

31. Scott, "Governing Prostitution."

32. Annemieke Van Drenth and Francisca de Haan, *The Rise of Caring Power: Elizabeth Fry and Josephine Butler in Britain and the Netherlands* (Amsterdam: Amsterdam University Press, 1999); Scott, "Governing Prostitution."

33. Van Drenth and Haan, *The Rise of Caring Power*; Faramerz Dabhoiwala, *The Origins of Sex: A History of the First Sexual Revolution* (New York: Oxford University Press, 2012).

34. Rebecca McCarthy, *Origins of the Magdalene Laundries: An Analytical History* (London: McFarland & Company, 2010), 2.

35. Annemieke Van Drenth, "Holy Beliefs and Caring Powers: Josephine Butler's Influence on Abolitionism and the Women's Movement in the Netherlands," in *Sex, Gender, and Religion: Josephine Butler Revisited*, ed. Jenny Daggers and Diana Neal (Oxford: Peter Lang, 2006), 73–96, 73.

36. Foucault, *The Will to Knowledge*, 39.

37. G. Simmons, *The Working Classes; Their Moral, Social, and Intellectual Condition; with Practical Suggestions for Their Improvement* (London: Partridge & Oakley, 1849), 56.

38. Van Drenth and Haan, *The Rise of Caring Power*; Van Drenth, "Holy Beliefs and Caring Powers."

39. James Miller, *Prostitution Considered in Relation to Its Cause and Cure* (Edinburgh: Sutherland and Knox, 1859), 6.

40. Scott, "Governing Prostitution."

41. William Tait, *An Inquiry into the Extent, Causes, and Consequences, of Prostitution* (Edinburgh: P. Rickard, 1840), 248–249.

42. A.J.B. Parent-Duchatelet, "A Short Account of the London Magdalene Hospital. London, 1846," *The Quarterly Review* 83 (1848): 367.

43. Tait, *An Inquiry into the Extent, Causes, and Consequences, of Prostitution*, 249–250.

44. Scott, "Governing Prostitution"; Drucker, *Warped*.

45. Scott "Governing Prostitution," 59.

46. Bell, *Reading, Writing, and Rewriting the Prostitute Body*; Scoular, *The Subject of Prostitution*.

47. Drucker, *Warped*.

48. Foucault, *The Will to Knowledge*, 64.

49. Jeffrey Weeks, *Sexuality and Its Discontents: Meanings, Myths and Modern Sexualities* (Abingdon, UK: Routledge, 1985).

50. Foucault, *The Will to Knowledge*; Weeks, *Sexuality and Its Discontents*.

51. Charles Darwin, *On the Origin of Species by Means of Natural Selection, or the Preservation of Favoured Races in the Struggle for Life* (London: John Murray, 1859). For an overview, see Weeks, *Sexuality and Its Discontents*.

52. Foucault, *The Will to Knowledge*; Weeks, *Sexuality and Its Discontents*; Jeffrey Weeks, *Sexuality* (Abingdon, UK: Routledge, 2016).

53. Darwin, *On the Origin of Species*, 12.

54. Foucault, *The Will to Knowledge*, 24.

55. Havelock Ellis, *Man and Woman: A Study of Human Secondary Sexual Characteristics* (London: Walter Scott Ltd., 1894).

56. Weeks, *Sexuality and Its Discontents*.

57. Ellis, *Man and Woman*, 395.

58. Darwin, *On the Origin of Species*, 459. What mattered for Darwin was the reproduction not of the individual but of the species very specifically: some insects such as worker ants, for instance, were "born capable of work, but incapable of procreation." Thus, nature did not determine that all creatures must be sexually reproductive, so long as they contributed to production. Darwin, *On the Origin of Species*, 236.

59. Federici, *Caliban and the Witch*; see also Jill Steans and Daniela Tepe, "Gender in the Theory and Practice of International Political Economy: The Promise and Limitations of Neo-Gramscian Approaches," ed. Alison J. Ayers, *Gramsci, Political Economy, and International Relations Theory: Modern Princes and Naked Emperors* (New York: Palgrave, 2008), 133–52.

60. Amanda Vickery, "Golden Age to Separate Spheres? A Review of the Categories and Chronology of English Women's History," *The Historical Journal* 36, no. 2 (1993): 383–414; Rosemary Hennessy, *Profit and Pleasure: Sexual Identities in Late Capitalism* (Abingdon, UK: Routledge, 2000); Federici, *Caliban and the Witch*; Roberts, *Gendered States of Punishment and Welfare*.

61. Weeks, *Sex, Politics and Society*.

62. Rev. J. Watts Lethbridge, *Woman the Glory of Man, Dedicated to the Ladies of England* (London: Thomas Richardson and Son, 1856), 30.

63. Bell, *Reading, Writing, and Rewriting the Prostitute Body*, 43; see also Weeks, *Sex, Politics and Society*.

64. Bell, *Reading, Writing, and Rewriting the Prostitute Body*, 41.

65. An English Mother, *An Appeal to the People of England on the Recognition and Superintendence of Prostitution by Governments, by an English Mother* (Banks: Nottingham, 1869), 4.

66. An English Mother, *An Appeal to the People of England*, 3.

67. Annie Besant, "The Legalization of Female Slavery in England," *National Reformer*, 4 (1876): 4.

68. Miller, *Prostitution Considered in Relation to Its Cause and Cure*, 20–23.

69. David F. Greenberg and Marcia H. Bystryn, "Capitalism, Bureaucracy and Male Homosexuality," *Contemporary Crises* 8, no. 1 (1984): 33–56. This is not to suggest that these discourses of self-restraint were unique to the nineteenth century. A century earlier, for example, Daniel Defoe had written an essay on *Conjugal Lewdness: Or, Matrimonial Whoredom* in which he argued that "Chastity in general is a Virtue, and a Christian Duty; and I affirm there is a particular Chastity, that is to say, a limited Liberty, which is to be observed and strictly submitted to in the conjugal State . . . that there is a needful Modesty and Decency requisite between a Man and his Wife after Marriage." Daniel Defoe,

Conjugal Lewdness: Or, Matrimonial Whoredom (London: T. Warner, 1727), 48, 73.

70. Greenberg and Bystryn, "Capitalism, Bureaucracy and Male Homosexuality."
71. Theo Van der Meer, "Medieval Prostitution and the Case of a (Mistaken?) Sexual Identity," *Journal of Women's History* 11, no. 2 (1999): 184.
72. Foucault, *The Will to Knowledge*.
73. Greenberg and Bystryn, "Capitalism, Bureaucracy and Male Homosexuality," 37.
74. Jeffrey Weeks, "Inverts, Perverts, and Mary-Annes," *Journal of Homosexuality* 6, no. 1–2 (1981): 113–134, 118.
75. Kevin Floyd, *The Reification of Desire: Toward a Queer Marxism* (Minneapolis: University of Minnesota Press, 2009), 59.
76. Weeks, *Sex, Politics and Society*.
77. Lethbridge, *Woman the Glory of Man*, 31, 34.
78. Floyd, *The Reification of Desire*.
79. These discourses were not new: John Locke, for instance, had written in his *Two Treatises on Government* that sodomy transgressed "the main intention of Nature, which wills the increase of Mankind, and the continuation of the Species in the highest perfection and the distinction of Families, with the Security of the Marriage Bed, as necessary thereunto." John Locke, *Two Treatises of Government: In the Former, the False Principles and Foundation of Sir Robert Filmer, and His Followers, Are Detected and Overthrown* (London: Printed for Awnsham and John Churchill, 1698), 57.
80. A.D. Harvey, "Prosecutions for Sodomy in England at the Beginning of the Nineteenth Century," *The Historical Journal* 21, no. 4 (1978): 939–48; Carlin, "The Roots of Gay Oppression"; Weeks, *Sex, Politics and Society*.
81. Carlin, "The Roots of Gay Oppression"; John Scott, "A Prostitute's Progress: Male Prostitution in Scientific Discourse," *Social Semiotics* 13, no. 2 (2003): 179–199.
82. "Offences Against the Person Act" (1861), http://www.legislation.gov.uk/ukpga/Vict/24-25/100/contents.
83. Weeks, "Inverts, Perverts, and Mary-Annes," 117.
84. William Thomas Stead, "The Maiden Tribute of Modern Babylon I: The Report of Our Secret Commission," *Pall Mall Gazette*, July 6, 1885.
85. "Criminal Law Amendment Act" (1885), http://www.irishstatutebook.ie/eli/1885/act/69/enacted/en/print.
86. Nicholas C. Edsall, *Toward Stonewall: Homosexuality and Society in the Modern Western World* (Charlottesville: University of Virginia Press, 2006), 112.
87. F. B. Smith, "Labouchere's Amendment to the Criminal Law Amendment Bill," *Historical Studies* 17, no. 67 (1976): 165–73.
88. Criminal Law Amendment Act.
89. Edsall, *Toward Stonewall*.
90. William A. Cohen, *Sex Scandal: The Private Parts of Victorian Fiction* (Durham, NC: Duke University Press, 1996), 123.
91. "Male Prostitution," *Reynold's Newspaper*, May 26, 1895; also cited in Kerwin Kaye, "Male Prostitution in the Twentieth Century: Psychohomosexuals, Hoodlum Homosexuals, and Exploited Teens," *Journal of Homosexuality* 46, no. 1–2 (2003): 17.
92. Weeks, "Inverts, Perverts, and Mary-Annes."
93. Weeks, "Inverts, Perverts, and Mary-Annes."
94. "Prostitution," *Northern Star*, July 1, 1848.
95. Weeks, "Inverts, Perverts, and Mary-Annes."

96. Weeks, "Inverts, Perverts, and Mary-Annes."

97. Weeks, "Inverts, Perverts, and Mary-Annes."

98. Scott, "A Prostitute's Progress."

99. Greenberg and Bystryn, "Capitalism, Bureaucracy and Male Homosexuality"; Jeffrey Weeks, *Making Sexual History* (Cambridge, UK: Polity Press, 2000).

100. Norman Lockyer, "Is Homosexuality Hard-Wired?," *Nature* 353 (1869): 13.

101. Greenberg and Bystryn, "Capitalism, Bureaucracy and Male Homosexuality"; Weeks, *Sexuality and Its Discontents*.

102. Kaye, "Male Prostitution in the Twentieth Century," 5.

103. Kaye, "Male Prostitution in the Twentieth Century," 5

104. Weeks, "Inverts, Perverts, and Mary-Annes"; Kaye, "Male Prostitution in the Twentieth Century"; Scott, "A Prostitute's Progress."

105. Weeks, "Inverts, Perverts, and Mary-Annes"; Scott, "A Prostitute's Progress."

106. Gert Hekma, "Wrong Lovers in the 19th Century Netherlands," *Journal of Homosexuality* 13, no. 2–3 (1987): 43–55; Gert Hekma, "Homosexuality and the Left in the Netherlands: 1890–1911," *Journal of Homosexuality* 29, no. 2–3 (1995): 97–116.

107. Richard von Krafft-Ebing, *Psychopathia Sexualis* (Philadelphia: F.A. Davis Company, 1894), 418. Similarly, in *Études de Pathologie Sociale: Les Deux Prostitutions* (1887), Carlier defended female prostitution on the grounds that it prevented rape but denounced male prostitution on the grounds that it "leads to the most monstrous pairings" and "whets the appetites of all evil-doers." Translated by Michael Sibalis, "Félix Carlier," in *Who's Who in Gay and Lesbian History: From Antiquity to World War II*, ed. Robert Aldrich and Garry Wotherspoon (London: Routledge, 2001), 87.

108. Kaye, "Male Prostitution in the Twentieth Century." For example, Krafft-Ebing wrote of "acquired homo-sexuality" that "in the milder cases, there is simple hermaphroditism; in more pronounced cases, only homo-sexual feeling and instinct, but limited to the vita sexualis; in still more complete cases, the whole psychical personality, and even the bodily sensations, are transformed to correspond with the sexual perversion; and, in the complete cases, the physical form is correspondingly altered." Indeed, the "final possible stage in this disease-process is the delusion of a transformation of sex." Krafft-Ebing, *Psychopathia Sexualis*, 187, 216.

109. Neil McKenna, *Fanny and Stella: The Young Men Who Shocked Victorian England* (London: Faber & Faber, 2013).

110. Anon., *The Lives of Boulton and Park: Extraordinary Revelations* (London: George Clarke, 1870), 2.

111. Jim Davis, "'Slap On! Slap Ever!': Victorian Pantomime, Gender Variance, and Cross-Dressing," *Theatre Quarterly* 30, no. 3 (2014): 218–230.

112. Cited in H. G. Cocks, *Nameless Offences: Homosexual Desire in the 19th Century* (London: I.B. Tauris, 2003), 107.

113. Cohen, *Sex Scandal*.

114. Christopher E. Forth and Ivan Crozier, *Body Parts: Critical Explorations in Corporeality* (Lanham: Lexington Books, 2005).

115. Neil Bartlett, *Who Was That Man? A Present for Mr Oscar Wilde* (London: Profile Books, 1988), 141. For a critique of contemporary accounts of Fanny and Stella's trial, see Simon Joyce, "Two Women Walk into a Theatre Bathroom: The Fanny and Stella Trials as Trans Narrative," *Victorian Review* 44, no. 1 (2018): 83–98.

116. Floyd, *The Reification of Desire*.

117. Foucault, *The Will to Knowledge*, 43; see also Bell, *Reading, Writing, and Rewriting the Prostitute Body*; Weeks, *Sex, Politics and Society*.
118. Hennessy, *Profit and Pleasure*.
119. Roberts, *Gendered States of Punishment and Welfare*, 71; see also Hennessy, *Profit and Pleasure*.
120. Hennessy, *Profit and Pleasure*.
121. Weeks, *Sexuality*.
122. Greenberg and Bystryn, "Capitalism, Bureaucracy and Male Homosexuality."
123. Henry Mayhew, *London Labour and the London Poor: Cyclopedia of the Condition and Earnings of Those That Will Work, Those That Cannot Work, and Those That Will Not Work, Volume 1* (London: G. Woodfall, 1851), 1–2.
124. Havelock Ellis, *The Criminal* (New York: Scribner & Welford, 1890), 208–210.
125. Jemima Repo, *The Biopolitics of Gender* (New York: Oxford University Press, 2015), 15.
126. Foucault, *The Will to Knowledge*.
127. Ann Laura Stoler, *Race and the Education of Desire: Foucault's History of Sexuality and the Colonial Order of Things* (Durham, NC: Duke University Press, 1995), 607; see also Luise White, *The Comforts of Home: Prostitution in Colonial Nairobi* (Chicago: University of Chicago Press, 1990); Anne McClintock, *Imperial Leather: Race, Gender and Sexuality in the Colonial Contest* (Abingdon, UK: Routledge, 1995); Zine Magubane, *Bringing the Empire Home: Race, Class, and Gender in Britain and Colonial South Africa* (Chicago: University of Chicago Press, 2004); Murat Aydemir, ed., *Indiscretions: At the Intersections of Queer and Postcolonial Theory* (Amsterdam: Colophon, 2011); Cynthia Weber, *Queer International Relations: Sovereignty, Sexuality and the Will to Knowledge* (New York: Oxford University Press, 2016).
128. Robbie Shilliam, *Race and the Undeserving Poor: From Abolition to Brexit* (Newcastle Upon Tyne, UK: Agenda, 2018).
129. Patrick Colquhoun, *A Treatise on the Wealth, Power, and Resources of the British Empire in Every Quarter of the World* (London: Printed for Joseph Mawman, 1815), 49.
130. "Slavery Abolition Act" (1833), http://www.irishstatutebook.ie/eli/1833/act/73/enacted/en/html.
131. Shilliam, *Race and the Undeserving Poor*.
132. Philippa Levine, *Prostitution, Race and Politics: Policing Venereal Disease in the British Empire* (Abingdon, UK: Routledge, 2003).
133. Levine, *Prostitution, Race and Politics*.
134. For example, Florence Nightingale dismissed claims that the aborigines in South Australia were "disappearing before a more highly civilized people" for "it is not civilization that has caused their deaths; it is rather the vices of the Europeans which they have imbibed." Florence Nightingale, *Sanitary Statistics of Native Colonial Schools and Hospitals, Volume 3* (London: G.E.Eyre & W.Spottiswoode, 1863), 62–63.
135. Levine, *Prostitution, Race and Politics*.
136. Stoler, *Race and the Education of Desire*; McClintock, *Imperial Leather*; Levine, *Prostitution, Race and Politics*.
137. Cynthia Enloe, *Bananas, Beaches and Bases: Making Feminist Sense of International Politics* (Oakland: University of California Press, 1990); Anna Agathangelou and Lily Ling, "Desire Industries: Sex Trafficking, UN Peacekeeping, and the Neo-Liberal World Order," *Brown Journal of World Affairs* 10, no. 1 (2003): 133–148;

V. Spike Peterson, "The Intended and Unintended Queering of States/Nations," *Studies in Ethnicity and Nationalism* 13, no. 1 (2013): 57–68.

138. Levine, *Prostitution, Race and Politics*; Ann Laura Stoler, *Carnal Knowledge and Imperial Power: Race and the Intimate in Colonial Rule* (Oakland: University of California Press, 2002).
139. Weber, *Queer International Relations*, 21, 30.
140. Levine, *Prostitution, Race and Politics*; Stoler, *Carnal Knowledge and Imperial Power*.
141. Grace Kyungwon Hong, "Existentially Surplus: Women of Color Feminism and the New Crises of Capitalism," *GLQ: A Journal of Lesbian and Gay Studies* 18, no. 1 (2012): 87–106; see also Cheryl Harris, "Whiteness as Property," *Harvard Law Review* 106, no. 8 (1993): 1707–1791; Brenna Bhandar, *Colonial Lives of Property: Law, Land, and Racial Regimes of Ownership* (Durham, NC: Duke University Press, 2018).
142. Leticia Sabsay, "The Ruse of Sexual Freedom: Neoliberalism, Self-Ownership and Commercial Sex," in *Global Justice and Desire: Queering Economy*, ed. Nikita Dhawan et al. (Abingdon, UK: Routledge, 2015), 180–194.
143. Levine, *Prostitution, Race and Politics*.
144. Federici, *Caliban and the Witch*; Janet R. Jakobsen, "Perverse Justice," *GLQ: A Journal of Lesbian and Gay Studies* 18, no. 1 (2012): 19–45; Imogen Tyler, *Revolting Subjects: Social Abjection and Resistance in Neoliberal Britain* (London: Zed, 2013).
145. Levine, *Prostitution, Race and Politics*.
146. Foucault, *The Will to Knowledge*, 54.
147. "The Knout of England," *Reynold's Newspaper*, February 20, 1870.
148. Michael Ryan, *Prostitution in London, with a Comparative View of That of Paris and New York, Etc* (London: H.Bailliere, 1839), 89. Likewise, tales of London's immorality also circulated on the continent. As the French physician Gustave Antoine Richelot argued, for instance:

> To satisfy the exhaustless demands of licentiousness, there has been organized in London a vast system of intrigues, of tricks, of traps of all sorts, a considerable commerce of indigenous and foreign importation, in a word, an immense industry, which has been established and developed, and is exercised, without hindrance, with such activity and impudence, that it may be truly said that nothing of the kind exists in any other European nation.

Gustave Antoine Richolet, *The Greatest of Our Social Evils: Prostitution, as It Now Exists in London, Liverpool, Manchester, Glasgow, Edinburgh and Dublin: An Enquiry into the Cause and Means of Reformation, Based on Statistical Documents* (London: Baillière, 1857), 82.
149. Mayhew, *London Labour and the London Poor*, 215.
150. "Editorial," *The Times*, February 25, 1858.
151. Alfred S. Dyer, *The European Slave Trade in British Girls: A Narrative of Facts* (London: Dyer Brothers, Amen Corner, Paternoster Row, 1880), 33.
152. Levine, *Prostitution, Race and Politics*.
153. John Campbell, *Church Fellowship, for Young People, With a Practical Essay on Marriage* (London: John Snow, 1840), 49.
154. "Editorial," *The Times*.
155. Levine, *Prostitution, Race and Politics*, 6.

156. Jemima Repo, "The Life Function: The Biopolitics of Sexuality and Race Revisited," in *Biopolitical Governance: Race, Gender and Economy*, ed. Hannah Richter (London: Rowman & Littlefield International, 2018), 42.

157. Foucault, *The Will to Knowledge*, 44. On homosexuality as an "alien strain," see also Weber, *Queer International Relations*, 19.

CHAPTER 4

1. Thomas Becon, *The Catechism of Thomas Becon: With Other Pieces Written by Him in the Reign of King Edward the Sixth* (Cambridge, UK: Printed at the University Press, 1844), 343.

2. Rosemary Hennessy, *Profit and Pleasure: Sexual Identities in Late Capitalism* (Abingdon, UK: Routledge, 2000); Kevin Floyd, *The Reification of Desire: Toward a Queer Marxism* (Minneapolis: University of Minnesota Press, 2009); Peter Drucker, *Warped: Gay Normality and Queer Anti-Capitalism* (Leiden: Brill, 2015).

3. Adam Smith, *An Inquiry into the Nature and Causes of the Wealth of Nations* (Edinburgh: Printed for Thomas Nelson and Peter Brown, 1827), 724.

4. Hennessy, *Profit and Pleasure*. On the rise of consumerism in Britain, see for instance Lorna Wetherill, *Consumer Behaviour and Material Culture in Britain 1660–1760* (Abingdon, UK: Routledge, 1996); Matthew Hilton, *Consumerism in Twentieth Century Britain: The Search for a Historical Movement* (Cambridge, UK: Cambridge University Press, 2003); Peter Gurney, *The Making of Consumer Culture in Britain* (London: Bloomsbury, 2017).

5. Krista Lysack, *Come Buy, Come Buy: Shopping and the Culture of Consumption in Victorian Women's Writing* (Athens: Ohio University Press, 2008), 17; see also Anne McClintock, *Imperial Leather: Race, Gender and Sexuality in the Colonial Contest* (Abingdon, UK: Routledge, 1995).

6. Miranda Joseph, *Against the Romance of Community* (Minneapolis: University of Minnesota Press, 2002).

7. John Angell James, *Female Piety: Young Woman's Friend and Guide Through Life to Immortality* (New York: Robert Carter & Brothers, 1853), 57.

8. Abraham Flexner, *Prostitution in Europe* (London: Grant Richards Ltd., 1914), 35.

9. Scott used interviews with sex workers to evidence these claims—in the words of Flossie, a "typical London street girl," for example: "A skivvy! Not on your life!" George Ryley Scott, *A History of Prostitution from Antiquity to the Present Day* (London: T. Werner Laurie Ltd., 1936), 26–29.

10. Flexner, *Prostitution in Europe*, 37.

11. Hennessy, *Profit and Pleasure*; Floyd, *The Reification of Desire*; Drucker, *Warped*.

12. Floyd, *The Reification of Desire*, 54.

13. Elizabeth Freeman, "Queer Belongings: Kinship Theory and Queer Theory," in *A Companion to Lesbian, Gay, Bisexual, Transgender, and Queer Studies*, ed. George E. Haggerty and Molly McGarry (Hoboken, NJ: John Wiley & Sons, 2007), 295–314.

14. Hennessy, *Profit and Pleasure*, 99.

15. Floyd, *The Reification of Desire*, 35–36.

16. Hennessy, *Profit and Pleasure*.

17. Sigmund Freud, *Three Essays on the Theory of Sexuality* (translated and newly edited by James Strachey) (London: The Hogarth Press, 1970), 1–2.

18. Hennessy, *Profit and Pleasure*.

19. Hennessy, *Profit and Pleasure*.

20. Jonathan Katz, *The Invention of Heterosexuality* (Chicago: University of Chicago Press, 2007); Jemima Repo, "The Life Function: The Biopolitics of Sexuality and Race Revisited," in *Biopolitical Governance: Race, Gender and Economy*, ed. Hannah Richter (London: Rowman & Littlefield International, 2018), 41–57.
21. Michelle M. Sauer, *Gender in Medieval Culture* (London: Bloomsbury, 2015), 7.
22. Michel Foucault, *The History of Sexuality: The Will to Knowledge* (translated by Robert Hurley) (New York: Pantheon, 1978), 156.
23. Hennessy, *Profit and Pleasure*; Jeffrey Weeks, *Making Sexual History* (Cambridge, UK: Polity Press, 2000); Drucker, *Warped*.
24. Foucault, *The Will to Knowledge*, 156.
25. Hennessy, *Profit and Pleasure*.
26. Louisa Allen, "Girls Want Sex, Boys Want Love: Resisting Dominant Discourses of (Hetero) Sexuality," *Sexualities* 6, no. 2 (2003): 224–225.
27. Hennessy, *Profit and Pleasure*; Drucker, *Warped*.
28. Hennessy, *Profit and Pleasure*, 104.
29. Floyd, *The Reification of Desire*, 35.
30. Hennessy, *Profit and Pleasure*; Drucker, *Warped*.
31. Hennessy, *Profit and Pleasure*.
32. Hennessy, *Profit and Pleasure*, 102.
33. Scott, *A History of Prostitution*, 7.
34. Drucker, *Warped*.
35. Havelock Ellis, *Studies in the Psychology of Sex: Sex in Relation to Society* (Philadelphia: F.A. Davis Company, 1910), 278.
36. Ellis, *Studies in the Psychology of Sex*, 272.
37. Drucker, *Warped*, 55.
38. Hennessy, *Profit and Pleasure*; Floyd, *The Reification of Desire*.
39. Lenore Kuo, *Prostitution Policy: Revolutionizing Practice Through a Gendered Perspective* (New York: New York University Press, 2002).
40. Lauren Gail Berlant, *Desire/Love* (New York: Dead Letter Office, 2012), 109–110.
41. Berlant, *Desire/Love*.
42. Sara Ahmed, *The Promise of Happiness* (Durham, NC: Duke University Press, 2010), 30.
43. Foucault, *The Will to Knowledge*, 156.
44. Linda Singer, *Erotic Welfare: Sexual Theory and Politics in the Age of Epidemic* (New York: Routledge, 1993), 48.
45. Alison Phipps, *The Politics of the Body: Gender in a Neoliberal and Neoconservative Age* (Hoboken, NJ: John Wiley & Sons, 2014).
46. Gargi Bhattacharyya, *Sexuality and Society: An Introduction* (Abingdon, UK: Routledge, 2005).
47. Bhattacharyya, *Sexuality and Society*, 62. On markets in women's sex toys, for example, see Lynn Comella, *Vibrator Nation: How Feminist Sex-Toy Stores Changed the Business of Pleasure* (Durham, NC: Duke University Press, 2017). For a feminist critique of consumerist discourses in Western popular culture, see Penny Griffin, *Popular Culture, Political Economy and the Death of Feminism: Why Women Are in Refrigerators and Other Stories* (Abingdon, UK: Routledge, 2015).
48. Foucault, *The Will to Knowledge*, 36.
49. Drucker, *Warped*.
50. Since destitution was a "disease," they argued, those afflicted should be "dealt with, not as paupers or as criminals, but definitely as mental defectives by an

Authority specializing in mental defectiveness." Sidney Webb and Beatrice Webb, *The Prevention of Destitution* (London: Longmans, Green and Co., 1916), 56–57.

51. C. F. Marshall, "Alcoholism and Prostitution," *British Journal of Inebriety* 8, no. 1 (1910): 30.

52. Freud, *Three Essays on the Theory of Sexuality*, 39.

53. Freud, *Three Essays on the Theory of Sexuality*, 42, 73.

54. Although, as Aimé Césaire wrote of the Holocaust in colonial discourse: "[T]hey hide the truth from themselves, that it is barbarism, the supreme barbarism, the crowning barbarism that sums up all the daily barbarisms; that it is Nazism, yes, but that before they were its victims, they were its accomplices; that they tolerated that Nazism before it was inflicted on them, that they absolved it, shut their eyes to it, legitimated it, because, until then, it had been applied only to non-European peoples." Aimé Césaire, *Discourse on Colonialism* (translated by Joan Pinkham) (New York: Monthly Review Press, 1955), 36.

55. Jemima Repo, *The Biopolitics of Gender* (New York: Oxford University Press, 2015), 28.

56. Repo, *The Biopolitics of Gender*.

57. W. Norwood East, "Sexual Offenders—a British View," *Yale Law Journal* 55, no. 3 (1946): 544.

58. Repo, *The Biopolitics of Gender*.

59. Rev. J. Watts Lethbridge, *Woman the Glory of Man, Dedicated to the Ladies of England* (London: Thomas Richardson and Son, 1856), 56. Indeed, the Victorian family was itself "an obligatory locus of affects, feelings, love" that served to "anchor sexuality and provide it with a permanent support." Foucault, *The Will to Knowledge*, 108–109.

60. Repo, *The Biopolitics of Gender*, 66–67.

61. "Of the New Britain," *Sunday Mirror*, April 6, 1941.

62. Penny Summerfield, *Women Workers in the Second World War: Production and Patriarchy in Conflict* (Abingdon, UK: Routledge, 2013), 1.

63. Stephanie Coontz, *Marriage, a History: How Love Conquered Marriage* (New York: Viking, 2005).

64. Registrar General, *The Registrar-General's Statistical Review of England and Wales for the Five Years 1946–1950* (London: Her Majesty's Stationary Office, 1954), 14.

65. Dolly Smith Wilson, "A New Look at the Affluent Worker: The Good Working Mother in Post-War Britain," *Twentieth Century British History* 17, no. 2 (2006): 206–229; Sara Horrell, "The Household and the Labor Market," in *Work and Pay in 20th Century Britain*, ed. Nicholas Crafts, Ian Gazeley, and Andrew Newell (Oxford: Oxford University Press, 2007), 117–141.

66. Smith Wilson, "A New Look at the Affluent Worker," 206.

67. Horrell, "The Household and the Labor Market."

68. To purloin Foucault's phrase regarding the homosexual. Foucault, *The Will to Knowledge*, 45.

69. Office for National Statistics, "Divorces in England and Wales: 2017," September 26, 2018, https://www.ons.gov.uk/peoplepopulationandcommunity/birthsdeathsandmarriages/divorce/bulletins/divorcesinenglandandwales/2017.

70. Foucault, *The Will to Knowledge*, 38.

71. Adrienne Roberts, *Gendered States of Punishment and Welfare: Feminist Political Economy, Primitive Accumulation and the Law* (Abingdon, UK: Routledge, 2016).

72. Roberts, *Gendered States of Punishment and Welfare*.

73. Drucilla K. Barker, "Querying the Paradox of Caring Labor," *Rethinking Marxism* 24, no. 4 (2012): 575, 578; see also Anca Parvulescu, *Traffic in Women's Work: East European Migration and the Making of Europe* (Chicago: University of Chicago Press, 2014).

74. Eleanor French, "Prostitution," *British Journal of Venereal Diseases* 31, no. 2 (1955): 114–116.

75. John Scott, "A Prostitute's Progress: Male Prostitution in Scientific Discourse," *Social Semiotics* 13, no. 2 (2003): 179–199; Julia Laite, *Common Prostitutes and Ordinary Citizens: Commercial Sex in London, 1885–1960* (Basingstoke, UK: Palgrave, 2012).

76. Kerwin Kaye, "Male Prostitution in the Twentieth Century: Psychohomosexuals, Hoodlum Homosexuals, and Exploited Teens," *Journal of Homosexuality* 46, no. 1–2 (2003): 1–77; Scott, "A Prostitute's Progress"; David S. Bimbi, "Male Prostitution: Pathology, Paradigms and Progress in Research," *Journal of Homosexuality* 53, no. 1–2 (2007): 7–35.

77. F. J. G. Jefferiss, "Venereal Disease and the Homosexual," *British Journal of Venereal Diseases* 32 (1956): 19.

78. Donald J. West, *Male Prostitution* (Abingdon, UK: Routledge, 1993), 3.

79. Alison Diduck and William Wilson, "Prostitutes and Persons," *Journal of Law and Society* 24, no. 4 (1997): 504–525.

80. Repo, *The Biopolitics of Gender*, 61.

81. John D'Emilio, "Capitalism and Gay Identity," in *Powers of Desire: The Politics of Sexuality*, ed. Ann Snitow, Christine Stansell, and Sharan Thompson (New York: Monthly Review Press, 1983), 108.

82. Thomas Egbert James, *Prostitution and the Law* (London: Heinemann Medical Books, 1951), 123.

83. Foucault, *The Will to Knowledge*, 32–33. As he asks, "What does the appearance of all these peripheral sexualities signify? Is the fact that they could appear in broad daylight a sign that the code had become more lax? Or does the fact that they were given so much attention testify to a stricter regime and to its concern to bring them under close supervision?" Foucault, *The Will to Knowledge*, 40.

84. "London's Morality," *St. James's Gazette*, May 15, 1901.

85. "The Vice of London," *London Daily News*, February 6, 1901.

86. Laite, *Common Prostitutes and Ordinary Citizens*.

87. International Congress on the White Slave Trade, *The White Slave Trade: Transactions of the International Congress on the White Slave Trade Held in London on the 21st, 22nd and 23rd of June, 1899* (London: Office of the National Vigilance Association, 1899), 70.

88. Royal Commission of Alien Immigration, *Report of the Royal Commission on Alien Immigration* (London: Her Majesty's Stationary Office, 1903), v, 12.

89. "Aliens Act" (1905), https://www.legislation.gov.uk/ukpga/1905/13/pdfs/ukpga_19050013_en.pdf.

90. Laite, *Common Prostitutes and Ordinary Citizens*.

91. George Greenwood, "Criminal Law Amendment (White Slave Traffic) Bill," (1912), c620. As the Labour politician Charles Bowerman put it: "Girls, young girls, are drawn through specious reasons into the net of these people. They do not know quite what they are going to . . . In every port of this country the police know very well what is being done so far as this traffic is concerned. They know the men; they know the uses to which these girls are brought." Bowerman, "Criminal Law Amendment (White Slave Traffic) Bill," c599.

92. Frederick Banbury, "Criminal Law Amendment (White Slave Traffic) Bill," (1912), c596.
93. Katherine Mullin, *James Joyce, Sexuality, and Social Purity* (New York: Cambridge University Press, 2003).
94. Helen J. Self, *Prostitution, Women and Misuse of the Law: The Fallen Daughters of Eve* (London: Frank Cass, 2003); Laite, *Common Prostitutes and Ordinary Citizens*.
95. Laite, *Common Prostitutes and Ordinary Citizens*.
96. The level of antipathy toward foreign sex workers in England was such that the Italian sociologist Robert Michels was prompted to write in 1914: "Not all Englishmen, be it understood, are moralists and adversaries of prostitution. But a large proportion of the English people is dominated by the jingo sentiment, and for this reason there exists in England a considerable animus against the foreign prostitutes who earn their living in that country. Thus it happens that to the ethical campaign against prostitution is superadded one of a 'nationalist' character." Robert Michels, *A Study of Borderland Questions: Sexual Ethics* (London: Transaction Publishers, 1914), 117.
97. Pringle in Royal Commission on Venereal Diseases, *Papers by Command, Reports and Minutes of Evidence, Volume 3* (Eyre and Spottiswoode: Her Majesty's Stationary Office, 1916), 113.
98. Rowland Hunt, "Commons Chamber: Oral Answers to Questions: Prostitutes of Alien Birth" (1917), c44.
99. Laite, *Common Prostitutes and Ordinary Citizens*.
100. "Women's International League," *The Woman's Leader*, May 18, 1923. Another argued: "A traffic of considerable dimensions is being carried on. It is a sinister business in which the traffickers seek to supply a demand with the greatest possible gain to themselves . . . Notorious vice centers and the system of licensed houses stimulates in a marked way the demand for foreign women, and also facilitates traffic in them, as where such vice areas or houses are tolerated it is found more profitable to move the women round." "Traffic in Women," *The Woman's Leader*, March 15, 1927.
101. Geoffrey De Freitas, "Commons Chamber: British Immigration Policy" (1951), c812.
102. Laite, *Common Prostitutes and Ordinary Citizens*; Jeffrey Weeks, *Sex, Politics and Society: The Regulations of Sexuality Since 1800* (Abingdon, UK: Routledge, 2014).
103. "A Colour Problem for Britain," *The Sphere*, October 30, 1954.
104. "Their New Life in Britain Pays," *Daily Herald*, May 8, 1958.
105. "Coloured People: Cheap Labour for Exploitation," *West London Observer*, February 17, 1956.
106. "Church Leader a Frank Speech," *Daily Mail*, July 6, 1956.
107. "How to Clean up the Shocking City," *Daily Mail*, May 18, 1956; see also Laite, *Common Prostitutes and Ordinary Citizens*.
108. "The Shocking City and the Silent Newspapers," *Daily Mirror*, May 28, 1956.
109. "The Street Girls," *Daily Mirror*, May 16, 1956.
110. Laite, *Common Prostitutes and Ordinary Citizens*.
111. "Vice War Hots Up," *Daily Herald*, February 25, 1954.
112. In 1928, the Street Offences Committee had also been set this task following the quashing of convictions of two men who had been arrested for importuning women in Hyde Park in London, which had led to public criticism that thousands of female sex workers were arrested and convicted annually without any condemnation. It did not result in new legislation at the time, however.

Self, *Prostitution, Women and Misuse of the Law*; Laite, *Common Prostitutes and Ordinary Citizens*.

113. Committee on Homosexual Offences and Prostitution, "Report of the Committee on Homosexual Offences and Prostitution" (London: HMSO, 1957), 87.

114. Committee on Homosexual Offences and Prostitution, "Report of the Committee on Homosexual Offences and Prostitution," 79–80.

115. Joanna Phoenix and Sarah Oerton, *Illicit and Illegal: Sex, Regulation and Social Control* (Abingdon, UK: Routledge, 2005); Laite, *Common Prostitutes and Ordinary Citizens*.

116. Phoenix and Oerton, *Illicit and Illegal*, 78.

117. Jane Scoular, *The Subject of Prostitution: Sex Work, Law and Social Theory* (Abingdon, UK: Routledge, 2015).

118. Phoenix and Oerton, *Illicit and Illegal*; Laite, *Common Prostitutes and Ordinary Citizens*.

119. Phoenix and Oerton, *Illicit and Illegal*; Scoular, *The Subject of Prostitution*.

120. Frank Pakenham, "Homosexual Offences and Prostitution" (1957), 735.

121. Julian Lee, *Policing Sexuality: Sex, Society and the State* (London: Zed, 2011).

122. "Criminal Law Amendment Act" (1912), http://www.irishstatutebook.ie/eli/1912/act/20/enacted/en/print.html.

123. Jeffrey Weeks, "Inverts, Perverts, and Mary-Annes," *Journal of Homosexuality* 6, no. 1–2 (1981): 113–134.

124. Lee, *Policing Sexuality*.

125. Committee on Homosexual Offences and Prostitution, "Report of the Committee on Homosexual Offences and Prostitution," 10.

126. Committee on Homosexual Offences and Prostitution, "Report of the Committee on Homosexual Offences and Prostitution," 11.

127. "Sexual Offences Act" (1967), http://www.legislation.gov.uk/ukpga/1967/60/pdfs/ukpga_19670060_en.pdf.

128. David Bell and Jon Binnie, *The Sexual Citizen: Queer Politics and Beyond* (Cambridge, UK: Polity, 2000), 3.

129. Committee on Homosexual Offences and Prostitution, "Report of the Committee on Homosexual Offences and Prostitution," 43–44.

130. Sexual Offences Act.

131. Brenda Cossman, *Sexual Citizens: The Legal and Cultural Regulation of Sex and Belonging* (Redwood City, CA: Stanford University Press, 2007), 8.

132. Margaret Thatcher, "Interview for *Woman's Own* (Commission of Enquiry Transcript)," Margaret Thatcher Foundation, September 23, 1987, https://www.margaretthatcher.org/document/106689. The original transcript of Thatcher's interview with *Woman's Own* differs from the published version (in which she is cited as having said, "There is no such thing as society").

133. Although this was on the specific condition that this did not "prohibit the doing of anything for the purpose of treating or preventing the spread of disease." "Local Government Act" (London: HMSO, 1988).

134. D'Emilio, "Capitalism and Gay Identity."

135. D'Emilio, "Capitalism and Gay Identity"; Julie Matthaei, "The Sexual Division of Labor, Sexuality, and Lesbian/Gay Liberation: Toward a Marxist-Feminist Analysis of Sexuality in US Capitalism," *Review of Radical Political Economics* 27, no. 2 (1995): 1–37.

136. Gay Liberation Front, *Gay Liberation Front Manifesto* (London: Gay Liberation Front Manifesto Group, 1971).

137. Such divisions were captured in *Spare Rib* magazine, for instance, which reported in 1977 that a London-based workshop to discuss commercial sex "revealed what an apparent lack of understanding there is between sisters in the movement . . . Many of those present felt too intimidated to speak." Nicola Rane, "Prostitution," *Spare Rib* 58 (1977): 13.

138. Kathleen Barry, *Female Sexual Slavery* (New York: New York University Press, 1979), 121, 134.

139. Carole Pateman, *The Sexual Contract* (Stanford, CA: Stanford University Pres, 1988), 203–204.

140. For a careful critique of abolitionist feminist discourses, see Leticia Sabsay, "The Ruse of Sexual Freedom: Neoliberalism, Self-Ownership and Commercial Sex," in *Global Justice and Desire: Queering Economy*, ed. Nikita Dhawan et al. (Abingdon, UK: Routledge, 2015), 180–194.

141. Alison Assiter and Avedon Carol, *Bad Girls and Dirty Pictures: The Challenge to Reclaim Feminism* (London: Pluto Press, 1993), 156.

142. Phipps, *The Politics of the Body*; Sabsay, "The Ruse of Sexual Freedom."

143. Suzanne, "Prostitution: Calling for an End to Repressive Laws," *Spare Rib* 231 (1992): 28.

144. Silvia Federici, "Prostitution and Globalization: Notes on a Feminist Debate," in *Poverty and the Production of World Politics: Unprotected Workers in the Global Political Economy*, ed. Matt Davies and Magnus Ryner (Basingstoke, UK: Palgrave, 2006), 113–136.

145. Silvia Federici, *Wages Against Housework* (London: Power of Women Collective, 1975), 4.

146. On which see Lisa Duggan, *The Twilight of Equality? Neoliberalism, Cultural Politics, and the Attack on Democracy* (Boston: Beacon Press, 2003); Cossman, *Sexual Citizens*.

CHAPTER 5

1. Michel Foucault, *The History of Sexuality: The Will to Knowledge* (translated by Robert Hurley) (New York: Pantheon, 1978), 54.

2. Sarah Dransfield, "A Tale of Two Britains: Inequality in the UK: Oxfam GB," 2014, http://policy-practice.oxfam.org.uk/publications/a-tale-of-two-britains-inequality-in-the-uk-314152; Equality Trust, "The Scale of Economic Inequality in the UK," 2019, https://www.equalitytrust.org.uk/scale-economic-inequality-uk.

3. Adrienne Roberts, *Gendered States of Punishment and Welfare: Feminist Political Economy, Primitive Accumulation and the Law* (Abingdon, UK: Routledge, 2016).

4. Joseph Rowntree Foundation, *UK Poverty 2018: A Comprehensive Analysis of Poverty Trends and Figures* (York: Joseph Rowntree Foundation, 2018).

5. Philip Alston, "Statement on Visit to the United Kingdom, by Professor Philip Alston, United Nations Special Rapporteur on Extreme Poverty and Human Rights" (London: United Nations, November 16, 2018), 1–2.

6. All-Party Parliamentary Group on Prostitution and the Global Sex Trade, *Behind Closed Doors: Organized Sexual Exploitation in England and Wales: An Inquiry by the All-Party Prostitution Group on Prostitution and the Global Sex Trade* (London: APPG, 2018); "Commercial Sexual Exploitation" (Hansard, July 4, 2018).

7. All-Party Parliamentary Group on Prostitution and the Global Sex Trade, *Behind Closed Doors*, 11.

8. All-Party Parliamentary Group on Prostitution and the Global Sex Trade, *Behind Closed* Doors, 11.
9. Alston, "Statement on Visit to the United Kingdom," 2.
10. The name popularly used to describe the Labour governments under the helm of Tony Blair and then Gordon Brown between 1997 and 2010.
11. Joanna Phoenix and Sarah Oerton, *Illicit and Illegal: Sex, Regulation and Social Control* (Abingdon, UK: Routledge, 2005).
12. Home Office, *Paying the Price: A Consultation Paper on Prostitution* (London: Home Office, 2004), 5, 84.
13. Home Office, *A Coordinated Prostitution Strategy and a Summary of Responses to Paying the Price* (London: Home Office, 2006), 1.
14. Phoenix and Oerton, *Illicit and Illegal*.
15. Jacqui Smith, "Policing and Crime Bill: Second Reading" (Hansard, January 19, 2009), c524.
16. Fiona McTaggart, "Policing and Crime Bill: Second Reading" (Hansard, January 19, 2009), c547.
17. Jane Scoular and Maggie O'Neill, "Regulating Prostitution: Social Inclusion, Responsibilization and the Politics of Prostitution Reform," *British Journal of Criminology* 47, no. 5 (2007): 764–778.
18. Phoenix and Oerton, *Illicit and Illegal*.
19. McTaggart, "Policing and Crime Bill," c546; see also Phoenix and Oerton, *Illicit and Illegal*.
20. Phoenix and Oerton, *Illicit and Illegal*.
21. Anthony Steen, "Policing and Crime Bill: Second Reading" (Hansard, January 19, 2009), c550.
22. Scoular and O'Neill, "Regulating Prostitution," 769.
23. Phoenix and Oerton, *Illicit and Illegal*; Sharron A. Fitzgerald, "Biopolitics and the Regulation of Vulnerability: The Case of the Female Trafficked Migrant," *International Journal of Law in Context* 6, no. 3 (2010): 277–294; Anna Carline, "Of Frames, Cons and Affects: Constructing and Responding to Prostitution and Trafficking for Sexual Exploitation," *Feminist Legal Studies* 20, no. 3 (2012): 207–225.
24. Carline, "Of Frames, Cons and Affects."
25. John Scott, "Governing Prostitution: Differentiating the Bad from the Bad," *Current Issues in Criminal Justice* 23, no. 1 (2011): 53–72.
26. "Policing and Crime Act" (2009), http://www.legislation.gov.uk/ukpga/2009/26/contents.
27. Scoular and O'Neill, "Regulating Prostitution," 765.
28. Sarah Kingston and Terry Thomas, "The Police, Sex Work, and Section 14 of the Policing and Crime Act 2009," *The Howard Journal of Criminal Justice* 53, no. 3 (2014): 255–269.
29. Smith "Policing and Crime Bill," c525.
30. English Collective of Prostitutes, "Bulletins: Raids, Arrests, and Prosecutions," 2019, http://prostitutescollective.net/bulletins/.
31. English Collective of Prostitutes, "Imprisoned for Working to Support Her Disabled Son," January 13, 2016, http://prostitutescollective.net/2016/01/13/imprisoned-for-working-to-support-her-disabled-son/.
32. English Collective of Prostitutes, "Facts About Sex Work," 2016, http://prostitutescollective.net/2016/11/facts-sex-work/; see also Molly Smith and Juno Mac, *Revolting Prostitutes: The Fight for Sex Workers' Rights* (London: Verso, 2018).

33. On material and symbolic violence vis-à-vis sex work, see for example Amalia L. Cabezas, *Economies of Desire: Sex and Tourism in Cuba and the Dominican Republic* (Philadelphia: Temple University Press, 2009); Yasmina Katsulis, *Sex Work and the City: The Social Geography of Health and Safety in Tijuana, Mexico* (Austin: University of Texas Press, 2009); Jennifer Suchland, *Economies of Violence: Transnational Feminism, Postsocialism, and the Politics of Sex Trafficking* (Durham, NC: Duke University Press, 2015); Sharron A. FitzGerald and Kathryn McGarry, eds., *Realizing Justice for Sex Workers: An Agenda for Change* (London: Rowman & Littlefield International, 2018); Sara Kallock, *Livable Intersections: Re/Framing Sex Work at the Frontline* (London: Rowman & Littlefield International, 2019).

34. Global Network of Sex Work Projects, "Briefing Paper: The Needs and Rights of Trans Sex Workers," 2014, https://www.nswp.org/sites/nswp.org/files/Trans%20SWs.pdf; International Committee on the Rights of Sex Workers in Europe, "Underserved. Overpoliced. Invisibilized. LGBT Sex Workers Do Matter: Intersection Briefing Paper #1," October 2015, https://www.sexworkeurope.org/sites/default/files/resource-pdfs/icrse_briefing_paper_october2015.pdf; Global Network of Sex Work Projects and MPact Global Action, "Briefing Paper: The Homophobia and Transphobia Experienced by LGBT Sex Workers," 2018, https://www.nswp.org/sites/nswp.org/files/bp_homophobia_transphobia_mpact_nswp_-_2018.pdf; Jasmine Sankofa, "From Margin to Center: Sex Work Decriminalization Is a Racial Justice Issue" (Amnesty International, 2019), https://www.amnestyusa.org/from-margin-to-center-sex-work-decriminalization-is-a-racial-justice-issue/; International Lesbian, Gay, Bisexual, Trans and Intersex Association, "LGBTI Organizations from across the World Call for Decriminalization of Sex Work," March 23, 2019, https://ilga.org/sex-work-lgbti-organisations-call-for-decriminalisation.

35. Women's Budget Group, "A Cumulative Gender Assessment of Ten Years of Austerity Politics" (London: Women's Budget Group, 2016), http://wbg.org.uk/wp-content/uploads/2016/03/De_HenauReed_WBG_GIAtaxben_briefing_2016_03_06.pdf.

36. Dawn Foster, "Mums Against Austerity," *Dissent* 63, no. 4 (2016): 47–52; Leah Bassel and Emejulu Akwugo, *Minority Women and Austerity: Survival and Resistance in France and Britain* (Bristol: Policy Press, 2017); Deborah Steinstra, "DisAbling Women and Girls in Austere Times," *Atlantis: Critical Studies in Gender, Culture & Social Justice* 38, no. 1 (2017): 154–167. For example, the UN reports that single parents (of whom nine in ten are women) represent two in three recipients of Universal Credit to have had their benefits capped. Special Rapporteur on Extreme Poverty and Human Rights, "Visit to the United Kingdom of Great Britain and Northern Ireland: Report of the Special Rapporteur on Extreme Poverty and Human Rights" (United Nations Human Rights Council, July 24, 2019), https://undocs.org/A/HRC/41/39/Add.1. Of course, the categories of single mothers, migrant women, etc. are not mutually exclusive but intersect to further compound disadvantage.

37. On which see Elizabeth Bernstein and Janet R. Jakobsen, "Introduction: Gender, Justice, and Neoliberal Transformations," *S&F Online* 11, no. 1 (2013), http://sfonline.barnard.edu/gender-justice-and-neoliberal-transformations/introduction/.

38. See for instance Phillips's speech in the House of Commons on February 26, 2019, which is being widely shared on social media at the time of writing. Jess Phillips, "Leaving the European Union" (Hansard, February 26, 2019).

39. Smith and Mac, *Revolting Prostitutes*, 150.

40. Gavin Shuker, "Commercial Sexual Exploitation" (Hansard, July 4, 2018), c 142WH.

41. Angela Crawley, "Commercial Sexual Exploitation" (Hansard, July 4, 2018), c157WH.

42. Sara Ahmed, *On Being Included: Racism and Diversity in Institutional Life* (Durham, NC: Duke University Press, 2012), 117.

43. Many thanks to Donna Lee for pointing me toward this example.

44. Department for Work and Pensions, "Housing Benefit: Size Criteria for People Renting in the Social Rented Sector: Equality Impact Assessment," 2012, 15, https://www.gov.uk/government/uploads/system/uploads/attachment_data/file/220154/eia-social-sector-housing-under-occupation-wr2011.pdf.

45. Tracey Jensen, "Tough Love in Tough Times," *Studies in the Maternal* 4, no. 2 (2012): 1–2.

46. Liam Stanley, "'We're Reaping What We Sowed': Everyday Crisis Narratives and Acquiescence to the Age of Austerity," *New Political Economy* 19, no. 6 (2014): 895–917; Liam Stanley, "The Idea of Austerity: An Alternative History" (University of Sheffield Political Economy Research Series, Sheffield, January 23, 2014); Angus Cameron, Nicola Smith, and Daniela Tepe-Belfrage, "Household Wastes: Disciplining the Family in the Name of Austerity," *British Politics* 11, no. 4 (2016): 396–417.

47. David Cameron, "Speech on the Big Society," May 23, 2011, https://www.gov.uk/government/speeches/speech-on-the-big-society; David Cameron, "Economy Speech," March 7, 2013, https://www.gov.uk/government/speeches/economy-speech-delivered-by-david-cameron; see also Stanley, "'We're Reaping What We Sowed'"; Stanley, "The Idea of Austerity: An Alternative History."

48. Johnna Montgomerie, "Austerity and the Household: The Politics of Economic Storytelling," *British Politics* 11, no. 4 (2016): 421.

49. Dani Tepe-Belfrage, "A Feminist Critique of the 'Politics of Community,'" in *The British Growth Crisis: The Search for a New Model*, ed. Jeremy Green, Colin Hay, and Peter Taylor-Gooby (Basingstoke, UK: Palgrave, 2015), 285.

50. For two extended explorations of this theme, see Nicola Smith, "Toward a Queer Political Economy of Crisis," in *Scandalous Economics: Gender and the Politics of Financial Crisis*, ed. Jacqui True and Aida Hozić (New York: Oxford University Press, 2016), 231–247; and Dani Tepe-Belfrage and Johnna Montgomerie, "Broken Britain: Post-Crisis Austerity and the Trouble with the Troubled Families Programme," in *Scandalous Economics: Gender and the Politics of Financial Crises*, 79–91.

51. David Cameron, "Troubled Families Speech," December 15, 2011, https://www.gov.uk/government/speeches/troubled-families-speech.

52. David Cameron, "PM's Speech on the Fightback after the Riots," August 15, 2011, https://www.gov.uk/government/speeches/pms-speech-on-the-fightback-after-the-riots.

53. "The Rich List: The Definitive Guide to Wealth," *Sunday Times*, May 18, 2014; "Britain Has the World's Most Billionaires per Capita," *The Guardian*, May 11, 2014; Jack Nickson, "Britain Is the Billionaire Capital of the World: Good or Bad?," *Huffington Post*, May 19, 2014.

54. Equality Trust, "The Equality Trust Warns of a Wealth Inequality Crisis, as UK Rich Increase Their Wealth by £274 Billion over Five Years," May 13, 2018, https://www.equalitytrust.org.uk/sites/default/files/FINAL%20Wealth%20Tracker%202018%20%28Press%20release%29.pdf.

55. Judith Butler, "Merely Cultural," *Social Text* 15, no. 3/4 (1997): 265.

56. Lisa Duggan and Richard Kim, "Beyond Gay Marriage: For the Right, This Campaign Is Not Just About Preventing Same-Sex Weddings," *The Nation* 281, no. 3 (2005): 24–27; Molly McGarry and George E. Haggerty, "Introduction," in *A Companion to Lesbian, Gay, Bisexual, Transgender, and Queer Studies*, ed. George E. Haggerty and Molly McGarry (Hoboken, NJ: John Wiley & Sons, 2007), 1–13; Jack Halberstam, *The Queer Art of Failure* (Durham, NC: Duke University Press, 2011).

57. Wendy Brown, "American Nightmare Neoliberalism, Neoconservatism, and De-Democratization," *Political Theory* 34, no. 6 (2006): 694; see also Michel Foucault, *The Birth of Biopolitics: Lectures at the Collège de France, 1978–1979* (translated by Graham Burchell) (Basingstoke, UK: Palgrave, 2008); Shannon Winnubst, "The Queer Thing about Neoliberal Pleasure: A Foucauldian Warning," *Foucault Studies*, no. 14 (2012): 79–97; Wendy Brown, *Undoing the Demos: Neoliberalism's Stealth Revolution* (Durham, NC: Duke University Press, 2015); Elisabeth Prügl, "Neoliberalizing Feminism," *New Political Economy* 20, no. 4 (2015): 614–631.

58. Jane Scoular, "What's Law Got to Do with It? How and Why Law Matters in the Regulation of Sex Work," *Journal of Law and Society* 37, no. 1 (2010): 12–39.

59. Duggan and Kim, "Beyond Gay Marriage"; Halberstam, *The Queer Art of Failure*. On the privatization of social reproduction, see for instance Isabelle Bakker, "Social Reproduction and the Constitution of a Gendered Political Economy," *New Political Economy* 12, no. 4 (2007): 541–556; Faranak Miraftab, "Contradictions in the Gender-Poverty Nexus: Reflections on the Privatization of Social Reproduction and Urban Informality in South African Townships," in *The International Handbook on Gender and Poverty: Concepts, Research, and Policy*, ed. Sylvia Chant (London: Edward Elgar, 2010), 644–649; Genevieve LeBaron, "The Political Economy of the Household: Neoliberal Restructuring, Enclosures, and Daily Life," *Review of International Political Economy* 17, no. 5 (2010): 889–912; Genevieve LeBaron and Adrienne Roberts, "Toward a Feminist Political Economy of Capitalism and Carcerality," *Signs* 40, no. 1 (2014): 19–44; Adrienne Roberts, "Household Debt and the Financialization of Social Reproduction: Theorizing the UK Household and Hunger Crises," in *Risking Capitalism*, ed. Susanne Soederberg (Bingley, UK: Emerald Group Publishing, 2016), 135–164; Tiina Vaittinen, Hanna-Kaisa Hoppania, and Olli Karsio, "Marketization, Commodification, and the Privatization of Care Services," in *Handbook on the International Political Economy of Gender*, ed. Juanita Elias and Adrienne Roberts (Cheltenham, UK: Edward Elgar, 2018), 379–391.

60. Elizabeth Freeman, "Queer Belongings: Kinship Theory and Queer Theory," in *A Companion to Lesbian, Gay, Bisexual, Transgender, and Queer Studies*, 298.

61. V. Spike Peterson, "The Intended and Unintended Queering of States/Nations," *Studies in Ethnicity and Nationalism* 13, no. 1 (2013): 57–68.

62. David Cameron, "Prime Minister's Speech at Lesbian, Gay, Bisexual and Transgender Reception," July 25, 2012, https://www.gov.uk/government/speeches/prime-ministers-speech-at-lesbian-gay-bisexual-and-transgender-reception.

63. Cameron himself had repeatedly opposed gay rights when in opposition, including voting against the repeal of Section 28 of the Local Government Act in 2003. Nicholas Watt, "David Cameron Apologizes to Gay People for Section 28," *The Guardian*, July 2, 2009.

64. Martin Mitchell et al., *Implications of Austerity for LGBT People and Services* (London: UNISON, 2013).

65. Stonewall Housing, "Home," Welcome, 2014, http://www.stonewallhousing.org/ ; Stonewall, *LGBT in Britain: Hate Crime and Discrimination* (London: YouGov/ Stonewall, 2019). For example, one fifth of LGBT people have "experienced a hate crime or incident due to their sexual orientation and/or gender identity in the last 12 months," a figure that increases to two fifths of trans people; and nearly a third of LGBT people "avoid certain streets because they do not feel safe there as an LGBT person." Stonewall, *LGBT in Britain*, 1.

66. Rosemary Hennessy, *Profit and Pleasure: Sexual Identities in Late Capitalism* (Abingdon, UK: Routledge, 2000).

67. Lauren Berlant and Michael Warner, "Sex in Public," *Critical Inquiry* 24 (1998): 553; see also Lisa Duggan, *The Twilight of Equality? Neoliberalism, Cultural Politics, and the Attack on Democracy* (Boston: Beacon Press, 2003).

68. Grace Kyungwon Hong, *Death Beyond Disavowal: The Impossible Politics of Difference* (Minneapolis: University of Minnesota Press, 2015); see also Roderick A. Ferguson, *Aberrations in Black: Toward a Queer of Color Critique* (Minneapolis: University of Minnesota Press, 2004); Jasbir Puar, *Terrorist Assemblages: Homonationalism in Queer Times* (Durham, NC: Duke University Press, 2008); David Eng, *The Feeling of Kinship: Queer Liberalism and the Racialization of Intimacy* (Durham, NC: Duke University Press, 2010); Leticia Sabsay, "The Emergence of the Other Sexual Citizen: Orientalism and the Modernisation of Sexuality," *Citizenship Studies* 16, no. 5–6 (2012): 605–623; Cynthia Weber, *Queer International Relations: Sovereignty, Sexuality and the Will to Knowledge* (New York: Oxford University Press, 2016).

69. Andrew Sullivan, *Virtually Normal: An Argument About Homosexuality* (New York: Vintage Books, 1995); see also David Eng, "Freedom and the Racialization of Intimacy," in *A Companion to Lesbian, Gay, Bisexual, Transgender, and Queer Studies*, 41.

70. Phoenix and Oerton, *Illicit and Illegal*.

71. John Scott, "A Prostitute's Progress: Male Prostitution in Scientific Discourse," *Social Semiotics* 13, no. 2 (2003): 179–199.

72. Jane Scoular, *The Subject of Prostitution: Sex Work, Law and Social Theory* (Abingdon, UK: Routledge, 2015), 69.

73. Phoenix and Oerton, *Illicit and Illegal*; Scoular, *The Subject of Prostitution*.

74. Don Kulick, "Four Hundred Thousand Swedish Perverts," *GLQ: A Journal of Lesbian and Gay Studies* 11, no. 2 (2005): 219; see also Scoular, *The Subject of Prostitution*.

75. Home Office, *A Coordinated Prostitution Strategy*, 2.

76. Smith, "Policing and Crime Bill," c525.

77. Anna Carline, "Criminal Justice, Extreme Pornography and Prostitution: Protecting Women or Promoting Morality?," *Sexualities* 14, no. 3 (2011): 313.

78. Policing and Crime Act.

79. Policing and Crime Act.

80. Smith, "Policing and Crime Bill," c526.

81. Sarah Kingston and Nicola Smith, "Sex Counts: An Examination of Sexual Service Advertisements in a UK Online Directory," *British Journal of Sociology* 71, no. 2 (2020): 328–348.

82. Home Office, *A Coordinated Prostitution Strategy*, 9.

83. Jo Doezema, "Ouch! Western Feminists' 'Wounded Attachment' to the 'Third World Prostitute,'" *Feminist Review* 67, no. 1 (2001): 28.

84. Nicola J. Smith, "The International Political Economy of Commercial Sex," *Review of International Political Economy* 18, no. 4 (2011): 530–549.

85. Nicola Smith, Mary Laing, and Katy Pilcher, "Being, Thinking and Doing 'Queer' in Debates about Commercial Sex," in *Queer Sex Work*, ed. Mary Laing, Katy Pilcher, and Nicola Smith (Abingdon, UK: Routledge, 2015), 1–9.

86. Carline, "Criminal Justice, Extreme Pornography and Prostitution," 315. For feminist critiques of such assumptions, see Laura J. Shepherd, *Gender, Violence and Popular Culture: Telling Stories* (London: Routledge, 2012); Laura Sjoberg, *Women as Wartime Rapists: Beyond Sensation and Stereotyping* (New York: NYU Press, 2016). On women as consumers of sexual services and products, see Jacqueline Sanchez Taylor, "Female Sex Tourism: A Contradiction in Terms?," *Feminist Review* 83, no. 1 (2006): 42–59; Katy Pilcher, *Erotic Performance and Spectatorship: New Frontiers in Erotic Dance* (Abingdon, UK: Routledge, 2017); Lucy Neville, *Girls Who Like Boys Who Like Boys: Women and Gay Male Pornography and Erotica* (Basingstoke, UK: Palgrave, 2018); Sarah Kingston, Natalie Hammond, and Scarlett Redman, *Women Who Buy Sex: Converging Sexualities?* (Abingdon, UK: Routledge, 2020).

87. Smith, "Policing and Crime Bill," c524.

88. On this shift, see Johanna Kantola and Judith Squires, "Discourses Surrounding Prostitution Policies in the UK," *European Journal of Women's Studies* 11, no. 1 (2004): 77–101; Ronald Weitzer, "The Movement to Criminalize Sex Work in the United States," *Journal of Law and Society* 37, no. 1 (2010): 61–84.

89. Ronald Weitzer, "The Social Construction of Sex Trafficking: Ideology and Institutionalization of a Moral Crusade," *Politics & Society* 35, no. 3 (2007): 447; Weitzer, "The Social Construction of Sex Trafficking," 61.

90. On which see for instance Vanessa E. Munro, "A Tale of Two Servitudes: Defining and Implementing a Domestic Response to Trafficking of Women for Prostitution in the UK and Australia," *Social and Legal Studies* 14, no. 1 (2005): 91–114; Ratna Kapur, *Erotic Justice: Law and the New Politics of Postcolonialism* (London: The Glass House Press, 2005); Julia O'Connell Davidson, "Will the Real Sex Slave Please Stand Up?," *Feminist Review* 83, no. 1 (2006), 4–22; Jo Doezema, *Sex Slaves and Discourse Masters: The Construction of Trafficking* (London: Zed Books, 2010).

91. Claudia Aradau, "The Perverse Politics of Four-Letter Words: Risk and Pity in the Securitisation of Human Trafficking," *Millennium: Journal of International Studies* 33, no. 2 (2004): 251; see also Doezema, "Ouch!"; Laura María Agustín, *Sex at the Margins: Migration, Labour Markets and the Rescue Industry* (London: Zed, 2007); Rutvica Andrijasevic, "Beautiful Dead Bodies: Gender, Migration and Representation in Anti-Trafficking Campaigns," *Feminist Review* 86, no. 1 (2007): 24–44.

92. Gargi Bhattacharyya, *Sexuality and Society: An Introduction* (Abingdon, UK: Routledge, 2005), 104.

93. Robin Bernstein, *Racial Innocence: Performing American Childhood from Slavery to Civil Rights* (New York: NYU Press, 2011); see also bell hooks, *Ain't I a Woman: Black Women and Feminism* (New York: Routledge, 2015).

94. Sabsay, "The Emergence of the Other Sexual Citizen"; Grace Kyungwon Hong, "Existentially Surplus: Women of Color Feminism and the New Crises of Capitalism," *GLQ: A Journal of Lesbian and Gay Studies* 18, no. 1 (2012): 87–106. On racialized discourses of prostitution as unfreedom, see also Leticia Sabsay, "The Ruse of Sexual Freedom: Neoliberalism, Self-Ownership and Commercial Sex," in *Global Justice and Desire: Queering Economy*, ed. Nikita Dhawan et al. (Abingdon, UK: Routledge, 2015), 180–194.

95. Home Office, *A Coordinated Prostitution Strategy*, 62. On white slavery and modern slavery discourses, see also Doezema, *Sex Slaves and Discourse Masters*; Smith and Mac, *Revolting Prostitutes*.

96. *Paying the Price*, for instance, pointed to the "effects of economic and political disruption in Eastern Europe and beyond," thus enabling a clear rhetorical focus on eastern Europe while collapsing the whole of the rest of the world into two words: "and beyond." As the report went on, this "creates markets in wealthy countries and people willing to supply those markets. Primarily young women but also teenage girls looking for a better life are promised work in the European Union, made to pay exorbitant charges for travel and forced into prostitution to pay their debts." Home Office, *Paying the Price*, 75.

97. Aradau, "The Perverse Politics of Four-Letter Words," 251.

98. Home Office, *A Coordinated Prostitution Strategy*, 64.

99. Claudia Aradau, *Rethinking Trafficking in Women: Politics out of Security* (Basingstoke, UK: Palgrave, 2008).

100. Home Office, *Victims of Modern Slavery: Frontline Staff Guidance* (London: Home Office, 2016), 18.

101. Aradau, *Rethinking Trafficking in Women*.

102. Jo Doezema, "Forced to Choose: Beyond the Voluntary v. Forced Prostitution Dichotomy," in *Global Sex Workers: Rights, Resistance and Definition*, ed. Kamala Kempadoo and Jo Doezema (Abingdon, UK: Routledge, 1998), 48; Doezema, *Sex Slaves and Discourse Masters*, 73.

103. Carline, "Of Frames, Cons and Affects."

104. Aradau, *Rethinking Trafficking in Women*.

105. Imogen Tyler, *Revolting Subjects: Social Abjection and Resistance in Neoliberal Britain* (London: Zed, 2013), 111; see also Anna Marie Smith, *New Right Discourse on Race and Sexuality: Britain, 1968–1990* (Cambridge, UK: Cambridge University Press, 1994).

106. Peterson, "The Intended and Unintended Queering of States/Nations," 62.

107. Phil Hubbard, Roger Matthews, and Jane Scoular, "Regulating Sex Work in the EU: Prostitute Women and the New Spaces of Exclusion," *Gender, Place and Culture* 15, no. 2 (2008): 137–152; Smith and Mac, *Revolting Prostitutes*.

108. Ferguson, *Aberrations in Black*, 87.

109. Andrijasevic, "Beautiful Dead Bodies." On the connections between family/intimacy and nation/sovereignty, see also V. Spike Peterson, "Family Matters: How Queering the Intimate Queers the International," *International Studies Review* 16, no. 4 (2014): 604–608; Weber, *Queer International Relations*.

110. Andrijasevic, "Beautiful Dead Bodies," 40.

111. Weber, *Queer International Relations*, 73.

112. Ferguson, *Aberrations in Black*.

113. Harriet Harman, "Commons Debate: Constitutional Affairs: Sex Trafficking" (2006), c407.

114. Kulick, "Four Hundred Thousand Swedish Perverts," 210, 224.

115. Shamim Miah, "The Groomers and the Question of Race," *Identity Papers: A Journal of British and Irish Studies* 1, no. 1 (2015): 54–66.

116. "Some of These Men Have Children the Same Age; They Are Bad Apples," *Times*, January 5, 2011.

117. Bhattacharyya, *Sexuality and Society*; Hubbard, Matthews, and Scoular, "Regulating Sex Work in the EU."

118. "Outlawed: Sex with Trafficked Prostitutes," *Independent*, November 19, 2008.

119. Tessa Jowell, "Commons Chamber: Oral Answers to Questions" (Hansard, November 9, 2009), c22. On the global politics of sport mega-events, see Jonathan Grix and Donna Lee, *Entering the Global Arena: Emerging States, Soft Power Strategies and Sport Mega-Events* (Basingstoke, UK: Palgrave, 2019).

120. Ronald Weitzer, "Flawed Theory and Method in Studies of Prostitution," *Violence Against Women* 11, no. 7 (2005): 229.

121. It also pointed to "significant evidence that national and international prostitution is inextricably linked . . . There are clear indications that brothels in London, and other cities, have seen an influx of foreign women." Home Office, *Paying the Price*, 75. Similarly, *A Coordinated Prostitution Strategy* emphasized the need to tackle off-street prostitution in order to counter "the trafficking of women from abroad" as "clearly a significant issue which can cause immense misery and harm to those involved." Home Office, *A Coordinated Prostitution Strategy*, 2, 12.

122. All-Party Parliamentary Group on Prostitution and the Global Sex Trade, *Behind Closed Doors*, 1.

123. All-Party Parliamentary Group on Prostitution and the Global Sex Trade, *Behind Closed Doors*, i.

124. All-Party Parliamentary Group on Prostitution and the Global Sex Trade, *Behind Closed Doors*, 3.

125. National Crime Agency, "Law Enforcement Steps up Response to Modern Slavery," August 10, 2017, http://www.nationalcrimeagency.gov.uk/news/1171-law-enforcement-steps-up-response-to-modern-slavery.

126. Bhattacharyya, *Sexuality and Society*, 112; see also Fitzgerald, "Biopolitics and the Regulation of Vulnerability."

127. Jasbir Puar, *The Right to Maim: Debility, Capacity, Disability* (Durham, NC: Duke University Press, 2017), 18.

128. Elizabeth Bernstein, *Temporarily Yours: Intimacy, Authenticity, and the Commerce of Sex* (Chicago: University of Chicago Press, 2007); Mark Padilla et al., *Love and Globalization: Transformations of Intimacy in the Contemporary World* (Nashville, TN: Vanderbilt University Press, 2008); Christine Chin, *Cosmopolitan Sex Workers: Women and Migration in a Global City* (Oxford: Oxford University Press, 2013); Megan Daigle, *From Cuba with Love: Sex and Money in the Twenty-First Century* (Oakland: University of California Press, 2015); Wanjohi Kibicho, *Sex Tourism in Africa: Kenya's Booming Industry* (London: Routledge, 2016).

129. Silvia Federici, "Prostitution and Globalization: Notes on a Feminist Debate," in *Poverty and the Production of World Politics: Unprotected Workers in the Global Political Economy*, ed. Matt Davies and Magnus Ryner (Basingstoke, UK: Palgrave, 2006), 123.

130. Federici, "Prostitution and Globalization."

131. Phoenix and Oerton, *Illicit and Illegal*; Weitzer, "Flawed Theory and Method."

132. Suchland, *Economies of Violence*; see also Cabezas, *Economies of Desire*; Prabha Kotiswaran, *Dangerous Sex, Invisible Labor: Sex Work and the Law in India*

(Princeton, NJ: Princeton University Press, 2011); Smith and Mac, *Revolting Prostitutes*.

133. Kallock, *Livable Intersections*, 42.

134. Teela Sanders and Kate Hardy, "Sex Work: The Ultimate Precarious Labour?," *Criminal Justice Matters* 93, no. 1 (2013): 16; see also Suchland, *Economies of Violence*.

135. Ann D. Jordan, "Human Rights of Wrongs? The Struggle for a Rights-Based Response to Trafficking in Human-Beings," *Gender & Development* 10, no. 1 (2002): 28–37; Carline, "Criminal Justice, Extreme Pornography and Prostitution"; Smith and Mac, *Revolting Prostitutes*.

136. Andrijasevic, "Beautiful Dead Bodies."

137. Caroline Robinson, "Claiming Space for Labor Rights Within the United Kingdom Modern Slavery Crusade," *Anti-Trafficking Review*, no. 5 (2015): 129; Andrijasevic, "Beautiful Dead Bodies."

138. Rutvica Andrijasevic, *Migration, Agency and Citizenship in Sex Trafficking* (Basingstoke, UK: Palgrave, 2010).

139. Anca Parvulescu, *Traffic in Women's Work: East European Migration and the Making of Europe* (Chicago: University of Chicago Press, 2014), 14. In Jasbir Puar's terms, they "are not necessarily or only tied to what has been historically theorized as 'race.'" Puar, *Terrorist Assemblages*, xii.

140. English Collective of Prostitutes, *Sex Workers Are Getting Screwed by Brexit* (London: English Collective of Prostitutes, 2019).

141. Robinson, "Claiming Space for Labor Rights."

142. "Modern Slavery Act" (2015), http://www.legislation.gov.uk/ukpga/2015/30/pdfs/ukpga_20150030_en.pdf.

143. Jason Haynes, "The Modern Slavery Act (2015): A Legislative Commentary," *Statute Law Review* 1, no. 1 (2015): 33–56.

144. Theresa May, "The Purpose of Reform," November 10, 2015, https://www.gov.uk/government/speeches/the-purpose-of-reform; Theresa May, "My Government Will Lead the Way in Defeating Modern Slavery," *The Telegraph*, July 30, 2016.

145. "Nationality, Immigration and Asylum Act" (2002), http://www.legislation.gov.uk/ukpga/2002/41; see also Munro, "A Tale of Two Servitudes."

146. "Sexual Offences Act" (2003), http://www.legislation.gov.uk/ukpga/2003/42/pdfs/ukpga_20030042_en.pdf; see also Munro, "A Tale of Two Servitudes;" Carline, "Of Frames, Cons, and Affects."

147. All-Party Parliamentary Group on Human Trafficking and Modern Slavery, "What Is Human Trafficking?," 2019, https://www.humantraffickingfoundation.org/theissue.

148. Home Office, *Victims of Modern Slavery*.

149. May, "The Purpose of Reform."

150. See for instance Genevieve LeBaron, "Women and Unfree Labor in the Global Political Economy," in *Handbook on the International Political Economy of Gender*, 353–364; Gary Craig et al., eds., *The Modern Slavery Agenda: Policy, Politics, and Practice in the UK* (Bristol: Policy Press, 2019).

151. Foucault, *The Will to Knowledge*, 148.

152. Luke De Noronha, "The Mobility of Deservingness: Race, Class and Citizenship in the Wake of the 'Windrush Scandal,'" *The Disorder of Things*, July 3, 2018, https://thedisorderofthings.com/2018/07/03/the-mobility-of-deservingness-race-class-and-citizenship-in-the-wake-of-the-windrush-scandal/.

153. All-Party Parliamentary Group on Prostitution and the Global Sex Trade, *Behind Closed Doors*, 3.

154. On racism and Brexit, see Gurminder K. Bhambra, "Brexit, Trump, and 'Methodological Whiteness': On the Misrecognition of Race and Class," *British Journal of Sociology* 68, no. 1 (2017): 214–232; Robbie Shilliam, *Race and the Undeserving Poor: From Abolition to Brexit* (Newcastle Upon Tyne, UK: Agenda, 2018); Aisha K. Gill and Nazneen Ahmed, "A New World Order?," in *Gender and Queer Perspectives on Brexit*, ed. Moira Dustin, Nuno Ferreira, and Millns Susan (Basingstoke, UK: Palgrave, 2019), 45–58.

155. Aida Hozić and Jacqui True, "Brexit as a Scandal: Gender and Global Trumpism," *Review of International Political Economy* 24, no. 2 (2017): 272.

156. Hozić and True, "Brexit as a Scandal," 278.

157. Parvulescu, *Traffic in Women's Work*, 12.

158. Phil Hubbard, "Cleansing the Metropolis: Sex Work and the Politics of Zero Tolerance," *Urban Studies* 41, no. 9 (n.d.): 1687–1702; Phil Hubbard, "Revenge and Injustice in the Neoliberal City: Uncovering Masculinist Agendas," *Antipode* 36, no. 4 (2004): 665–686; see also Sabsay, "The Ruse of Sexual Freedom"; Kallock, *Livable Intersections*.

159. Noah D. Zatz, "Sex Work/Sex Act: Law, Labor, and Desire in Constructions of Prostitution," *Signs* 22, no. 2 (1997): 277–308; Hubbard, "Revenge and Injustice in the Neoliberal City."

160. Hubbard, Matthews, and Scoular, "Regulating Sex Work in the EU," 137.

161. Michael Warner, *The Trouble with Normal: Sex, Politics and the Ethics of Queer Life* (Cambridge, MA: Harvard University Press, 2000), 161–162.

162. On the modern-day enclosures, see Silvia Federici, *Re-Enchanting the World: Feminism and the Politics of the Commons* (San Francisco: PM Press, 2018).

163. Brett Christophers, *The New Enclosure: The Appropriation of Public Land in Neoliberal Britain* (London: Verso, 2019).

164. David Harvey, "The 'New' Imperialism: Accumulation by Dispossession," *Socialist Register* 40 (2004): 63–86; see also Silvia Federici, *Caliban and the Witch: Women, the Body and Primitive Accumulation* (New York: Autonomedia, 2004); LeBaron and Roberts, "Toward a Feminist Political Economy"; Silvia Federici, "Feminism and the Politics of the Commons," in *The Wealth of the Commons: A World Beyond Market and State*, ed. David Bollier and Silke Helfrich (Amherst, MA: Levellers Press, 2014); Sutapa Chattopadhyay, "Caliban and the Witch and Wider Bodily Geographies," *Gender, Place & Culture* 24, no. 2 (2017): 160–173; Yuliya Yurchenko, *Ukraine and the Empire of Capital: From Marketization to Armed Conflict* (London: Pluto Press, 2018).

165. Foucault, *The Will to Knowledge*, 44.

166. Puar, *Terrorist Assemblages*, xvii.

167. Dean Hochlaf, Harry Quilter-Pinner, and Tom Kibasi, *Ending the Blame Game: The Case for a New Approach to Public Health and Prevention* (London: Institute for Public Policy Research, 2019).

168. Lauren Berlant, "Slow Death (Sovereignty, Obesity, Lateral Agency)," *Critical Inquiry* 33, no. 4 (2007): 154; see also Puar, *The Right to Maim*.

169. Federici, "Feminism and the Politics of the Commons."

170. As some anti-prostitution feminists infer—see for instance Sheila Jeffreys, *The Industrial Vagina: The Political Economy of the Global Sex Trade* (Abingdon, UK: Routledge, 2008); Julie Bindel, *The Pimping of Prostitution* (London: Palgrave, 2017).

CONCLUSION

1. Molly Smith, "On March 8th—WE STRIKE!", *Verso* (blog), February 15, 2019, https://www.versobooks.com/blogs/4243-on-march-8th-we-strike.

2. Silvia Federici, *Caliban and the Witch: Women, the Body and Primitive Accumulation* (New York: Autonomedia, 2004), 97.

3. See for instance Jacqueline O'Reilly et al., "Equal Pay as a Moving Target: International Perspectives on Forty Years of Addressing the Gender Pay Gap," *Cambridge Journal of Economics* 39, no. 2 (2015): 299–317; Tanja van der Lippe, Judith Treas, and Lukas Norbutas, "Unemployment and the Division of Housework in Europe," *Work, Employment & Society* 32, no. 4 (2018): 650–669.

4. Heather Love, *Feeling Backward: Loss and the Politics of Queer History* (Cambridge, MA: Harvard University Press, 2009), 9.

5. International Committee on the Rights of Sex Workers in Europe, "Sex Workers Strike for Decriminalization," Sex Work Europe, 2018, https://www.sexworkeurope.org/ru/news/general-news/sex-workers-strike-decriminalisation.

6. Sage Woodford, "Why British Sex Workers Are Striking This Friday," *Vice*, March 6, 2019, https://www.vice.com/en_uk/article/59xqp5/why-british-sex-workers-are-striking-this-friday.

7. Lisa Duggan and Richard Kim, 'Preface: A New Queer Agenda,' *S&F Online* 10, no. 1–2 (2012): 1, http://sfonline.barnard.edu/a-new-queer-agenda/preface/.

8. Joey L. Mogul, Andrea J. Ritchie, and Kay Whitlock, *Queer (In)Justice: The Criminalization of LGBT People in the United States* (Boston: Beacon Press, 2011); Joseph DeFilippis, "Common Ground: The Queerness of Welfare Policy," *S&F Online* 10, no. 1–2 (2012), http://sfonline.barnard.edu/a-new-queer-agenda/common-ground-the-queerness-of-welfare-policy/; Nikita Dhawan et al., eds., *Global Justice and Desire: Queering Economy* (Abingdon, UK: Routledge, 2015).

9. Mary Laing, Katy Pilcher, and Nicola Smith, eds., *Queer Sex Work* (Abingdon, UK: Routledge, 2015); Brooke M. Beloso, "Queer Theory, Sex Work, and Foucault's Unreason," *Foucault Studies* 23 (2017): 141–166. For example, queer history has largely written out the pivotal role of Sylvia Rivera, a trans sex worker of color, in the Stonewall riots of 1969. Melinda Chateauvert, *Sex Workers Unite: A History of the Movement from Stonewall to SlutWalk* (Boston: Beacon Press, 2014).

10. International Lesbian, Gay, Bisexual, Trans and Intersex Association, "LGBTI Organizations from Across the World Call for Decriminalization of Sex Work," March 23, 2019, https://ilga.org/sex-work-lgbti-organisations-call-for-decriminalisation.

11. On the "politics of recognition" and the "politics of redistribution," see Nancy Fraser, *Justice Interruptus: Critical Reflections on the "Postsocialist" Condition* (Cambridge, UK: Cambridge University Press, 1997), 6. For examples in sex work research on the politics of refusal, recognition, and/or redistribution, see Heather Berg, "An Honest Day's Wage for a Dishonest Day's Work: (Re) Productivism and Refusal," *WSQ: Women's Studies Quarterly* 42, no. 1 (2014): 161–177; Sharron A. FitzGerald and Kathryn McGarry, eds., *Realizing Justice for Sex Workers: An Agenda for Change* (London: Rowman & Littlefield International, 2018); Sara Kallock, "Livability: A Politics for Abnormal Lives," *Sexualities* 21, no. 7 (2018): 1170–1193.

12. Kathi Weeks, *The Problem with Work: Feminism, Marxism, Antiwork Politics, and Postwork Imaginaries* (Durham, NC: Duke University Press, 2011), 13.

13. Berg, "An Honest Day's Wage," 161–162.

14. Lisa Downing, *Selfish Women* (Abingdon, UK: Routledge, 2019).

15. Jack Halberstam, *The Queer Art of Failure* (Durham, NC: Duke University Press, 2011), 110; see also Lisa Downing, "Antisocial Feminism? Shulamith Firestone, Monique Wittig and Proto-Queer Theory," *Paragraph* 41, no. 3 (2018): 364.

16. Wanda Vrasti, "Work and the Politics of Refusal," *The Disorder of Things* (blog), June 13, 2013, http://thedisorderofthings.com/2013/06/13/work-and-the-politics-of-refusal/.

17. Drucilla K. Barker, "Querying the Paradox of Caring Labor," *Rethinking Marxism* 24, no. 4 (2012): 574–591.

18. For example, the "queer art of failure" advocated by Jack Halberstam offers an important corrective to the cult of individual success that neoliberal capitalism feeds on, but the question of who, and who is not, "entitled" to fail may warrant further deliberation. Halberstam, *The Queer Art of Failure*. Significantly, the hierarchies involved in refusal were explicitly acknowledged in the sex workers' strike of March 8, 2019: "Those of us who can strike are striking on behalf of everybody who can't . . . Those of us who are able to take the streets, who have less to fear, will be doing so in solidarity for people who maybe don't have the option. It is to highlight everybody's needs." Woodford, "Why British Sex Workers Are Striking This Friday."

19. Jasbir Puar, *The Right to Maim: Debility, Capacity, Disability* (Durham, NC: Duke University Press, 2017), xix.

20. Vrasti, "Work and the Politics of Refusal."

21. Michel Foucault, *The History of Sexuality: The Will to Knowledge* (translated by Robert Hurley) (New York: Pantheon, 1978), 96.

22. Jack Halberstam, "You Are Triggering Me! The Neo-Liberal Rhetoric of Harm, Danger and Trauma," Bully Bloggers, July 5, 2014, https://bullybloggers. wordpress.com/2014/07/05/you-are-triggering-me-the-neo-liberal-rhetoric-of-harm-danger-and-trauma/.

INDEX

For the benefit of digital users, indexed terms that span two pages (e.g., 52–53) may, on occasion, appear on only one of those pages.